Navigating the Transition

A Guide for Veterans Moving into Civilian Life

Edward Young

Contents

Transition and Renewal: From Service to Home

Resilience and Self-Love: Strength Beyond Service

Reconnection and Bridges: Relationships Across Worlds

Post-Service Realities: Life, Family, and Forward Momentum

Foundations, Prompts, and Practical Tools

Carrying Forward the Strength Within

Transition and Renewal: From Service to Home

Transition Realities and Reintegration Rituals

Military life follows a powerful, regular pattern that shapes emotions, relationships, and identity — understanding and moving with it turns turbulence into intentional flow.

Understanding deployment cycles and homecoming dynamics

Military life follows recurring, structured patterns that shape daily experience — training schedules, deployment cycles, and the ebb of duties and emotions. Predictability is the sense of knowing what to expect next, the assurance that a routine will arrive on time. This book begins by naming those waves so you can move with them instead of being slammed by them. To make that possible, it maps the three predictable stages of service life—or its civilian equivalent—pre deployment, and post deployment — just as a season has a clear weather cycle. Understanding where you are in that cycle helps you act, not react. During pre deployment you can plan small rituals: a "goodbye dinner" with a favorite playlist, a weekly video call slot, and a mutual note exchange for when one of you needs extra encouragement.

For instance, consider Sergeant Maria Lopez and her partner, Carlos. Before Maria's first deployment, they carved out a Friday night ritual: they cooked a meal together, set aside a small table for a quiet chat, and then Maria packed her gear while Carlos showered to decompress. This simple routine anchored both of them. When deployment began, Maria used the same ritual — calling Carlos at 7 p.m., sharing a quick message about the day's events, and then listening as he talked about home. At homecoming, they extended the ritual into a full evening, reviewing their lists of "three things I miss" and "three things I want back" from the previous chapter. The ritual grounded them through the transition.

During deployment, the emotional tempo shifts. The first weeks can feel like a freight train; the middle is oddly calm. Toward the end, excitement, anxiety, and the fear of change spike as return plans collide. Homecoming is both glorious and tricky; it demands patience because the person who left and the person who returns have both shifted. Partners often adjust at different speeds — one may wrestle with sleep, hyper alertness, or a need for solitude, while the other may have restructured daily life and expect the same flow to continue. That mismatch can create friction, so the book offers prompts such as the Reintegration Reflection, where each partner lists three daily tasks they relied on during deployment and three they want back, then shares and ranks them together to set small, practical goals for the first month — low pressure conversation: shared errand, or a ten minute check-in. Navigating post deployment reality also requires rediscovery and reconnection. It isn't automatic; it's work with pay-offs. Schedule small shared wins: a monthly "new thing" date, a weekly ritual of brief check-ins where each partner shares appreciation, a brief check-in, or a concrete way the other could be supportive that week. By understanding the rhythms and planning ahead, you'll be better equipped to thrive through the tides of deployment and homecoming.

In military life, predictable sequences of tasks, emotions, and responsibilities unfold in each phase. The pre deployment phase involves packing, juggling last-minute tasks, and feeling a mix of excitement and dread. Deployment breaks into sub phases: the raw, loud initial separation; the adjustment period as you find a new normal; and the final stretch when both sides rehearse home life in their heads. Knowing what to expect lets you plan.

One practical tool is a short, honest conversation right at the start of the deployment. Ask each partner to list three things they expect in the first month home and to identify what they need most right now. Sample prompts:

The goal of these prompts is to elicit concrete, actionable expectations—specific requests for support, boundaries, or goals—so that both partners have a clear, realistic picture of the first month.

- What are three things you expect in the first month home? Examples: extra affection, help with household chores, and predictable downtime.
- What will feel most supportive to you in the first week, and the first month?
- Which household tasks or responsibilities should we plan to share, and which can wait?

- How will we handle child care, work demands, and visits with extended family?
- When do you want low-pressure conversation: a shared errand, a short walk, or coffee?
- How will we check in emotionally—daily, weekly, or as needed—and who initiates?
- What do I need most right now? (Quiet time, physical closeness, help with kids, fewer questions about the deployment)
- How can we support each other? . This way you align expectations with the realities of each deployment phase.

Building a stronger partnership

To continue building a stronger partnership, here are concrete steps that build trust and closeness. Communicating openly and honestly helps establish transparency. Cultivating empathy encourages deeper understanding. Seeking support strengthens resilience.

- Communicate openly and honestly: practice intentional shared activities every evening.
- Cultivate empathy: use "I" statements and ask, "What's one part of this that surprised you?" Instead of assuming motives.
- Seek support: lean on peers, family, or a counsellor who understands military life.

These are tools for handling the cycles you already know.

Planning pre-return communication and boundary setting

Reintegration and Reconnection: Aligning Expectations and Building a Stronger Bond

As discussed in Transition Realities and Reintegration Rituals: Understanding deployment cycles and homecoming dynamics, the next step is to set the stage. The goal here is simple: talk about what each of you expects, set clear personal boundaries, and start rebuilding daily life together with intention.

Aligning Expectations and Defining Personal Space

As discussed in Transition Realities and Reintegration Rituals: Understanding deployment cycles and homecoming dynamics, we can look at practical examples like chores and decision making.

- What do I expect from my partner around chores and decisions?

Practical example:

- Reintegration Reflection – Each partner lists three "non negotiable" for alone time and three for together time.
- Communication Channels and Emotional Safety – Partners discuss preferred check-ins and schedules to maintain emotional safety.
- Plan – They wrote a short, concrete action plan: "I will set a reminder to lock the garage door at 6 pm, so the space stays quiet for you" and "I'll send a calendar invite for our next two hour 'hangout' nights." The plan also included a quick check-in the following Friday to see how the plan was working.

As discussed in Transition Realities and Reintegration Rituals: Understanding deployment cycles and homecoming dynamics, Mike

(Army) came home craving quiet after shift like deployments, while his partner, Jenna, desired extended hangouts to feel secure.

They agreed on the following boundaries:

- Mike would take an hour after work to decompress in the garage with headphones.
- Two evenings a week would be reserved for one on one time.

By creating separate decompress zones and scheduled together time, both avoided feeling boxed in.

To deepen their adjustment, they incorporated the Reintegration Reflection process at the end of each deployment cycle. Every Sunday evening, they sat in the living room with a cup of tea and a shared notebook. The reflection followed a simple three step template:

- Review – Mike and Jenna each answered two prompts: "What moments felt most real this week?" And "Which tasks or responsibilities felt out of sync?" This helped surface both the quiet needs of Mike and the social needs of Jenna.
- Decide – Using the answers, they jointly mapped out chores and decision making priorities for the coming week. For example, Mike committed to preparing dinner on Mondays to give Jenna a break, while Jenna agreed to handle bill payments on Wednesdays to reduce Mike's post deployment fatigue.

During the reflection, they used a "Reintegration Checklist" that listed recurring tasks (laundry, grocery shopping, meal prep, budgeting) and flagged any new responsibilities that arose after Mike's return. By turning the checklist into a conversation, they turned chore management from a silent expectation into a shared, negotiated partnership. The reflection process also served as a safe space for Mike to voice feelings of restlessness and for Jenna to express her desire for quality time—both of which were incorporated into the upcoming week's plan.

Through this structured yet flexible routine, the couple ensured that each decision about chores and daily life was a product of intentional reflection, not an afterthought. This method reinforced mutual respect, reduced friction, and allowed the home to become a true sanctuary for both of them.

Reintegration Reflection: Use the following three-step process to turn reintegration considerations into clear agreements about alone time, together time, communication channels, and emotional safety.

- List non negotiable – Each partner lists three "non negotiable" for alone time and three for together time.
- Establish communication channels and emotional safety – Agree on preferred channels (text, call, in person), timing, and intentional check-ins or schedules to create emotional safety during transitions.
- Plan – They wrote a short, concrete action plan: "I will set a reminder to lock the garage door at 6 pm, so the space stays quiet for you" and "I'll send a calendar invite for our next two hour 'hangout' nights." The plan also included a quick check-in the following Friday to see how the plan was working.

Share and rank them.

In line with our discussion on navigating challenging moments and shared responsibilities, we can begin by speaking aloud about triggers. As discussed in the section Communication Adaptations for Military Couples: Emotional safety and active listening, names, smells, phrases, or sudden loud noises can bring up reactions. Map them: write down what triggers show up and what helps—deep breaths, leaving the room for five minutes, calling a buddy. If a trigger points to a deeper issue, agree on a next step: pause the conversation and schedule a time with a counsellor or trusted support person.

Household duties need written agreements. Use a simple chore chart or sticky note chart: list who does laundry, who handles bills, who takes kids to bed on which nights. Pair each chore with a quick micro celebration—fold the laundry together, then spend five minutes chatting or listening to music. Check the chart at two and six weeks, adjust roles as needed.

Intentional Shared Activities and Reconnection

- Create intentional shared activities to reconnect.
- Explore low pressure activities like model building, running, or streaming a show.
- Schedule intentional time together, such as a short weekend getaway or a 45 minute mini date, at least twice a month.
- Try a night of model building, running, or streaming a show—pick something low pressure. This low stress activity keeps the evening light, allows shared focus, and builds a routine.
- Plan intentional time together: schedule a short weekend getaway or a 45 minute “mini date” at home at least twice a month to break routine, create new memories, and keep romance alive.
- Give one specific appreciation, schedule a mini date, and set one shared anchor for tomorrow.
- Then, schedule three shared activities for the next month: one emotional (deep conversation), one physical (walk or gym), one fun (game night).
- Commit, then check in weekly about how each felt.
- Keep lists short, check tanks often, and treat the first months as a series of small experiments to find what works for both of you.

Rebuilding Life Together: Rituals, Routines, and Reconnection

Reentry after a separation—especially military service—can feel like learning to drive a new vehicle: the road is the same, but the controls have changed. That's okay. The goal here is clear: discuss each partner's expectations, set firm personal boundaries, and begin crafting a daily life together with intention. Think of this as the "how" that follows the "what": small rituals, shared routines, and scheduled moments of reconnection.

Homecoming Ritual

- When you return home, take a small folded flag.
- Place the flag in a specific spot on your dresser.
- Each time you do this, it signals the end of separation and the beginning of shared life again.

In this chapter we weave together the ideas of intentional rituals, shared daily routines, and moments of reconnection to help couples create a steady post deployment rhythm.

The first building block is selecting a ritual that marks the transition from deployment back into shared life. It should be simple, repeatable, and emotionally resonant.

Reintegration reflection provides a structured pause to process emotions, assess intentions, and align on shared goals before moving forward.

Building on your reintegration reflection, carve a brief window after work or arrival to settle in before starting shared routines—use this time to take a quick walk, stretch, grab a coffee, review the day's agenda, or share a highlight from the day.

Consider this prompt: What kind of symbolic objects or shared activities would make your homecoming feel "official"? List three such items and pick one to repeat each time.

Dedicated transition time is a short, intentional buffer that helps partners shift from separate schedules into a shared rhythm before engaging in joint activities.

- Weekly Transition Talk: 45 minute, interruption free. One partner speaks for 10 minutes while the other listens, then swap. Use a timer. The goal is to align priorities and emotions for the coming week.
- Reset Ritual: Sunday evening, tech free hour with tea, or a beer, where you name one stress and one hope for the week. This creates a shared moment of reflection that helps reduce anxiety and encourages hopeful anticipation.

Prompt: Block it on the calendar now—what day and time will be your Transition Talk?

Rhythms are the structured moments you build into daily life, and predictability is the sense that each moment will occur when you expect it. With the date for your Transition Talk confirmed, we now turn to the "Love Tank Check." This exercise uses brief, focused conversations—your regular check-ins—to keep both partners on the same cadence throughout the transition. See the Love Tank concept for guidance on how to rate and refill your emotional tank.

Scheduling Regular Check-in Conversations

Short, regular check-ins—integrated into the "Love Tank Check"—beat surprise blow ups. Keep them crisp and focused:

To keep check-ins crisp and focused, try this daily format as part of the "Love Tank Check":

- Share two things: what you're doing tomorrow and one highlight from today (or briefly one word about your day and one thing you need).

- Daily check-in: Five minutes—share two things: what you're doing tomorrow and one highlight from today (or briefly one word about your day and one thing you need).

- The Monthly Big Picture: An hour to revisit finances, childcare, or shifts in work/school, plus a "Love Tank" check: rate your emotional tank from 1–10. If one partner is under a 6, the other picks one small action to help refill it.

- Use a coloured banana on the fridge door as a neutral signal to indicate when you need space versus when you want company.

When you return from a shared hobby session, you can also schedule a brief "rewind" moment to honour the space you earned during the activity, ensuring the hobby doesn't blur personal boundaries.

Building on the idea of reintroducing shared hobbies and interests, bring back small pleasures together before trying big new things: By reintroducing light activities first, you allow each partner to experience the joy of shared time while still respecting their need for individual recharge.

- Micro Missions: Reconnect by dedicating six weeks to a shared hobby—biking Tuesdays, cooking Wednesdays—then evaluate progress.

- Buddy System: If one partner lost civilian friendships, plan one social outing each month with a civilian friend and attend together the first time. After each micro mission, give each partner a brief reflection period to honour how the shared hobby either refreshed or stretched their personal space.

- Buddy System: If one partner lost civilian friendships, plan one social outing each month with a civilian friend and attend together the first time. Allow a few minutes after the outing for each person to step back, reflect, and return to their solo recharge hour.

Action Plan: Pick one homecoming ritual, one weekly routine, and one shared hobby to start this month. After six weeks, schedule a check-in to see what's working and what needs change. Use the check-in to confirm that the shared hobby respects each person's space and that individual needs are still met.

Stress management during transition and normalization of triggers

The Transition: A Stressful but Normal Part of Reintegration

Building on the idea that the transition is stressful yet normal, consider how everyday situations trigger those lingering effects. If you've noticed your chest tighten walking into a crowded grocery store, or you flinch at a loud truck in the street, that's not weakness — it's how your brain keeps tally of what it's been through. Transition from service to civilian life can be stressful in predictable and surprising ways. Naming that stress as a normal part of reintegrating reduces shame and gives you something usable to work with.

Understanding Triggers and Stress Responses

Building on that understanding, let's look at the everyday cues that trigger these responses. Triggers are often leftovers from time in uniform: a sudden noise, a tight space, an argument that escalates too fast. Those reactions aren't "just in your head." They're your body responding to cues that once kept you safe. Many vets can point to one small thing—sirens, a certain smell, a type of handshake—that can pull them back into high alert. That clarity helps you plan.

Identifying Personal Triggers — Reintegration Reflection

Now that we've identified your personal triggers, let's put them into practice.

- Take 10 minutes alone or with your partner. List three situations in the last month that led to unexpected anxiety or startle responses. For instance, imagine stepping into a crowded elevator and feeling your chest tighten; you might think, "What if I can't breathe?" Note where you were, what you were doing, and who was with you. Then share one item aloud with your partner, saying, "This is a trigger for me." Keep it short; this is data gathering, not a therapy session.

Stress-Reduction Strategies (Practical, tested, and simple)

Building on the stress-reduction strategies discussed above, here are specific techniques:

- Mindfulness: Try a 1minute body scan—notice where tension sits, then breathe out; or the 54321 grounding technique, naming 5 things you see, 4 you hear, 3 you feel, 2 you smell, 1 you taste. See the self care section for short, practical exercises.

- Deep breathing: Paced, intentional breathing can create a pause before you respond to a stress or. Refer to the self care section for specific patterns and instructions.

Physical activity: Short walks or brief, focused bursts of movement can help reset your nervous system. Practical routines and recommendations are provided in the Self Care section.

- Social support: Create a mini support plan. Who gets a online text: "Need ten minutes" when something spikes? Name that person now.

Self-love Techniques for Men and Women Who Served

Below is a specific technique tailored to the topic of self-love discussed in the previous section:

- For men: Practice progressive muscle relaxation before bed—clench shoulders, then release—three sets. It signals your body that tension can be turned off.

- For women: Try grounding with the "54321" technique (name five things you see, four things you feel, etc.) in situations that feel crowded or loud. This technique shifts focus from overwhelming sensations to concrete sensory details, calming the nervous system and fostering a sense of control.

Both: set a "do not disturb" buffer on your phone for an hour after returning home to reduce immediate demands.

When to Reach Out — The "Red Flag" Check

After reviewing the red flag indicators in the previous section, if you're using the breathing, walks, and heart-to-heart check-ins and still find you're avoiding places you used to enjoy, having trouble sleeping more than a few weeks, or feeling numb around your partner, that's a signal to get professional support. Reaching out is strength; professionals offer tools that speed recovery.

Practicing Self-Care: Short Prompts

Here's a practical example that builds on those prompts:

- The "Love Tank" Check: Once a week, with your partner, each names one thing that filled their tank this week and one thing that drained it. This helps you see what made you feel seen and what you'd like more of.

- Ranking Needs: Each partner ranks their top three self care needs by impact (e.g., quiet time, help with bills, date night). Swap lists, agree on two small actions you can do this week.

Building on the idea of ranking needs as a self care practice, final thought: transition brings stress, but with identification of triggers, practical coping steps, and clear support plans, you can lower the spikes and give each other room to heal. Small, repeatable practices create stability; use them out loud, together, and with a little humour when you can.

Building a new daily routine post-service

Embracing Flexibility and Building a New Routine

These anchors are foundational self-care practices and are also addressed in the self-care section.

These anchors are foundational self care practices that keep you steady when the rest of your day varies. For example, schedule a fixed start time for a shared hobby but let its length vary, and pair that with a personal wind down anchor—such as a 10 minute journal or a solo walk—to honour individual recharge.

Treat these anchors as foundational self-care practices; you'll find them explored further in the self-care section.

- Physical activity – Treat it like a "duty time" on your phone calendar. Schedule two 30 minute sessions each week: a purposeful walk at 0700 and a 20 minute kettle bell set (three times a week) or a local intramural team. Treat these as non-negotiable duties so the shared wins and stress reduction become automatic.

- Physical activity – Aim for a short, daily movement: a 10 minute walk, stretching routine, or a simple bodyweight set. Small, consistent movement stabilizes energy and sleep.

Having identified your foundational anchors, you can now enrich them with quiet reflection. Use reflection prompts to assess whether each anchor effectively balances the joy of shared hobbies with respect for personal space, adjusting as needed. If you're looking to integrate physical activity, aim for a short, daily movement—such as a 10 minute walk, a brief stretching routine, or a simple bodyweight set—without the need for a gym or special equipment.

- Quiet reflection – Try a two minute breathing check when you wake up and a five minute journal prompt at bedtime. Prompt example: "One thing I handled well today" and "One thing I'll try tomorrow."

Combine this quiet reflection with physical activity and reading as a cohesive self-care routine.

Try a two minute breathing check each morning and a five minute journal prompt at bedtime—e.g., "One thing I handled well today" and "One thing I'll try tomorrow." Pair that quiet reflection with physical activity and reading to create a cohesive self care routine. Jot the emotion you felt, the trigger, your response, and a lesson you learned.

As these anchors create a predictable skeleton for your day, they also serve as essential elements of your self care plan; they are discussed further in the self care section.

- Reading – Set a five page minimum each night. That's small, measurable, and doable even after a long day. Choose a mix—one practical book, one novel to give the brain different kinds of rest.

These are core self-care practices.

Read a minimum of five pages each night.

Choose a mix—one practical book, one novel—to give the brain a different kind of rest.

Use these prompts as intentional self-care tools; answer them privately and revisit regularly. These reflective habits are also part of the self-care section.

- Which two anchors could you commit to this week?
- Treat the anchors you choose as self-care commitments.
- Choose anchors and put them in the calendar now.
- Blocking time for them is a practical self-care action.

Blocking time for anchors in your calendar—a practical self care action—prepares you to recreate shared rhythms.

Co-Creating Shared Rhythms

Co-creating rhythms with household members or colleagues supports these self-care anchors and increases the likelihood they'll stick.

By co creating rhythms that honour both needs, you lay a shared framework that naturally embeds each partner's self care practices, making them easier to maintain and less likely to be overlooked.

Applying that collaborative rhythm to the kitchen, here are some mealtime practices that weave self care into everyday nourishment:

- Meal times: Aim for at least three shared meals each week. When schedules differ, set Sunday dinner as a sacred, low pressure tradition. Rotate cooking duties to keep it enjoyable.
- Daily partner check-in: Use the "state of the tank" prompt—each partner reports emotional and practical "tank" status, shares one win, one challenge, and the next day's top three priorities. This routine establishes a shared emotional language and a sense of safety by making feelings visible and predictable.
- Probed routine: Follow it with a calming probed routine (dim lights, screens in a basket, 10 minutes of chat) that reinforces nightly self care.
- Weekly mission brief: Schedule a weekly "mission brief" dinner for deeper discussion, anchoring the rhythm framework.

Building on the shared rhythms we've set up with daily partner check-ins and meal times, let's transition to the "Love Tank" Check, a practice that turns self care into a tangible, shared metric.

- Tonight: each partner rates their current love tank on a 1-10 scale and suggests one small action—such as a hug, a brief phone call, or a quick chore—to help the other tomorrow. This nightly micro-check of the "Love Tank Check" keeps both partners attuned.

Prioritizing Non Negotiable Self Care

As we discussed earlier, prioritizing self care as a non-negotiable part of your routine is essential. Treat the three core habits—sleep, nutrition, and social connection as mission critical tasks that you cannot skip. Pick one routine for each habit and stick to it every day. Sleep—aim to be in bed between 10:30 p.m.–11:30 p.m. and wake within 30 minutes of that target most days; food—follow a simple rule of two meals each day, each containing a vegetable and a protein; social connection; schedule a regular catchup with a friend or veteran buddy (coffee or video call) so you keep your social muscles active.

Ranking Needs

- Identify top three self care needs
- Each partner writes their top three self care needs for the next month, ranking them by expected impact.
- Add a one sentence reason for each need.
- Compare the lists
- Line up the items side-by-side.
- Mark common needs and note any unique ones.
- Choose two concrete actions, document them, set a reminder.
- Discuss priorities
- Discuss why each partner prioritised their top choice.
- Select concrete actions
- Choose two concrete actions that address both partners' highest impact needs.
- Examples include carving out quiet time, offering to handle a bill, or scheduling a short date night.
- Document and follow up
- Document the agreed actions.

- Set a reminder to check in on progress next week.

Ranking Needs

- After ranking your needs, use the shared rhythm you've created to decide which self care need to prioritize, ensuring both partners agree on a single focus for the coming week.
- Morning routine: Replace roll call with a short practice—5 min of mobility, 5 min of planning, and one quick win (make the bed). It signals readiness.
- Marking dates: Commemorate your transition anniversary with a handwritten note to yourself or a small ceremony—maybe a favourite meal or a hike to a meaningful spot.
- List your top three self care needs and rank them by impact. Which one will you safeguard first?
- List your top three self care needs and rank them by impact. Decide which one you will safeguard first.
- Schedule when you will do them: put them in your calendar now.

After deciding which self care need to prioritize, test new rituals that reinforce that choice. For example, if the chosen need is sleep, you might add a nightly wind down ritual—no screens 30 minutes before bed, a short stretch, and a gratitude note. If the need is social connection, schedule a recurring video catchup with a friend. These rituals become part of your shared rhythm, keeping self care front and centre.

Choose two concrete connection actions, document them, and set reminders.

- Choose: pick two specific actions — one small daily practice (for example, a 2 minute appreciation or a brief "Love Tank" check) and one weekly shared activity (for example, a twice monthly date night or a 45 minute mini date at home).
- Document: write the chosen actions where you both can see them (shared calendar, notes app, or a visible checklist) and note who will lead each action.

- Schedule: create recurring calendar events and reminders so the actions happen predictably and consistently.
- Review: after two weeks, briefly check how the actions are going, adjust as needed, and recommit to the plan.

Daily 5 (share two things):

- Tomorrow – what you're doing next day.
- Highlight – one moment from today that made you smile, helped you overcome a challenge, taught you a new skill, or was a favourite memory.
- Need – if you prefer sharing a need, name something you'd like support with (e.g., help on a task, a decision you're weighing, or a request for more quality time or listening).
- "Appreciate, Schedule, Anchor" prompt:
- Appreciate – say something you appreciate about your partner.
- Schedule – set a brief catchup or a task to tackle together.
- Anchor – agree on a single takeaway or action to carry into the next day.
- Keep the whole check-in under five minutes.

This is a streamlined version of the "Love Tank Check."

- Try a new recipe together using pantry staples.
- Have a boardgames or card game marathon.
- Build a blanket fort and watch a classic movie.
- Do a DIY spa night with homemade face masks and scented candles.
- Visit a free museum or art gallery on a designated free entry day.
- Explore a local farmers market or street fair.
- Have a "back to school" snack night where you make fun finger

foods.

- Stroll in the park and share a small picnic.
- Host a themed karaoke night at home.

Every few months, plan a short weekend getaway or even a one night motel reset to break routine and make new memories. Whether it's a mini date or an overnight trip, schedule it in advance, rotate who plans it, and protect the time. This rhythm is part of the "Love Tank Check" and helps refill emotional reserves.

- Small experiments, repeated, become habits.
- Pick one anchor, one shared rhythm, and one ritual to try this week.
- To keep momentum, jot the anchor, rhythm, and ritual in a simple log or app, marking each day you hit the target, and celebrate each milestone with a small reward—perhaps a favourite coffee, a short walk, or a brief moment of silence.
- After six weeks, schedule a check-in to see what's working and what needs change.

Steady steps and small agreements make civilian life feel less like a free for all and more like a life you can predict, shape, and actually enjoy. This process is the "Love Tank Check" in action.

Sleep, grounding, and mental health basics

Prioritizing Sleep and Mental Health for a Healthy Reintegration

Building on the emphasis of prioritizing sleep and mental health, sleep is a cornerstone of stress management; this section outlines why you should prioritize it early in your journey.

The Impact of Sleep Deprivation on Close Partnerships

Understanding sleep deprivation's impact early aligns with stress management principles.

Prioritizing sleep—making it a non-negotiable part of your routine—is essential; without it, relationships can suffer.

Prioritizing sleep—making it a non-negotiable part of your routine—is essential; without it, relationships can suffer.

Early in your reintegration, consider these effects as part of stress management.

- Increased irritability and emotional reactivity: little things feel huge.
- Decreased empathy and understanding: it's harder to step into each other's shoes.
- Poor communication and conflict resolution: words get harsher; tone gets clipped.
- Reduced intimacy and connection: tired bodies, tired brains, less interest in closeness.

Quick Practical Fixes for Better Sleep

Implementing these fixes early supports stress management and overall well-being.

Building on the Quick Fixes: Consistency Is Key

Quick Practical Fixes for Better Sleep

- Create a wind down routine – Establish a consistent pre sleep ritual (e.g., reading or gentle stretching). A predictable routine cues your nervous system to shift into rest mode, making it easier to fall asleep.

- Limit blue light exposure – Turn off screens at least an hour before bed. Blue light suppresses melatonin, the hormone that regulates sleep cycles, so reducing exposure helps your body produce the right amount.

- Keep the bedroom cool and dark – Aim for 60–67 °F (15–19 °C) and use blackout curtains or a sleep mask. Cooler temperatures and minimal light signal your body that it's time to sleep, improving sleep quality.

- Watch caffeine and alcohol – Avoid stimulants after mid afternoon and limit alcohol to no more than one drink before bedtime. Both can disrupt sleep architecture, causing lighter, less restorative sleep.

- Exercise earlier in the day – Regular activity promotes deeper sleep, but vigorous workouts close to bedtime can raise core body temperature and keep you alert.

These quick fixes are not just tricks; each targets a specific physiological cue that drives sleep onset and maintenance. Consistency turns them into habits, making the benefits long lasting.

- Pick a target bedtime and wake time and stick with them, even on weekends.

- Avoid naps that last longer than 20 minutes, especially in the late afternoon.

- Use a "safety net" cue: set an alarm to remind you when it's time to prepare for sleep.

- Treat your sleep plan like a mission: hold yourself accountable and celebrate small wins.

Begin with consistency, a principle also critical in stress management.

Choose a consistent bedtime and wake time—even on weekends—and treat this routine like a mission: hold yourself accountable and celebrate small wins while grounding the practice in the stress management principle of consistency.

To find your personal sweet spot, note the times you feel most rested after a night's sleep and the times you naturally fall asleep when left to yourself. Set a bedtime that allows you to get 7–9 hours before that wake time. For example, if you feel most alert at 6 am, aim for a 10–11 pm bedtime. Create a wind down routine—such as reading or gentle stretching—to cue your nervous system into rest mode, making it easier to fall asleep. Ask yourself a quick self assessment: "When do I naturally feel sleepy?" And "When do I feel refreshed after waking?" The answers will help you lock in realistic, sustainable sleep targets.

Limit naps to 20 minutes, especially in the late afternoon, and turn off screens at least one hour before bedtime to support melatonin production.

- Build a short bedtime routine: dim lights, quiet the house for 30 minutes, read a paper book or listen to a slow podcast.

- Create a 30 minute wind down routine—dim lights, quiet the house, read a paper book, or listen to a slow podcast, and set a recurring alarm to remind you to power down screens.

- Keep the bedroom cool, dark, and quiet—aim for 60–67 °F (15–19 °C), use blackout curtains, a fan or white noise machine, and a sleep mask if needed.

- Build a short bedtime routine: dim lights, quiet the house for

30 minutes, read a paper book or listen to a slow podcast.

Treat your sleep plan like a mission—hold yourself accountable and celebrate small wins.

Ensure the bedroom is cool, dark, and quiet (60–67 °F). Invest in blackout curtains and a fan or white noise machine if needed.

- Early day exercise: Begin each morning with 10–20 minutes of light aerobic movement—brisk walking, gentle stretching, or a short yoga sequence—to lower stress hormones, boost mood, and ground your attention for the day ahead.

- Exercise earlier in the day – Regular activity promotes deeper sleep and helps regulate stress hormones. Vigorous workouts close to bedtime can raise core body temperature and keep you alert, counteracting the calming effect of grounding practices. Aim for light to moderate activity in the morning or early afternoon to support both sleep quality and stress relief.

A brief overview of grounding: simple practices that return attention to the present so you can respond rather than react. This section offers high-level context; detailed, step-by-step grounding exercises are presented in the practical self-care material.

Grounding is a set of simple practices that bring your attention back to the present, allowing you to respond rather than react. Detailed, step by step grounding exercises are provided in the practical self care material.

- Deep breathing: use slow, paced breaths to steady your heart rate and nervous system; grounding with this practice helps anchor the mind and calm the nervous system. (Detailed breathing exercises are provided in the practical self-care material.)

- Progressive muscle relaxation: briefly tense and then release major muscle groups to reduce physical tension; guided sequences are available in the practical self-care material. Short mindfulness practices: one- to three-minute breath checks or sensory scans during a break to reset attention; longer guided practices are found in the practical self-care material.

- Exercise earlier in the day—light to moderate activity in the morning or early afternoon promotes deeper sleep and regulates stress hormones.

Prioritizing Mental Health Without the Shame

As we move from the principle of prioritizing mental health without shame, let us look at practical ways to make it a reality. Seeking help is courage in plain clothes. That includes talking with friends, using counselling resources, or seeing a therapist. Small routine practices keep you steady too: for instance, schedule a weekly "reset" activity that brings you joy—gardening, woodworking, running drills at the gym, painting. Practice self compassion by noting one thing you did well when a plan falls apart. Challenge negative thoughts with a quick reality check: rate how likely the worst case thought actually is, then list two facts that contradict it. For example, if you think 'I will fail', rate the likelihood on a scale of 1–10, then write down two facts that prove otherwise, such as 'I have succeeded before' and 'I prepared thoroughly'.

Developing Healthy Coping Mechanisms — Practical Ideas

Building on the ideas introduced in the previous section, "Developing Healthy Coping Mechanisms — Practical Ideas", here are concrete habits to replace numbing behaviours:

- Swap numbing habits for life holding habits:
- These habits build on the ideas from the previous section, "Developing Healthy Coping Mechanisms — Practical Ideas":
- Swap numbing habits for life holding habits. Life holding habits are activities that nourish your mind, body, and relationships, helping you feel present and energized. For example:
- Daily movement: a 30 minute walk, a short yoga routine, or a home workout that gets your blood flowing.
- Mindful breathing or meditation: a few minutes of focused breathing to reset the nervous system.

- Creative expression: drawing, writing, playing music, or crafting something that feels meaningful.
- Social connection: a phone call with a friend, a quick coffee meet up, or a group hobby that keeps you linked to others.
- Skill building: learning a new language, practicing a musical instrument, or working on a personal project that expands your capabilities.
- Journalling prompt: "What three things went okay today?" Write quickly for five minutes.

These habits build on the ideas from the previous section, "Developing Healthy Coping Mechanisms — Practical Ideas".

Swap numbing habits for life holding habits:

- Daily movement: take a 30 minute walk, do a short workout, or stretch each day to boost energy and mood.
- Mindful breathing: practice a 5 minute breath focus routine to calm the nervous system.
- Creative expression: journal, draw, play music, or engage in a hobby that brings joy.
- Social connection: reach out to a friend or family member, join a community group, or volunteer to strengthen bonds.
- Skill building: dedicate time to learning a new skill or deepening an existing one, whether it's cooking, coding, or a language.
- Journalling prompt: end each day with a reflective prompt such as, "What moments made me feel alive today, and why?"

Swap numbing habits for life holding habits

Life holding habits are activities that nourish your mind, body, and relationships, helping you feel present and energized.

- Example: Take a 15 minute walk, practice mindful breathing, or share a meal with a friend.

Journal Prompt

"What three things went okay today?" Write quickly for five minutes.

- Create a music list for different moods—workout, chill, or "I need to calm down right now."
- Move together: a partner walk or partner stretch session replaces scrolling and reconnects you.
- Reach out: set a weekly call with a civilian friend and a weekly check-in with a military buddy.

These habits build on the ideas from the previous section, "Developing Healthy Coping Mechanisms — Practical Ideas":

- Daily movement: a 30 minute walk, a short yoga routine, or a home workout that gets your blood flowing.
- Move together: a partner walk or partner stretch session replaces scrolling and reconnects you.
- Move together: Engage in low impact, steady pace movement such as walking, gentle yoga, or tai chi.
- Move Together: a partner walk or partner stretch session replaces scrolling and reconnects you.

These habits build on the ideas from the previous section, "Developing Healthy Coping Mechanisms — Practical Ideas": practice mindful breathing or meditation—a few minutes of focused breathing to reset the nervous system—and reach out by setting a reminder to contact a trusted friend, family member, or counsellor at least once a week—e.g., a brief phone call or supportive text on Friday evenings—to share how you're feeling and receive encouragement.

- Reach out: set a weekly call with a civilian friend and a weekly check-in with a military buddy.

Reintegration Reflection:

- Move together: partner walks, stretches, or shared chores to rebuild connection.

- Move Together: Combine the previously separate "Move Together" suggestions into a single coordinated activity that includes shared physical movement and cooperative tasks — for example, a group walk, gentle stretching or dance, paired exercises, and collaborative chores — to help rebuild connection, rhythm, and mutual support during reintegration.

- Creative expression: drawing, writing, playing music, or crafting something that feels meaningful.

Building on your Reintegration Reflection, tonight's focus is:

- Tonight, rank your sleep habits from 1–5 and choose one small change for the week (bedtime, screen curfew, room adjustment).

- With your partner: once a week do a "Love Tank Check" —

- Rate your love tank on a scale of 1–10.

- Each names one thing that filled their tank and one that drained it; keep responses brief and non-judgemental.

- Choose a specific small action that can boost your tank, such as:
- Sharing a short 5 minute gratitude note,

- Planning a 15 minute walk together, or

- Setting a daily 2 minute reflection ritual.

You don't have to fix everything all at once. Small, steady changes to sleep and stress care make you calmer, kinder, and more available to the people you love. You got this—one restful night at a time.

Role negotiation and household responsibilities

Rebuilding Domestic Harmony: Equitable Household Responsibilities

By first defining clear expectations about who does what, you lay the groundwork for a workable system that ensures responsibilities are shared fairly.

Rebuilding domestic harmony, you can make the chore chart a daily ritual—e.g., start each day together with a quick 5 minute review of the colour coded chart, assigning tasks and celebrating completion with a shared toast. This turns the routine of household chores into a tangible, shared practice that reinforces partnership.

Start by articulating the expectations for each role; when these are explicit, they become the building blocks of a functional household system.

These practices dovetail with the daily rituals you create together, helping to weave a new routine that feels fair and sustainable.

From Military Structure to Mutual Partnership

Start by articulating expectations. Capture them in a simple mission sheet or checklist and fold them into shared rituals. This concise framework keeps everyone aligned, ensures clarity of purpose, and embeds accountability into everyday practices.

Start by articulating expectations for each role. When responsibilities are explicit, they become the building blocks of a functional household system. Capture them in a simple mission sheet or checklist, then fold that document into the rituals you practice together — a shared morning run-through, an evening review, or a weekly planning session. By translating structured check lists into shared rituals, you turn discipline into a joint practice that reinforces a routine which feels fair, sustainable, and strengthens your partnership.

Imagine Sarah and Tom, a military couple, who started their day at dawn with a rigorous training schedule. While Tom was up early for a 5am briefing, Sarah was trying to catch up on sleep after her night shift on the base medical unit. Their calendars were a collage of mission briefings, flight deck rotations, and family appointments, each ticking at different tempos. One evening, after a hectic week of deployments, they sat on the porch with mugs of coffee, realizing that their routines were out of sync. They decided to map out their schedules side by side, marking where their obligations overlapped and where they could carve out shared time. By naming these differences and planning together, they turned a potential source of friction into a collaborative partnership that strengthened both their relationship and their readiness for service.

The transition begins by negotiating expectations; these agreements naturally evolve into a practical system that mirrors the reliability of military organization but serves a partnership.

By translating structured check lists into shared rituals, you can turn discipline into a joint practice that strengthens partnership.

After moving from strict military schedules to a cooperative partnership, the next step is to see how daily routines influence your shared life. Identify the differences: one partner may be accustomed to fixed shifts, check lists, and clear roles ("you do this, I do that"), while the other has managed many home tasks alone. Discuss these roles without judgment—think of it as a practical briefing, not a court martial. List who handles groceries, vehicle maintenance, bills, child pickup, pet care, and home repairs, and arrange them in a simple task sheet.

Once you have outlined these differences, use them to define expectations, which then form the blueprint for a daily system of shared duties.

As you draft this mission sheet, weave it into the rituals you'll practice each day to reinforce the new routine.

Reintegration Reflection

Use reflection not only to understand past roles but also to crystallize expectations that will drive a sustainable household system.

Use reflection not only to understand past roles but also to crystallize expectations that will drive a sustainable household system. Building on the ideas presented in Reintegration Reflection, the most powerful way to translate reflection into shared action is to pair it with rituals you establish together. For example, try journalling or a structured conversation to crystallize expectations.

By embedding the defined expectations into those rituals, you create a living system that keeps responsibilities balanced.

Discussing Expectations and Resentments

Explicitly mapping expectations uncovers resentments and, once addressed, gives you the clarity needed to establish a clear, workable system for daily tasks.

Addressing expectations and resentments becomes a shared practice when integrated with the daily rituals you cultivate as a couple.

List five household tasks you currently do most days. Which two tasks feel most draining? Which one gives you satisfaction?

Make a dedicated time to talk—20 minutes, uninterrupted, no scoring. Each partner speaks for five minutes while the other listens. Use "I" statements: "I felt burned out handling X" instead of "You left me to do X." If resentment has built up, name it; naming clears fog and stops passive aggressive logrolling. List the chores you find draining or satisfying, and ask why each feels that way—this insight helps address underlying issues. Use this 5 minute ritual regularly to name resentments and examine chores.

When the expectations are clearly stated, you can design a system that allocates tasks smoothly, preventing future resentment.

Pair this conversation with a ritual you perform together each week, so the dialogue remains a living habit.

This ritual should reinforce the expectations that underpin the system of shared responsibilities, keeping it dynamic and responsive.

Defining Expectations and Creating a System

By articulating and agreeing on expectations, you immediately craft a practical system that organizes household duties, ensuring both partners feel heard and accountable.

Turn your task list into a living plan. Options:

□Make the plan a shared ritual—review it together at the same time each week so the system becomes a routine part of your partnership.

□Use the plan as a cue to launch your daily rituals, aligning responsibilities with shared moments of connection.

By articulating and agreeing on expectations, you immediately craft a practical system that organizes household duties, ensuring both partners feel heard and accountable. Turn your task list into a living plan. Options:

□A shared digital chore chart that uses a visual board—think of a Trellolike grid with colour coded cards and a rotating schedule that everyone can update in real time.

- Chore chart on the fridge with weekdays and responsibilities.

This visual cue can double as a ritual trigger, reminding you to check in on your shared routine each day.

- Shared calendar reminders for bill payments, car checks, and doctor visits.

Integrating these reminders into your daily rituals keeps financial and health responsibilities as shared habits.

- Task swaps: If one partner hates mowing but doesn't mind dishes, trade accordingly.
- Set up a two week trial:
- Assign tasks.
- Hold a review.
- Ensure skills are taught, such as a quick tutorial on:
- How to fold laundry the "right" way.
- How to change the oil.

(This helps avoid future complaints.)

- Support the task swap idea:
- Set up a shared tracker (for example, a Google Sheet) where employees log swaps.
- Use a rotation schedule or swap points to keep fairness and prevent overburdening anyone.

Ranking Needs

To operational the ranking of needs discussed in the previous section, each partner follows this method:

- Each partner lists household areas (cleaning, cooking, finance, childcare, yard) with a priority rank from 1 (highest) to 5 (lowest). Next, compare the two lists by summing the priority scores for each area; the partner with the lower total for an area takes primary responsibility, while the other serves as backup. If the totals are equal, discuss and negotiate until a consensus is reached.

The Importance of Flexibility and Compromise

Building on the importance of flexibility and compromise discussed in the previous section, here are concrete ways to weave those principles into your daily routine. Life throws new orders—new job, schooling, physical therapy. When you build your daily routine, leave room for these changes. Add a "sick week" rule: if one partner is overwhelmed, the other steps up for seven days without score keeping. For example, if Partner A is on a long recovery after surgery and can't cook or clean for a week, Partner B takes over meals, laundry, and yard work for those seven days, and no points are recorded for that period. A points system can also help—tasks earn points, and when one partner racks up too many, the other accepts extra points to equalize. For instance, washing dishes earns 2 points, vacuum 3, and mowing the lawn 5. If Partner A earns 15 points in a month and Partner B earns 8, Partner B would take on an extra chore or two to bring the totals closer. Schedule a monthly household review: ask "Are you feeling supported around the house?" And rate from 0–10. If either score is under 6, schedule a 30 minute reset: swap tasks, adjust expectations, or bring in outside help (cleaner, lawn service) for a short burst.

The 'Love Tank' Check

Use it as a weekly pulse to gauge how the shared routine is affecting each partner's emotional capacity. Adjust tasks if the score drops.

Revisiting and Adjusting Responsibilities

First, reflect on the Love Tank check to understand how the routine is affecting your emotional balance.

After setting your daily routine, schedule a check-in to tweak the split of chores. Look for patterns that cause resentment and refine the schedule so it stays fair and realistic.

First, conduct a brief "Love Tank Check" to gauge how your routine is affecting your emotional balance. Then set a recurring "household review" on your calendar — 30 minutes monthly. Connect it to your daily routine: look at what's working, what's brewing resentment, and what needs a new plan. Small adjustments now prevent bigger blow ups later.

Now that your monthly household review is set, follow this quick script for each check-in:

- Start with the Love Tank Check—rate your current emotional balance on a 1-10 scale.
- Review the household review agenda: list what's working, what's brewing resentment, and any new tasks.
- Adjust the chore split if patterns of resentment surface.
- Confirm the plan for the next month.

This keeps the review grounded in practical, fair, and realistic adjustments.

Quick script for a check-in

Use this short script during your routine check-in to keep conversations focused and productive.

Effective communication involves sharing direct, needs based statements and responsive offers. Example: Partner A says, "I'm feeling tapped at a 4 this week because of work hours." Partner B responds, "Okay — I can take two week day dinners can handle Saturday yardwork for the next two weeks."

Effective communication involves sharing direct, needs based statements and responsive offers. Example: Partner A says, "I'm feeling tapped at a 4 this week because of work hours." Partner B responds, "Okay — I can take two weekday dinners and handle Saturday yardwork for the next two weeks."

Try practicing this exchange as a brief role-play: give each partner a role, rehearse the dialogue, then switch roles. Make this exchange a regular part of your daily routine to keep energy levels aligned.

Wrap up prompt:

At the end of each routine review, ask yourself: What did we learn? What will we try next week? Fit this reflection into the rhythm of your daily routine.

Building on the wrap up prompts,

- Schedule your first 20 minute household chat, create a simple chore list, and nail down two changes to try for 14 days.

Do this as part of setting your initial daily routine.

Practical teamwork at home is less about perfect fairness and more about reliable sharing. With honest talk, clear assignments, and periodic review, you'll get to a cadence that works for both of you — no orders needed. Keep a simple log of who does what and pause to celebrate each task you finish together.

Fit this cadence into your daily routine and let it evolve naturally.

Financial literacy and benefits navigation for transition

Having set up a rhythm for sharing at home, you're ready to tackle the next essential area:

Addressing these foundational topics early in your transition helps you navigate the challenges that come with leaving military life—home repairs, grocery budgets, mortgage timelines—and the unfamiliar financial terrain many veterans face. Think of it not as an overwhelming obstacle, but as a solvable mission. Together, we'll chart a clear strategy and give you quick prompts you can use solo or with your partner.

Navigating Income Changes and Building a Civilian Budget

Action example:

Start by mapping your cash flow for the past three months—every pay check and every bill, plus irregular costs such as vehicle maintenance, licensing, and training.

- Start by mapping your actual cash flow for three months—every pay check, every bill, and irregular costs (vehicle maintenance, licensing, training).
- Use a ready made spreadsheet template such as the free Google Sheets "Personal Cash Flow Tracker" (or create your own) with columns for Date, Category, Income, Expense, and Running Balance.
- Create a three column list—Fixed (rent/mortgage, utilities), Variable (groceries, gas), Irregular (uniforms, vet bills).
- Track for 90 days, then draft a budget that keeps a cushion equal to one month of fixed expenses.

Veteran Specific Benefits: Use What's Available

As you consider the veteran specific benefits mentioned earlier, these foundational topics are best addressed early in your transition. Programs designed for people who served—including education support, home loan programs, and VA medical services—can change the financial picture significantly, but often require paperwork and patience.

These foundational topics are best addressed early in your transition. Concrete steps:

- For education: gather your discharge paperwork and school acceptance letters before applying for GI Bill benefits so you avoid back and forth delays.
- For a VA home loan: talk to a VA loan officer early. Even if you plan to rent at first, knowing your entitlement and certificate of eligibility helps you plan credit and savings goals.
- For healthcare: list current medical needs and check what the VA covers vs. Private insurance gaps.
- For a VA home loan: talk to a VA loan officer early. Ask about your current entitlement, the minimum credit score required, and how much you need to save for a down payment. Bring your recent pay stubs, W2s, a copy of your credit report, and your Certificate of Eligibility (COE).
- For healthcare: list current medical needs and check what the VA covers vs. Private insurance gaps.

Creating a Joint Financial Plan with Your Partner

Building on the joint financial plan you created earlier, the next step is to address money fights. Money fights are often about mismatched assumptions. Make the money talk routine concrete by following these steps:

- Schedule a recurring 30 minute meeting on the first Sunday of every month.
- Follow this simple agenda:

- Review bills due this month.
- Track progress on goals.
- Decide on one financial decision for the upcoming month.
- Use a shared spreadsheet or a dedicated app that lists net income, who paid what, and the current emergency fund balance.
- If you need external help, schedule a call with a VA or financial counsellor by the end of the week and pick a firm date.

This routine establishes the foundation that will be expanded in the next section on shared tasks.

- One partner handles bill payments, the other handles savings and investments.
- Swap roles every six months.
- After each swap, hold a joint review meeting where both partners discuss what they learned and set goals for the next period.
- This shared reflection ensures that both partners actively acquire the skills, not just one.

Ranking Your Financial Priorities

Ranking Needs:

- Write down goals
- Three short term goals (for example, pay off a credit card, build a \$3 k emergency fund, save \$5 k for a car).
- Three long term goals (house down payment, retirement account, education fund).
- Score each goal
- Assign a score from 1 to 5 for urgency and a score from 1 to 5 for impact.
- Multiply the two scores to get a priority score.

- Order the goals
- Arrange the goals from highest to lowest priority.
- Agree on concrete actions
- Decide how much extra money each month will go toward the top ranked goal (for instance, $200 toward the credit card payoff).
- Set a realistic deadline.

We now build on the idea of developing financial skills by exploring the specific vocabulary of civilian finance. This area includes credit scores, APRs, and the choice between Roth and traditional retirement accounts. Pick one topic a month to study.

Civilian finance has its own vocabulary—credit scores, APRs, Roth vs. Traditional retirement accounts. Pick one topic a month to study, such as credit scores. Read a concise guide, then put the following steps into practice:

- Check your score
- Correct errors
- Lower credit utilization

When you're ready to tackle debt, choose a strategy: use the "snowball" (smallest balance first) or "avalanche" (highest interest first) method—pick one and commit. To make the learning stick, turn it into a challenge: invite a friend, create a short quiz, or track your progress in a shared spreadsheet so you can compare notes and celebrate milestones together.

Insurance: What You'll Need Outside Military Coverage

Having addressed the insurance needs outside military coverage, you might wonder when professional guidance becomes essentialist get help: Professional Guidance

A financial advisor who understands military transitions can speed things up and prevent costly mistakes. Look for accredited counsellors who have experience with VA programs and veteran finances—search the VA Office of Financial Management, the National Association of Personal Financial Advisors (NAPFA) directory, or the Military Friendly network. Qualified advisors often hold certifications such as CFP, CLU, or are registered VA financial planners. Even one session can help you map benefits, tax issues, and investment basics.

Now that you've explored the benefits of professional guidance, it's time to examine your insurance options. Look at three basic policies: health, life, and auto. If you're leaving a system that included certain coverage, list what gaps appear and get quotes from two providers before choosing. Term life insurance is usually straightforward and affordable for most veterans; compare quotes and beneficiaries during your monthly money meeting. The 'Money Map' Check:

- Do we have 3 months of spending saved?
- Who understands our VA benefits?
- What's our next financial goal?

To make this review actionable, use tools like the VA's benefits portal to track eligibility, a budgeting app such as Mint or YNAB to monitor savings, or a simple spreadsheet template to log and update your three month buffer.

These steps are practical, short, and repeatable. Use them with the household tools you already put in place—chore charts, monthly reviews, and honest conversations—to make the financial side of civilian life one less thing to argue about and one more thing you tackle together.

Accessing healthcare and mental health resources

Prioritizing Wellbeing through Effective Healthcare Navigation

Following the emphasis on wellbeing, let's dive into the practical steps of navigating healthcare. Okay—time for the part every caregiver and partner notices quickly: healthcare is its own mission set. If you've been helping a veteran through appointments, refill chaos, or one too many phone trees, this section is your field manual for getting the care you both need without burning out.

Understanding and Maximizing VA Healthcare System Benefits

Now that you understand the scope of VA benefits, the next step is to determine eligibility and enrolment. For example, John, a 38 year old Army veteran, pulled his DD214, called his local VA centre, and discovered he was already enrolled in dental and mental health benefits he hadn't realized. His quick check saved him months of paperwork.

First, make sure you know where your veteran stands with VA eligibility and enrolment. The VA healthcare system benefits go beyond primary care: mental health, dental, prosthetics, rehab, and Healthcare are all on the roster for those who qualify.

Practical steps:

- Pull out the veteran's service records and DD214.
- Have your social security number, current address, and phone number ready.
- Call the closest VA medical centre's enrolment office and ask, "What am I signed up for, and what do I need to change?"
- Ask about Healthcare options—many clinics now do video visits that save travel time and stress.

Reflection:

- List three VA healthcare system benefits you think apply to your partner.
- Call the enrolment office to confirm one of them today.

Exploring and Securing Suitable Civilian Healthcare Options and Insurance Plans

Building on the exploration of civilian options in the previous section, here are practical steps to evaluate and choose a plan. Some couples mix VA care and civilian providers—and that can be smart. When you look at Civilian healthcare options and insurance plans, compare networks to confirm that your preferred specialists are in network, out of pocket costs, and coverage for mental health or prosthetic care.

- Items to check:
- ACA marketplace plans for gaps if VA isn't available locally.
- VGLI for life insurance continuity after service.
- Concrete move:
- Set a 30 minute "insurance hour" where you compare two plans side-by-side—include premiums, deductibles, and a quick call to any specialist you need to keep seeing.

The "Ranking Needs" prompt: Rank healthcare priorities from 1–5 (primary care, mental health, specialty care, dental, prescriptions). After ranking, build a simple spreadsheet: list each plan in a column, each priority in a row, assign a score (e.g., 010) for how well the plan covers that priority, multiply by a weight that reflects the priority's importance, and sum the weighted scores. The plan with the highest total, or the one that meets your top three priorities most fully, is the logical choice. Discuss the results together, noting any trade offs, and agree on the final plan.

Recognizing the Critical Importance of Seeking Mental Health Support

As we highlighted in the previous section, recognizing the critical importance of seeking mental health support sets the stage for this next step. Mental health isn't optional. Whether it's PTSD, depression, or anxiety, early support makes a big difference. Both the VA and civilian therapists offer evidence based care—CBT, exposure therapy, medication management, and group therapy. If a veteran resists help, that's normal—it happens to many. Reframe the hesitation: going to therapy is mission preparation, a strategic asset that strengthens resilience, not a sign of weakness.

Love Tank Check (Mental Health Adaptation): A short, regular ritual to share what fills each partner's emotional "tank" and to plan concrete support when stress or crisis hits. How to do it:

- Start by asking a concrete, actionable question such as: "If you're feeling overwhelmed in the next hour, what would you like me to do right away?"
- Follow up with a specific trigger question: "When you notice your stress level rising, can you tell me what's causing it—work, home, or something else?"

These examples keep the focus on immediate, tangible steps the partner can take and the support the other can provide.

- Set aside a few minutes regularly (weekly, nightly, or whenever it feels useful).
- Ask two core prompts, one focused on everyday connection and one on stress/crisis:
- Regular prompt: "What helps me feel loved or connected?" (Or "What's one small thing I can do this week to fill your love tank?")
- Mental Health Edition prompt: "What helps me when I'm stressed?" And "If I'm in crisis, what are two specific things you can do to help me?"

- Each partner writes down two clear, actionable things the other can do in a crisis (examples: call and stay on the phone for 10 minutes, give 30 minutes of quiet time, help with a chore, bring a comforting item, or contact a trusted support person).
- Revisit and update these answers as needs change. Keep responses specific, practical, and non-judgemental.

Learning Practical Steps to Access Therapy and Counselling Services (Mental Health Adaptation). Building on the Love Tank Check, the following steps help partners navigate therapy and counselling services.

Learning Practical Steps to Access Therapy and Counseling Services (Mental Health Adaptation)

Building on the practical steps to access therapy discussed above, here are concrete actions you can take.

Start simple: call the VA mental health clinic or search for community therapists who accept your insurance. Ask whether they offer teletherapy. If you need quick help, consider peer support groups, crisis hotline, or online therapy platforms that connect you with licensed clinicians quickly. Create a small roster: primary care physician, at least one specialist, a mental health provider, and a pharmacy you trust. Keep contact info in one place (a paper card and a shared note on your phone). Include caregivers and support groups—these are part of the team too. Practical example: schedule a quarterly "care huddle"—a 20-minute check-in where you review prescriptions, upcoming appointments, and any care concerns.

Building a Trusted and Reliable Network of Healthcare Providers

Now that you've built a trusted network, the next step is to reach out for care. Start simple: call the VA mental health clinic, or search for community therapists who accept your insurance. Ask whether they offer teletherapy. If you need care quickly, consider interim options—peer support groups, crisis hotline, or online therapy platforms that connect you with licensed clinicians quickly. For instance, your partner could:

Tip: when contacting a therapist, ask if they have experience with military culture—small detail, big difference.

- Call the VA toll free number 18008271000 and request a mental health triage.
- Text 988 to the Suicide and Crisis Lifeline to start a chat with a trained volunteer.
- Open the VA Direct app to locate the nearest VA mental health clinic and schedule an appointment.

Tip: when contacting a therapist, ask if they have experience with military culture—small detail, big difference.

Create a small roster: primary care physician, at least one specialist, a mental health provider, and a pharmacy you trust. Keep contact info in one place (a paper card and a shared note on your phone). Include caregivers and support groups—these are part of the team too.

Practical example: schedule a quarterly "care huddle"—a 20-minute check-in where you review prescriptions, upcoming appointments, whether mental health supports are meeting needs, and any other care concerns.

Actively Engaging in Self Care and Preventative Health Measures

Self care keeps caregivers and veterans capable. Turn each routine—regular movement, decent sleep, and simple stress tools—into a personal reward instead of a chore. For example, after a five minute walk, treat yourself to a favourite podcast or a small snack; after a deep breath session, reward yourself with a few minutes of your favourite hobby. Routine screenings (blood pressure, cholesterol, dental checks) catch things early. For fitness, try partner based activities: a short hike, a mobility routine, or a weekly bike ride. When you and your partner maintain this foundation, you build the mental stamina needed for the job hunt, networking calls, and interviews that follow a deployment.

Learning Practical Steps to Access Therapy and Counselling Services

(Mental Health Adaptation). Building on the Love Tank Check, you can help your partner navigate healthcare by attending appointments together, keeping a shared medication list, and setting up reminders for follow up. This creates a stable home life and lets a partner focus on their own job search. The shared sense of well being reduces stress that otherwise hampers performance in new roles.

Schedule a quarterly "care huddle" to review progress. During each huddle, attend appointments together, keep a shared medication list, set reminders for follow up, celebrate small wins such as a week of good sleep or a successful therapy session, and connect with local caregiver groups for peer tips.

Caregiver Action Sheet: Pick one appointment to attend this month, set reminders for two medications, and join one support group meeting. Use this action sheet as a daily reminder that your own organization skills will translate to a structured résumé and interview preparation. Each completed step builds confidence for your career transition. Reflect on how these actions benefit both you and the veteran; consider how your organized approach supports their care and your own career goals.

Building on the practical steps outlined in the caregiver action sheet, here's how to navigate the larger healthcare system. Seeking care takes courage. When you and your partner use these steps—confirm VA benefits, compare civilian plans where needed, prioritize mental health, build a reliable provider network, and protect your own well being—you create a sustainable path to better health. Treat this as regular maintenance: small, repeated actions add up to big improvements. These habits of proactive health management also mirror the proactive planning required for a successful career shift.

Prioritized mental health resources:

- VA Suicide Prevention Lifeline: 988
- National Suicide Prevention Lifeline: 988
- Crisis Text Line: Text HOME to 741741
- Local crisis centre: 123-456-7890

Translating military skills to civilian work and identity

Re-framing Military Skills for Civilian Roles

You did hard things in service. Now the trick is making civilian employers see those hard things as exactly the strengths they want. This section turns military experience into clear, marketable assets and gives you quick, usable ways to talk about them—on a resume, in an interview, or at a networking event.

Identifying Transferable Skills

Start by listing what you actually did, not just your rank or MOS. Pick three examples for each skill and put numbers on them where possible.

Problem solving: Coordinated delivery of parts for 12 vehicles in 36 hours, reducing mission delay from 48 to 6 hours.

Leadership: Led a 10 person team, instituted weekly after action reviews and increased on time task completion by 25 %.

Communication: Developed a one page SOP that cut training time for new operators from 5 days to 3 days.

Translating Military Communication Styles

Civilian workplaces often expect softer edges when giving feedback or making requests. You don't have to lose clarity—just flex the style.

- Active listening practice: Try this in a meeting—repeat back a colleague's point in one sentence before offering your idea. ("So you're saying X; I think Y might help because…") It signals respect and cuts down on friction.

Editor note: Place this section near the book's discussion of translating military skills to civilian work and identity.

As discussed earlier, the key is to translate your hard service experiences into the strengths employers want. Treat this as an early framing step—turn your military experience into clear, marketable assets and use these quick, usable ways to talk about them on a resume, in an interview, or at a networking event. This framing is most effective when you are physically and mentally rested, so your communication is sharp and your confidence high.

Tip: when contacting a therapist, ask if they have experience with military culture—small detail, big difference.

Editor note: Place this paragraph near the material on translating military skills to civilian work and identity.

Identifying Transferable Skills

Begin here as one of your first steps in the transition process: inventory the capabilities you used that civilian employers value.

Editor note: This belongs alongside the section on translating military skills to civilian work and identity.

Having identified your transferable skills, start by listing what you actually did, not just your rank or MOS. For example, a combat engineer (MOS 12B) might phrase their experience as "construction and demolition specialist with 5 years of experience managing large scale projects and ensuring safety compliance." Do this early—make it one of your first tasks when preparing civilian materials. Pick three examples for each skill and put numbers on them where possible. Doing this while you practice self care routines—e.g., journalling after a workout—helps solidify memory and boosts your ability to articulate these skills under interview pressure.

Editor note: Include this guidance near the discussion of translating military skills to civilian work and identity.

- 42hour savings verified by cross checking shipment timestamps from the automated logistics system against on site receipt logs.
- Document examples like this up front so you can use the metrics in applications.
- The more you can quantify outcomes, the more persuasive your story becomes.
- When you approach this task with a clear head—after a restful sleep and a mindful breathing session—you're less likely to forget key figures and more likely to convey them confidently.

Editor note: Position this concrete example next to the section on translating military skills to civilian work and identity.

- Led a 10 person team.
- Instituted weekly after action reviews that began with a brief stand up.
- Used a shared template to capture lessons learned.
- Assigned owners to each action item.
- Tracked completion in a live dashboard.

These structured reviews reduced confusion, accelerated knowledge transfer, and increased on time task completion by 25 %. Capture these leadership outcomes early when building your resume and interview stories.

Editor note: Place this leadership example with the content on translating military skills to civilian work and identity.

- Reduced training time for new operators from 5 days to 3 days.

Editor note: Include this communication example near the section on translating military skills to civilian work and identity.

Translating Military Communication Styles

- Quantify results: people managed, budgets overseen, time saved, error rate reduced.

When Captain Lisa Nguyen transitioned from leading platoon briefings to consulting on corporate communication, she found that the same concise, mission oriented style that had kept her unit on point also made her reports crystal clear to executives. By cutting jargon and focusing on actionable next steps, her team's project turnaround time dropped from 12 weeks to 6 weeks, and client satisfaction scores rose by 15%. This quick adaptation demonstrates how disciplined communication can translate into measurable civilian success.

Address this early in your transition: adapting how you give feedback and make requests helps civilian employers see your communication as a strength.

Editor note: Place this guidance adjacent to the material on translating military skills to civilian work and identity.

Civilian workplaces often expect softer edges when giving feedback or making requests. You don't have to lose clarity—just flex the style. Start practicing these adjustments from the beginning of your civilian networking and onboarding.

Place this guidance near the translating military skills section.

- Active listening practice: Try this in a meeting—repeat back a colleague's point in one sentence before offering your idea (e.g., 'So you're saying X; I think Y might help because…'). This signals respect and cuts friction.

- Active listening practice: Try this in a meeting—repeat back a colleague's point in one sentence before offering your idea. ("So you're saying X; I think Y might help because…") It signals respect and cuts down on friction.

- 42hour savings verified by cross checking shipment timestamps with on site receipt logs.

- Collaboration prompt: Give one measurable example of cross unit work. ("Coordinated with logistics and medical teams to deliver X support to Y beneficiaries, showing ability to work across departments.").

Translating Military Experience into Civilian Success

The first step in this journey is to inventory your military skills and translate them into civilian language. Once you have a clear, concise mapping of those skills, you are ready to present them confidently to potential mentors.

- Replace service specific titles with plain English role descriptions. For example, instead of "squad leader" say "supervised a 10 person team responsible for operations and training, resulting in X outcome."

- Put a online impact statement under each position.

- Use numbers: people managed, budgets overseen, time saved, error rate reduced.

- Swap jargon for results. Quick swaps you can use: Use these swaps when talking to mentors to translate your experience into outcomes they understand.

Common military terms and civilian equivalents:

- Mission – Project goal

- Tactics – Operational plan

- Deployment – Implementation

- Briefing – Presentation

- Command – Leadership

- Use plain English role descriptions, e.g., instead of "squad leader" say "supervised a 10-person team responsible for operations and training, resulting in X outcome."

- Instead of listing equipment or acronyms, describe the skill:

"managed sensitive equipment maintenance schedules, reducing downtime by 15%."

- Branch courses often include technical certs or specialty tasks useful in civilian roles. Make those obvious.
- Short resume checklist:
- Convert every military title to a civilian friendly phrase.
- Include a quantified impact statement for each role.
- Highlight transferable skills and certifications earned.
- Replace equipment lists or acronyms with clear skill statements, such as "managed sensitive equipment maintenance schedules, reducing downtime by 15%."
- Include a short resume checklist to confirm all essential elements are covered.
- Replace service specific titles with plain English role descriptions.
- Add a online impact statement beneath each position, formatted consistently as: Impact: [concise, quantified result] (e.g., "Impact: Reduced training time for new operators from 5 days to 3 days.").
- Quantify results: specify number of people managed, budgets overseen (amount or percentage), time saved (hours or percentage), and reduction in error rates (absolute number or percentage).

Tip: When contacting a therapist, ask whether they have experience with military culture—small detail, big difference.

Recognizing the value of training: Technical angle – If you completed avionics, cybersecurity, or diesel engine training, list the exact systems or software and any certifications. Add an outcome: "conducted maintenance on C-130 avionics, lowering fault reports by 20%." Soft-skill angle – Highlight training scenarios that built leadership under pressure, cross culture communication, or project planning.

Before you can seek civilian mentors, the first step is to inventory your military skills and translate them into civilian language. The first step in this journey is to inventory your military skills and translate them into civilian language. Once you have a clear, concise mapping of those skills, you can present them confidently to potential mentors. When describing your experience, replace service specific titles with plain-English role descriptions—for example, instead of "squad leader" say "supervised a 10 person team responsible for operations and training, resulting in X outcome."

- Document examples up front so you can use the metrics in applications.

When describing your past roles, avoid military jargon and replace service specific titles with plain English role descriptions.

For example:

- "Combat Engineer" → "Construction Engineer" or "Project Manager – Field Construction"
- "Supply Officer" → "Supply Chain Manager"
- "Intelligence Analyst" → "Business Analyst"
- "Flight Crew" → "Operations Manager – Aviation"
- "Non-commissioned Officer" → "Team Leader" or "Operations Supervisor"

These translations help recruiters instantly recognize the relevance of your experience.

Additionally, highlight soft skills such as communication, adaptability, teamwork, leadership, and problem solving—qualities that may not be obvious in military roles but are highly valued in civilian ones. Discuss how your training and experiences have cultivated resilience, time management, and conflict resolution, positioning you as a well rounded candidate in the civilian workforce. Building on the collaboration example above, we now seek civilian mentors.

Seeking Civilian Mentors

Identify at least two civilian mentors: one in your target field and one in general professional development. Use your mapped skill set to seek mentors who can advise on averaging those skills, while another provides broader career guidance.

- When you approach this task with a clear head—after a restful sleep and a mindful breathing session—you're less likely to forget key figures and more likely to convey them confidently.
- Networking prompt for couples: Attend one community or industry event together. One partner practices small talk while the other practices a 60-second impact story about service skills.

Reintegration Reflection.

After reflecting on your reintegration, think about how your translated skills will be discussed with mentors.

Reflecting on your reintegration, consider the following: Use this list as a foundation for your upcoming mentor discussions.

- Common military terms and civilian equivalents:
- Mission – Project goal
- Tactics – Operational plan
- Deployment – Implementation
- Briefing – Presentation
- Command – Leadership
- Identify three military skills you want to emphasize.
- For each skill, write one concise sentence that explains its relevance in civilian terms, pointing out how specific branch courses you took can be mapped to civilian job functions. This concise statement will serve as a talking point during mentor conversations.

- Use plain English role descriptions; for example, instead of "squad leader" say "supervised a 10 person team responsible for operations and training, resulting in X outcome."
- Instead of listing equipment or acronyms, describe the skill: "managed sensitive equipment maintenance schedules, reducing downtime by 15%."

Choose someone to review your résumé this week—ideally a mentor or a trusted professional who can ensure it speaks to civilian employers. Tailor your résumé for each job by emphasizing the experience can skills most relevant to the position.

Short résumé checklist:

- Translate every military title into a civilian-friendly phrase.
- Include a quantified impact statement for each role.
- Highlight transferable skills and certifications earned.

As you engage mentors, consider sharing your Love Tank insights with your partner to keep communication aligned.

Love Tank Check for partners:

Use the prompts below to celebrate military strengths that help at home, identify habits to soften for civilian life, and agree on one small household change to practice together this week.

- Which strengths from service help at home (planning, discipline, steady under pressure)?

Use the Love Tank Check for partners prompts to surface each other's needs. If disagreements or differing needs arise, pause, restate what each person values, then brainstorm a compromise that respects both perspectives.

- Which habits need softening for civilian life (direct commands, blunt feedback)?

- Pick one household habit to tweak together this week.

The end result: a short, honest pitch that translates your service into clear, practical value for employers—and a few small steps you can take with your partner to make the transition smoother.

Self-care, boundaries, and social support networks

Prioritizing Intentional Self-Care Practices

Transitioning out of service takes energy—physical, emotional, mental—and if you treat self-care like optional, the tank runs dry fast. This section gives specific, doable habits you can adopt and adapt with a partner or on your own, so you stay steady during the chaos of change.

Treat personal time like a mission briefing you can't miss. Block it on your calendar as "Personal Ops" and protect it. Pick a predictable window: 20–30 minutes after lunch for a walk, 10 minutes before bed for quiet reflection, or a Sunday morning gym session. To help others respect this time, explicitly communicate its purpose. For example, add a short note such as "Personal maintenance – please do not schedule meetings during this time" to the meeting invite or calendar note, and inform key collaborators or your manager so they understand the importance of keeping the slot free.

Scheduling Dedicated Personal Time

Continuing from the discussion of the energy required for self-care during transition in the previous section, we now turn to the next steps.

Treat personal time like a mission briefing that you can't miss. Block it on your calendar as "Personal Ops" and protect it. Pick a predictable window: 20–30 minutes after lunch for a walk, 10 minutes before bed for quiet reflection, or a Sunday morning gym session. If you were an early morning type in the military, keep that rhythm for a solo hour of reading or journalling.

Concrete examples

Placement note: Integrate this material alongside the section on stress management and normalizing triggers to keep related strategies together and preserve a cohesive narrative flow.

- For men who prefer action: 30 minutes of kettle bell swings followed by a five minute breath count. Log it in your planner as non-negotiable.

Following our discussion on scheduling dedicated personal time, it is also essential to consider how to integrate stress management techniques into daily routines. For men who prefer action, set aside 30 minutes for kettle bell swings followed by a five minute breath count - log it in your planner as non-negotiable. If you don't have a kettle bell, try bodyweight squats or a brisk walk instead.

- For women who want calm: guided yoga or a 20 minute meditation app session after drop-off or before lights-out.

Prompt: Schedule three "Personal Ops" blocks this week. Treat them like training—no substitutions without prior approval.

Establishing Boundaries

Building on the boundaries you established earlier in the previous section,

Placement note: place this material alongside the section on stress management and normalizing triggers.

Boundaries are the polite way to hold ground. Say "I can do X after 6 p.m." or "Weekend mornings are family time" and stick to it. Communicating limits works best when short and direct—no long explanations needed. For example: "I appreciate your invitation, but I must decline." "I'd love to help, but I need to finish my report first." "I'm happy to join, but I have a prior commitment." These polite statements keep the tone respectful. How to practice: At work interviews, specify availability: "I'm available weekdays 9–5; I reserve evenings for family." Clear, civilian friendly, firm. At family events, use a simple script: "I'll stay two hours; I need rest after that." Rehearse it with a partner.

Now that you know how to communicate limits clearly, rank your top three non-negotiables using "The Boundaries List" (sleep, family dinner, gym, uninterrupted work time). Post it where others can see it.

Building a Social Support Network

Friends who get the post service shift matter, especially civilian friends who can help bridge everyday life back into your routine. Look for groups that match an interest—carpentry club, running group, veterinarian meet ups that include civilians—or join a community class where civilians attend. The goal is new contacts who can talk civilian talk and share ordinary experiences while you practice reintegration. Practical steps: join one local club this month and attend two meet ups before deciding if it fits; intentionally introduce yourself to at least one civilian member at each event; pair up with a fellow veteran or a civilian friend for a weekly coffee walk to compare notes.

Having laid out the importance of building a social support network, the next step is to find friends who can help ease the post service transition. Friends who get the post service shift matter, especially civilian friends who can bridge everyday life back into your routine. Seek out mixed groups—community classes, interest clubs, veterinarian meet ups that include civilians, or carpentry clubs and running groups that attract civilians—so you can build bridges between military and civilian life. The goal is to meet new contacts who can talk civilian talk, share ordinary experiences, and help you practice reintegration. Shared joyful activities—like cooking together, hiking, attending a local art class, playing board games, volunteering at a community garden, or joining a language exchange—serve as natural conversation starters and create lasting bonds. Practical steps: join one local club this month, attend two meet ups before deciding if it fits; intentionally introduce yourself to at least one civilian member at each event; pair up with a fellow veteran or a civilian friend for a weekly coffee walk to compare notes.

Reintegration Reflection — Write down three people who make you feel understood and one new type of person you want to meet. Add a civilian friend if you haven't already. Note one small step you can take this week to reach out to each person. Consider that joyful activities can introduce you to new people who share your interests, turning moments of fun into opportunities to expand your support network. Try answering in bullet points or short sentences for clarity.

Joyful Activities — Build on the insights from your Reintegration Reflection by engaging in activities that bring you joy. These moments of fun not only boost your satisfaction but also attract like minded individuals, expanding your support network.

Engaging in Joyful Activities

Do things that light you up that have nothing to do with being productive. Try a hobby from your pre service life or something you've always wanted to attempt. Joy refills morale. Ideas to try. Engaging in these activities with civilian friends can deepen connections and give you low pressure ways to practice everyday conversation.

Recharging Energy Reserves — Do things that light you up that have nothing to do with being productive. Try a hobby from your pre service life or something you've always wanted to attempt. Joy refills morale. Engage in these activities with civilian friends to deepen connections and practice everyday conversation. Choosing a hobby that also connects you with civilian friends—join a class or community group to meet people outside the veteran community—can increase the likelihood of forming friendships outside the veteran circle.

Here's a practical way to bring those ideas to life:

- Weekly "try night" with your partner or a new civilian friend:
- One week: a new recipe
- Next week: a pottery class
- Then a hike
- Rotate ideas and invite civilians to join so the activity becomes a bridge between veteran and civilian life.
- After each try night, pause for reflection:
- Jot what you enjoyed

- What you might change next time
- How it shapes future activities.

Inviting civilians to your "try night" transforms a fun evening into a shared experience that strengthens bonds.

- Solo joy: build a model plane, learn guitar chords, or binge a feel good TV show with zero guilt, and share it with a civilian friend if you wish. Occasionally invite a civilian along to an activity or show to strengthen the connection.

Sharing a solo joy with a civilian friend turns a solitary moment into a bridge toward deeper connection.

Prompt The "Joy List" — list five small things you can do this month that make you grin. Commit to at least two. When you share your joy list with a new friend, it invites them into your world and opens doors for ongoing support.

Building on the Joy List, let's shift our focus to recharging your energy reserves.

Recharging Your Energy Reserves

Recharging your energy reserves is essential for staying connected to civilian friends; when you are rested and grounded, you can show up consistently and authentically in those relationships. Schedule rest and set boundaries so social time feels sustainable, not draining.

Short resets win over dramatic ones. Power naps, breathing pauses, and weekly slow mornings add up. They help you recharge your energy reserves, keeping you rested and grounded so you can show up consistently and authentically in civilian interactions. Short resets keep you refreshed, so you're more present during social interactions that build your network. By giving your brain brief breaks that reset attention, reduce cortisol, and restore quick bursts of alertness, short resets make regular social contact easier to maintain. Schedule rest and set boundaries so social time feels sustainable, not draining.

Continuing from short resets, we now consider simple routines for recharging. Simple routines

Include simple routines that schedule regular contact with civilian friends: a weekly text check-in, a monthly coffee meet up, or a shared hobby night. Small, regular touches make friendships grow without overwhelming your energy reserves.

- Micro-reset: 3 deep breaths at your desk when you feel tense; follow it with a brief text check-in to a civilian friend to keep a simple routine of regular contact.
- Weekly reset: 90minute downtime on Sunday afternoon—no screens, low stimulation.

If you found the micro reset useful, you can carry the same idea into your relationship. Partner practice: The "Love Tank" Check – twice a week, ask your partner: "What filled your tank this week? What drained it?" Use their answers to plan for the next week. For instance, you could say: 'What moments made you feel most loved and supported this week?' And 'What situations left you feeling depleted or unheard?'

Schedule one micro-reset and one weekly reset this week and note the difference after seven days.

Now that you've scheduled a micro reset and a weekly reset, you can bring self care into your routine. Make self-care part of the standard operating rhythm so you and your partner stay functional, connected, and ready for whatever civilian life throws at you next.

Documenting transition: journaling and storytelling

Reintegration Reflection (Prompt)

Journal Prompt:

- Describe a specific moment during your transition when you felt your identity shift.
- Reflect on how that moment influenced your values, goals, or habits.
- Writing this helps you see how journalling and storytelling map your evolving identity.

In light of the reflection prompt above, consider how documenting your transition informs your evolving identity. By consistently journaling, you create a narrative that shows how your values, goals, and habits change over time. This practice clarifies both individual and shared identities for you and your partner.

Couples Prompt: The "Role Check"

A brief explanation of how to conduct the comparison aloud and what kind of space is most helpful: each partner writes a short paragraph on what they thought their role would be after service, and another paragraph on what their role actually is now. Then, together, they sit in a quiet, comfortable space and take turns sharing their paragraphs aloud, using "I" statements. The goal is to listen without correcting, interrupting, or judging. Each partner should respond with reflective listening—acknowledging the other's feelings before offering their own perspective. This creates a safe, non-judgemental environment that encourages empathy and reduces assumptions.

Instructions:

- Each partner writes a short paragraph describing what they thought their role would be after service, and another paragraph describing what their role actually is now.
- Together, sit in a quiet, comfortable space and take turns sharing these paragraphs aloud, using "I" statements.
- The goal is to listen without correcting, interrupting, or judging.
- After each sharing, the other partner responds with reflective listening—acknowledge the other's feelings before offering their own perspective.
- This creates a safe, non-judgemental environment that encourages empathy and reduces assumptions.

Storytelling is a powerful tool for building intimacy. By sharing your experiences, you weave a shared narrative that clarifies how each of you has evolved. Use storytelling to illustrate identity changes and strengthen your bond.

Storytelling is a powerful tool for building intimacy. By sharing your experiences you weave a shared narrative that clarifies how each of you has evolved, illustrating identity changes and strengthening your bond. As a practical exercise, pick a pivotal day from your service and write it in vivid sensory detail—what you saw, heard, smelled, felt. Afterward, reflect on how that memory influences your present choices and the way you see yourself. Share even a small excerpt with a trusted friend or partner; consider how this shared story might shape your current identity or future decisions, deepening empathy and illuminating your evolving identity.

The Habit: Make It Stick

Commit to a brief daily writing habit—just ten minutes. Even short entries build a continuous thread of your identity journey, making it easier to see growth over time.

The Habit: Make It Stick

- Pick a consistent time—right after morning coffee, before bed, or during a transit ride.
- Commit to 10 minutes—whether daily or three times a week; consistency beats intensity.
- Start with simple prompts like "Describe a memory that still feels vivid" or "Write about something that made you smile today."
- Even short entries build a continuous thread of your identity journey, making it easier to see growth over time.
- Pick a time: right after morning coffee, before bed, or during a transit ride. Consistency beats intensity.

After each brief session, reflect: how did this small commitment help you progress toward your bigger goal?

Tips for Strong Documentation

- Keep a dedicated journal or digital app for transition notes.
- Write consistently; even brief updates reinforce identity continuity.
- Review past entries periodically to track how your values and goals evolve.
- Share selected reflections with your partner to foster mutual understanding.
- Write honestly and without editing.
- Use imagery or metaphors to express complex feelings (e.g., "my patience is a worn field jacket").
- Reflect on specific service events and follow-up impacts on work, intimacy, or sleep.
- Note how your individual identity and couple roles are shifting—documenting this helps you adapt communication

and expectations.

Continuing from the previous section on tips for strong documentation, we emphasize:

- Review past entries periodically to track progress and identify patterns.

Write honestly and without editing

- Write consistently; even brief updates reinforce identity continuity.
- Reflect on specific service events and follow-up impacts on work, intimacy, or sleep.
- Note how your individual identity and couple roles are shifting—documenting this helps you adapt communication and expectations.
- For service experiences, imagine describing a support agent as "a lighthouse in a storm, steady and guiding," to capture calm and clarity.

Review your entries periodically and write honestly without editing. The end result is a clearer head, better conversations with your partner, and a record of progress. Keep the notebook private or share parts—it's your story. For example, "my patience is a worn field jacket".

Diversity: incorporating varied veteran experiences into transition

Those gains from keeping a clear record of your service—whether a brief 18month enlistment or a 20 year career—also help you navigate a new career path.

- For example, an Army infantry squad leader who previously led a squad of 12, coordinated rapid deployments, and managed supply logistics might transition into a project coordinator role at a logistics firm, averaging leadership, rapid decision making, and cross functional communication skills.
- Look for transitional positions that offer flexible schedules or contract work, giving you time to adjust.
- A former Air Force technician, familiar with specialized equipment, can seek civilian employers who value certifications and offer retraining credits.
- After outlining your career goals, use a Love Tank Check with your partner: set aside 5–10 minutes to share one concrete way you want to feel supported during this transition and agree on a small action—perhaps a research call or a skill sharing session to try before the next check-in.

Veterans of any gender may feel pressure to "tough it out" when mental health support would help. Those who have experienced sexual trauma, childcare challenges, or hiring bias also benefit from tailored resources. For female veterans who have experienced sexual trauma informed therapies—such as EMDR or CBT—along with specialized support groups and the VA's Women Veterans Program, can be beneficial. Heavy combat exposure can leave complex effects for all veterans; those with prolonged deployments often benefit from therapies that focus on bodily experiences—like somatic therapy, controlled breathing techniques, or graded re exposure—alongside talk therapy. A Love Tank

Check can surface these unique needs: each partner names one concrete way they want support—perhaps a childcare referral or a therapy appointment—and commits to one small action to honour that need before the next check-in.

Example Action:

- Pair a trauma informed therapist with a peer support group where members have similar levels of combat exposure.
- If hyper vigilance is an issue, practice a "safe room" drill at home with your partner:
- Identify one low stimulation space.
- Time a five minute grounding routine.
- Repeat until the body learns the cue.

This drill teaches the nervous system to recognize the environment and routine as safe, thereby reducing hyper vigilant arousal and promoting calm.

- Returning with children or having served while single changes the logistics and the emotion:
- Parents need childcare solutions, re-entry routines, and ways to rebuild trust with kids.
- LGBTQ+ veterans may need support navigating civilian workplaces and accessing services that respect their identity.
- During a Love Tank Check, partners can identify one concrete action to support hyper vigilance management—like scheduling a safe room drill or arranging childcare—and commit to practicing it before the next check-in.

Veterans' reintegration needs vary widely by factors such as:

- Combat exposure
- Tempo of deployment

- Family and dependent responsibilities
- Identity factors such as being LGBTQ+

Tailor supports to those differences by combining targeted clinical care, peer connections, and family or identity informed resources. For instance, a single veteran parent might receive a structured parenting support group that integrates trauma informed care with practical childcare resources. During a Love Tank Check, partners can discuss which specific support categories resonate most—for example, a veteran who served for 10 years may focus on identity exploration, while a recently deployed single veteran may prioritize peer connection—and agree on a small, actionable step to pursue.

Match tempo and exposure: When combat exposure matters, pair veterans with peer support groups whose members share similar deployment lengths and experiences. Matching on exposure reduces isolation and makes peer strategies more relevant. This matching approach is further supported by the Love Tank Check, which tailors brief check-ins to each veteran's deployment history.

- Love Tank Check adaptation: Use the weekly check-in to identify one concrete support needed for your specific deployment tempo and agree to one small action—such as arranging a group meeting or scheduling a counselling session—to honour that need before the next check-in.
- Targeted clinical supports: Offer somatic therapies (body-focused trauma work), trauma-informed psychotherapy, and evidence-based treatments (e.g., CBT, EMDR) as appropriate. Coordinate care so clinicians understand family dynamics and identity-related stressors.

Practical household drills for hyper vigilance:

- Identify a low stimulation space.
- Time a five minute grounding routine: breathing, a 54321 sensory check, and a simple progressive muscle relaxation.

- Repeat until the body learns the cue.
- After each drill, use a Love Tank Check to discuss how the routine felt, what adjustment could help, and one small commitment—such as setting a timer or inviting a friend for support—to implement before the next session.

Following the practical household drills for hyper vigilance, next consider involving family, dependence, and partners. During a Love Tank Check, the group can follow these steps:

- Each family member shares one concrete need—such as a childcare plan, a trust building activity, or a communication cue.
- The group agrees on a small, actionable step to honour that need before the next check-in.

This keeps the entire household engaged in the transition and reinforces mutual support across diverse veteran experiences.

- Family, dependence, and partners: Involve partners and caregivers in planning and education (with the veteran's consent). Offer couples or family therapy, childcare and schooling supports, and clear guidance on phased responsibilities to avoid overwhelming a reintegrating veteran.
- LGBTQ+–affirming care and community: Ensure access to clinicians and peer groups that are explicitly LGBTQ+–affirming. Address safety, confidentiality, and disclosure decisions sensitively; help connect veterans to local LGBTQ+ veteran networks and legal/social resources when needed.
- Practical wraparound services: Include benefits navigation, employment transition supports that consider parental responsibilities, and community connections that respect identity and family roles.
- Safety and pacing: Create phased reintegration plans that build in decompression time, anticipate tempo-related triggers (anniversaries, loud noises, crowded environments), and integrate

grounding or somatic practices into daily routines.

Use these approaches in combination and adapt them to the veteran's priorities: matching peers by exposure, providing somatic and trauma-informed therapies, involving families appropriately, and ensuring LGBTQ+–affirming supports where relevant.

Building on the discussion of the varying needs of veterans, the Love Tank Check is a brief weekly check-in to top up connection. Set aside 5–10 minutes, give each person uninterrupted time to speak, name one concrete thing that would make them feel cared for, and agree on one small action to try before the next check-in. When combat exposure levels matter, match tempo and exposure by connecting veterans with peer support groups whose members have similar experiences and deployment tempo; shared exposure reduces comparative isolation and makes peer strategies more relevant. The check-in can be tailored to deployment length, identity, and current support needs: a 20 year veteran might focus on identity redefinition, while a short term veteran might prioritize peer connection. For example, a veteran who served six months might discuss feelings of isolation and ask for help finding local support groups, whereas a 20 year veteran might talk about redefining their identity post service. For LGBTQ+ veterans, the check-in can surface unique needs around safe spaces or community resources. Use the weekly check-in to identify one concrete support needed for your specific deployment tempo and agree to one small action—such as arranging a group meeting or scheduling a counselling session—to honour that need before the next check-in. Finally, offer targeted clinical supports such as somatic therapies (body focused trauma work), trauma informed psychotherapy, and evidence based treatments (e.g., CBT, EMDR) as appropriate, and coordinate care so clinicians understand family dynamics and identity related stressors. The Love Tank Check thus adapts to each veteran's service history, identity, and current support needs.

Use one of these tailored prompts depending on your situation:

These prompts help you prioritize your needs and tasks. Ranking emotional and practical needs is especially useful for LGBTQ+ veterans, who often face unique challenges in integrating identity and military identity; focusing on top needs can guide support and reduce overwhelm.

- For couples: list one household task and one emotional need you want help with this week.
- For parents: write a 10-minute bedtime ritual you can try this month to reconnect with your child.
- For LGBTQ+ vets: identify one local or online resource that explicitly lists supportive services; reach out this month.

Close the check by repeating back what you heard, confirming the small action you'll take, and setting the next brief check-in.

Duration and Nature of Service: Identity Beyond the Uniform. The length and character of service shape identity, leading to varying shifts. Short enlistments and 20 year careers produce different identity shifts. Those who served long may feel loss of purpose; those who served briefly may struggle to claim veteran identity. A Love Tank Check can surface these identity concerns: each partner names one way they want to feel recognized—perhaps a ceremony, a new role, or a community connection—and commits to one small action to pursue that recognition before the next check-in.

- Family, dependence, and partners: Involve partners and caregivers in planning and education (with the veteran's consent). Offer couples or family therapy, childcare and schooling supports, and clear guidance on phased responsibilities to avoid overwhelming a reintegrating veteran.
- LGBTQ+–affirming care and community: Ensure access to clinicians and peer groups that are explicitly LGBTQ+–affirming. Address safety, confidentiality, and disclosure decisions sensitively; help connect veterans to local LGBTQ+ veteran networks and legal/social resources when needed.

As highlighted in the previous section, the length and character of service shape identity, leading to varying shifts. Short enlistments and 20 year careers produce different identity shifts. Those who served long may feel a loss of purpose; those who served briefly may struggle to claim veteran identity. During a Love Tank Check, partners can discuss how their service length influences their sense of purpose and agree on a concrete action to honour their unique identity trajectory before the next check-in. Concrete actions include:

- Joining a veteran organization
- Creating a memory box
- Setting a personal goal

Exercise — "Ranking Needs"

- Safety: Ensure the environment is free of hazards, provide clear sign age, and post emergency contact information.
- Pacing: Gradually increase task duration and intensity; monitor for signs of fatigue and allow regular rest breaks.
- Planning: Create a step by step routine that includes check-in points and feedback sessions.
- Routine Building: Encourage consistent scheduling, use visual planners, and reinforce positive behaviours.

This exercise helps you prioritize needs across diverse veteran experiences. Use three broad categories to organize what matters most to you:

- Purpose (meaning, goals, career, skills)
- Finances (income, benefits, housing, debt)
- Connection (family, friendships, community, health care, social supports)

As you work, explicitly consider how the duration and nature of your service and your identity (era, role, combat vs. Support, reserve vs. Active, gender, race, LGBTQ+ status, caregiver status, etc.) shape these needs—some needs may be more pressing because of when or how you served or because of your identity.

Steps

- Under each category, list 3–5 specific needs that feel important to you.
- Make a note beside any need that is influenced by your service duration/nature or by identity factors.
- Rank all listed needs across the three categories from highest to lowest priority.
- Pick the top two and create one small, concrete step for each (e.g., join a skills class, schedule a budgeting meeting, book a physical exam).

Branch-Specific Transition Nuances

Army-specific transition realities (active duty and reserve)

Transition & Resilience: From Army Habits to Civilian Rhythms

This section focuses on shifting routines and identity after service. It also ties directly into stress management and the normalization of triggers: many habits formed in uniform help regulate stress responses, so intentionally rebuilding routines supports resilience and reduces reactive responses to reminders of military life.

Leaving the Army is more than a change of address; it's a reshuffle of daily habits, identity cues, and decision making. For many soldiers, the mission first mindset—orders, a shared purpose, and tight routines—feels natural and comforting. In civilian life, employers expect initiative, social groups don't run on command, and your calendar may suddenly contain large, unscheduled blocks of time. That mismatch can cause frustration, restlessness, or a sense that something missing. These reactions are normal stress responses; acknowledging them and applying grounding and routine building strategies can reduce the intensity.

The start stop mindset is the alternating pattern of high intensity focus (the "start") and brief pause or lower energy periods (the "stop"). It is a natural rhythm in military life: a mission may demand relentless execution for a short window, then shift to downtime for reflection, recovery, or awaiting the next directive. This rhythm can feel disorienting in civilian life, where such clear cycles are rarer. This exercise helps you prioritize needs across diverse veteran experiences. Use three broad categories to organize what matters most to you: When using the Ranking Needs exercise, first identify your highest priority need, keeping in mind how your era, role, combat versus support status, reserve versus active duty, gender, race, LGBTQ+ identity, or caregiver role may shape that priority. Then craft one concrete, measurable step and set a realistic deadline so progress can be tracked.

Rhythms in the Army are the structured cadence of training, operations, and command, while predictability is the assurance of knowing what to expect next. Understanding the Army's collective approach helps make the shift less jarring. One practical antidote is to create micro missions—daily check lists with three non-negotiable tasks, a 20 minute sprint on a hobby, or a time bound role in a community organization. These micro missions establish small, predictable cycles that mirror the start–stop rhythm: you "start" with a focused task, then "stop" by moving to the next micro mission or resting. Pair each micro mission with a civilian equivalent of an Army habit: replace a chain of command meeting with a project team check-in, translate a training rhythm into a weekly personal schedule, or substitute on the spot leader feedback with regular mentor check-ins. These intentional pockets of urgency keep the nervous system engaged without causing burnout. Framing these tools as part of stress management and trigger normalization helps: micro missions act as short, predictable anchors that reduce hyper vigilance and make unpredictable civilian rhythms feel safer.

Hurry Up and Wait: Managing the Start-Stop Mindset

This heading introduces strategies for managing the start-stop rhythm common after service. Recognize that the "hurry up and wait" pattern can produce heightened arousal and reactivity; treating those responses as normal and using structured small tasks, scheduled rest, and brief grounding exercises can smooth the transition and lower stress.

Rhythms are the predictable sequences you relied on in uniform; predictability is the sense of assurance those sequences provided. Understanding the Army's collective approach helps make the shift less jarring. That classic "hurry up and wait" rhythm doesn't switch off automatically, and you may find yourself on edge during long stretches without a mission. In the broader discussion of family and social integration, it is clear that the same sense of predictability can strengthen home life. Start by identifying three behaviours you relied on in uniform that you miss now—examples: clear chain of direction, predictable training rhythm, immediate feedback from leaders. Next to each, write one civilian equivalent you can experiment with: join a project team at work to recreate clear direction; set a weekly personal training schedule to preserve predictable rhythm; ask a mentor or supervisor for regular check-ins to get feedback. Practical antidotes include creating micro missions—daily check lists with three non-negotiable tasks; scheduling a practice alert (a 20 minute sprint on a hobby); or volunteering for time bound roles at a community organization. These intentional pockets of urgency satisfy the nervous system without creating burnout, helping you preserve strengths you gained while practicing new patterns and supporting a steady rhythm at home. Remember, feeling on edge or impatient is a common trigger during this period—naming the feeling and using a short grounding practice (breathing, movement, or a micro mission) normalizes the experience and reduces its hold.

Mitigating the Impact on Families

These practices—clear priorities, short concrete steps, and regular check-ins—help families adjust by reducing uncertainty, clarifying roles, and creating shared routines. Use brief, mission-style planning for household goals (finances, parenting, social life): set three priorities, assign one time line, and define clear roles so tasks remain actionable and shared.

Family dynamics shift dramatically when a member transitions out of the Army. To keep the household stable, begin by mapping the current family routine and pinpointing gaps that arise when the regimented schedule dissolves. Use a simple three step approach: (1) Identify priority areas—finances, childcare, social connection; (2) Set realistic goals for each area; (3) Assign clear roles and timeliness. This mirrors the mission planning process discussed earlier but applies it to the domestic sphere. Frequent short check-ins, such as "What's one thing I can do this week to make home easier?" Keep communication specific and doable. By integrating these steps into the broader family integration framework, partners and children feel supported and involved in the transition. Also normalize stress reactions within the family—share that irritability, restlessness, or withdrawal can be expected during adjustment, and pair role assignments with simple coping strategies so everyone knows what to do when triggers appear.

Adapting to Civilian Career Paths

Career transitions affect not only individual identity but also family stability. Translate military skills into civilian terms: team leader = project manager, logistics planner = supply chain coordinator, communications NCO = operations coordinator. Build a professional network by attending two local industry events in the next month and reaching out to one alumni or veteran contact for informational coffee. Create a simple 90day plan: identify one certification, one networking goal, and one project to demonstrate your capabilities. Pair each goal with a family discussion—share progress, ask for input, and celebrate milestones together. Because career change can trigger anxiety or self-doubt, include at least one stress management element in the 90day plan (scheduled downtime, a mentor check-in, or a short grounding routine before interviews) to normalize and mitigate those responses.

Without rank structure, career advancement looks different. Translate military skills into civilian terms: team leader = project manager, logistics planner = supply chain coordinator, communications NCO = operations coordinator. Build a professional network by attending two local industry events in the next month and reaching out to one alumni or veteran contact for informational coffee. Create a simple 90day plan: identify one certification, one networking goal, and one project to demonstrate your capabilities. Acknowledge that the lack of formal rank can be a trigger for uncertainty; add small regular actions (weekly progress notes, mentor feedback) to the plan to reduce stress and keep momentum.

Building on the momentum from career advancement, the next focus is rebuilding community. Rebuilding community takes both courage and small rituals. Join one civic group, one hobby club, or a veterans' meet up within the next six weeks. Pair outward steps with inward practices: a weekly self-check (The "Love Tank" Check) where you note emotional fuel levels—social, physical, and purpose—and share results with your partner. Reintegration Reflection: What three things give you a sense of belonging? Rank them and pick the top two to pursue this month. These actions reinforce the family and social integration narrative by embedding community engagement into the household routine. Also treat community steps as graded exposure: small, repeatable rituals reduce social anxiety and normalize triggers related to belonging and identity.

Army specific family and community integration: After a deployment ends, frequent moves have taken a toll on partners and kids. To rebuild civilian support networks, start with a "mission planning" chat to set household goals (finances, parenting, social life) with clear roles and timeliness. Use military style brevity—three priorities, one time line—to keep it actionable. Concrete steps: map current support (neighbours, schools, friends) and identify one gap—childcare, social connection, or medical care. Then pick one action: enrol in a local parent group, set a standing weekly family night, or schedule a meet up with new neighbours. If your partner struggles, use short check-ins: "What's one thing I can do this week to make home easier?" Keeps communication specific and doable. This plan dovetails with the broader discussion on family cohesion by translating mission style clarity into everyday life.

Navy-specific transition realities

This section focuses on shifting routines and identity after service, and it ties directly into stress management and the normalization of triggers: many habits formed in uniform help regulate stress responses, so intentionally rebuilding routines supports resilience and reduces reactions to reminders of military life.

Understanding the Unique Transition Realities for Navy Veterans

One practical antidote is to create micro missions—daily check lists with three non-negotiable tasks, a 20 minute sprint on a hobby, or a time bound role in a community organization.

The familiar "hurry up and wait" pattern is a core part of that rhythm. It can trigger heightened arousal and reactivity when the mission stops but the expectation of the next task remains. Treat those responses as normal and use structured small tasks, scheduled rest, and brief grounding exercises to smooth the transition and lower stress.

Identify three behaviours you relied on in uniform that you miss now—for example: a clear chain of direction, a predictable training rhythm, and immediate feedback from leaders. For each, experiment with a civilian equivalent: join a project team at work to recreate clear direction; set a weekly personal training schedule to preserve predictable rhythm; ask a mentor or supervisor for regular check-ins to get feedback.

Practical antidotes include:

- Creating micro missions—daily check lists with three non-negotiable tasks;
- Scheduling a practice alert—a 20 minute sprint on a hobby;
- Volunteering for time bound roles at a community organization.

These intentional pockets of urgency satisfy the nervous system without creating burnout, helping you preserve strengths gained while adapting to new patterns and supporting a steady rhythm at home. When you feel on edge or impatient, name the feeling, then use a short grounding practice (breathing, movement, or a micro mission) to normalize the experience and reduce its hold.

Rhythms are the structured patterns of watches, turnovers, and readiness that define naval life; predictability is the confidence that these patterns will repeat. Having outlined the unique transition realities for Navy veterans, we now turn to how the distinct rhythms of naval service influence your adjustment. Building on the concepts of managing the start–stop mindset, if you served on a ship or shore duty, you know the rhythm: watches, turnovers, standing by for the next evolution. That structure becomes part of who you are. Leaving that behind is more than switching jobs; it's stepping out of a shared lifestyle where daily life, social life, and mission life overlapped. For many sailors, the resulting gap feels like being unmonitored. The good news: there are practical steps to steady the boat. These steps illustrate how Navy specific routines can serve as templates for anyone adjusting to new daily life.

Rhythms are predictable patterns you relied on in uniform. Predictability is the confidence that those sequences will repeat. The "hurry up and wait" rhythm doesn't switch off automatically. In the Army, the start–stop mindset alternates focused action with deliberate pause, keeping the nervous system engaged. To bring that cadence into civilian life, create micro missions: tasks with a clear start and stop that fit your day. For example:

- Identify three behaviours you relied on in uniform that you miss now (e.g., clear chain of command, predictable training rhythm, immediate feedback from leaders). For each, write one civilian equivalent you can experiment with: join a project team for clear direction; set a weekly training schedule to preserve rhythm; ask a mentor for regular check-ins to get feedback.
- Practical antidotes include daily check lists with three non-negotiable tasks; scheduling a 20 minute sprint on a hobby; or volunteering for time bound roles at a community organization.

These intentional pockets of urgency satisfy the nervous system without leading to burnout, preserving strengths while building new patterns.

- Morning stretch: a 5 minute stretch routine before breakfast to wake up the body.
- Coffee break brainstorm: a 10 minute mind dump of ideas while sipping coffee.
- Evening reflection: a 3 minute gratitude jot down at bedtime.
- Weekend hike: a 30 minute nature walk on Saturdays to reset the week's energy.
- Mid afternoon stretch: a quick desk stretch cycle that breaks long sessions of work.

These micro missions can be tailored to different interests—creative, physical, mental—and to varying time constraints, helping you maintain consistent rhythm and predictability in your life.

Translating rhythms into a weekly personal schedule

- Identify your priority domains (e.g., health, creativity, reflection).
- Assign each micro mission to a domain and pick a specific time slot that naturally fits your daily flow.
- Use a colour coded calendar: blue for physical, green for mental, orange for creative.
- Set a recurring event in your digital calendar for each micro mission and include a brief reminder (e.g., "Stretch: 5 Min").
- Review and adjust weekly: at the start of each week, move or swap events as needed to keep the rhythm balanced and realistic.
- Track completion by ticking off the event each day; this visual feedback reinforces predictability and motivates consistency.
- Schedule regular mentor check-ins: If you usually rely on the

spot leader feedback, consider replacing it with planned mentor sessions. Reach out with a concise note—e.g., "Hi [Mentor], could we schedule a 15 minute chat next week to review my progress?" Propose a specific date and time, and highlight the topics you'd like feedback on. Keep the meetings brief (1015 Min) and focus on concrete goals to maximize the benefit.

The start–stop mindset is the alternation between focused action (the "start") and deliberate pause (the "stop") that military service in stills. It is why the familiar "hurry up and wait" cadence can feel disorienting when civilian life does not provide those built in cycles. Micro missions—short, time bounded tasks with clear start and stop points—recreate that rhythm, offering predictable anchors that keep the nervous system engaged without leading to burnout.

Understanding the Unique Transition Realities for Navy Veterans: Reintegration Reflection Building on the strategies discussed above for easing the transition, let's focus on establishing reliable routines that ground your daily life. As you transition into civilian life, building reliable routines can be a key foundation. Start small and concrete. For example, a Navy veteran might reintroduce a "shore watch": set a two hour block each morning for non-negotiable tasks—mail, bills, exercise. Treat it like a duty and check it off. Use a simple checklist app or a sticky note system on the kitchen counter. These tiny anchors reduce the overwhelm that can turn grocery lists into Everest sized problems.

Normalize stress reactions within the family by acknowledging that everyone experiences anxiety or frustration. For instance, the family could hold a brief nightly conversation where each person shares one thing that stressed them and one coping strategy they used, fostering empathy and support.

To tailor the routine to your family, first map the current family routine and pinpoint gaps. A visual method, such as a family calendar or a flowchart, helps you see where responsibilities overlap or where time is unallocated, making it easier to adjust and integrate everyone's needs.

- What three daily tasks would make your day feel stable?

- Reflect on the routines you've outlined:

Rhythms are the structured patterns of watches, turnovers, and readiness that define naval life; predictability is the assurance that these patterns will repeat.

- Identify three community groups or non-unit contacts you would like to reconnect with.

Reflect on the routines you've outlined: Consider how each routine creates predictability, where start–stop moments occur, and which micro missions can smooth transitions between activities.

- Which of those can you commit to for the next 30 days?

These practices—clear priorities, clear, concrete steps, and regular check-ins—help families adjust by reducing uncertainty, clarifying roles, and creating shared routines.

These practices—clear priorities, concrete steps, and regular check-ins—help families adjust by reducing uncertainty, clarifying roles, and creating shared routines.

Building on the discussion of reintegration, when returning from Navy duty, Reintegrating into Family and Community Life can feel like stepping onto unfamiliar ground. Use these Navy specific relationship building tools to ease the transition. These tools illustrate how routine based communication can support anyone's return to everyday life.

Rebuilding Relationships

Hold a "House Huddle"—a 20 minute weekly sit down where each person lists one need and one offer for the coming week. Keep it low drama and practical: "I need morning coffee made twice this week" or "I'll handle carpool Monday and Thursday." This is an example of using routine based strategies to strengthen family and community ties.

Repair work is mostly small acts: consistent check-ins, showing up once more, apologizing for missed calls. Hold a "House Huddle" – a

20 minute weekly sit down where each person lists one need and one offer for the coming week. Keep it low drama and practical: "I need morning coffee made twice this week" or "I'll handle carpool Monday and Thursday." This routine based strategy helps strengthen family and community ties. If reconnecting feels awkward, try a shared micro project—planting a small herb garden with your partner, joining a local volunteer shift with an old friend. The project gives you conversation fuel and a visible result.

By blending these tactics, you can renegotiate roles and rebuild trust.

Frequent moves, long deployments, and unpredictable ship schedules leave loose ends in families, friendships, and partnerships. Reconnecting is largely practical work: accept that things have changed, then renegotiate roles and routines.

Start a simple weekly ritual—try a 20-minute "House Huddle" where each person names one need and one offer for the coming week. Keep it low-drama and specific (for example: "I need morning coffee made twice this week" or "I'll handle carpool Monday and Thursday"). The structure makes expectations clear, shares responsibility, and prevents resentment from building.

Repair also happens in small, consistent acts: regular check-ins, showing up one more time, returning missed calls, and offering a brief, sincere apology when needed. If conversation feels awkward, use a shared micro-project to create natural interaction and a visible result—plant a small herb garden with your partner, join a local volunteer shift with an old friend, or tackle a home task together after a port call. These projects provide conversation fuel and tangible progress.

Tailor your approach to Navy life: communicate upcoming watch rotations, deployments, or PCS moves so loved ones can plan; create arrival rituals to mark returns; use available family-support resources when reintegrating children and partners; and be patient—reconnection is gradual. Small, predictable gestures and a bit of structure go a long way toward rebuilding trust and routines.

Beyond rank and rate, what sparks you now? Try three one month experiments: a class, a weekend hobby group, and a short volunteering stint. Treat them like reckon—collect information, not verdicts. After each experiment, reflect: what did you learn? Do you want to keep this activity going? Journalling prompts: "What felt most like mine this week?" And "What did I enjoy without pressure?" Use a shared calendar or chore chart to renegotiate roles and routines. Remember, life changes—accept that things may shift, and renegotiate responsibilities as you reconnect.

Adapting to Different Paces and Communication Styles

Reconnecting is largely practical work: accept that things have changed, then renegotiate roles and routines. Translate commands into invitations to ease collaboration, adapting your communication pace to match others and being open to adjusting your style. This pragmatic approach—paired with concrete gestures like friendly greetings and eye contact—keeps relationships resilient.

Translate commands into invitations to ease collaboration.

Instead of the hard edge "Bring your report to the meeting," try "Would you mind bringing your report to the meeting?"

In a training context, change "Please review this module" to "Could you review this module at your convenience?"

When setting deadlines, transform "Finish the code by Friday" into "Could you finish the code by Friday so we can test it?"

These subtle shifts invite participation and show respect for others' autonomy, fostering smoother interactions across varied communication styles.

Building on the experiments you just began to rebuild relationships, the next step is to adapt how you move and communicate.

Shipboard talk is efficient and direct. Civilians often use softer language and indirect cues.

- Translate commands into invitations: when a sailor says "I'll think about it could mean yes, maybe, or no.

- Ask clarifying questions without judgment: "Do you plan to do this, or would you like my help making it happen?"

Practice this with a partner—one plays civilian, one plays sailor—and swap feedback.

Just as you translate commands into invitations to ease collaboration in those experiments, you can do the same with your crew connections by applying concrete communication strategies: start each conversation with a friendly greeting, maintain steady eye contact, nod to signal active listening, and mirror the other person's posture to build rapport. Use non verbal cues like an open hand gesture when sharing ideas or a slight lean forward to show interest. The crew is more than co-workers; it's a built in family. Rebuild that community gradually: reconnect with former shipmates through occasional informal reunions, join a veteran social group, explore online communities or forums dedicated to your fleet, or try a civilian club that aligns with your interests. Aim for three meaningful social contacts in three months—coffee, a walk, or a phone call.

Building on the tailored approach to Navy life discussed in the previous section, we now explore the themes of the "Lost Family" and Building New Communities

Continuing from the discussion of the "Lost Family" and Building New Communities, we now turn to the relationship dynamics addressed in the "Love Tank" Check (for couples).

Here's a simple weekly routine to apply the Love Tank Check: each partner rates the other's Love Tank on a scale of 1-10, names one way they felt especially supported, and identifies one missed element that would most strengthen their connection (e.g., quality time, affectionate touch, attentive listening).

- Weekly: each partner names one way they felt supported and one thing they missed (Love Tank Check).

- Weekly: Hold a 20 minute House Huddle where each person lists one need and one offer for the coming week. Keep it low drama and practical.
- Monthly: Schedule a no-technology date night to practice civilian-style downtime together?
- Monthly: schedule a no-technology date night to practice civilian-style downtime together.

These steps are practical, repeatable, and forgiving. The goal is steady progress—little anchors that restore rhythm, rebuild bonds, and help you claim a civilian identity that fits who you are now.

Understanding the Air Force Transition with a Focus on Self Care, Boundaries, and Support Networks

If you thought swapping flight suits for civilian clothes would be the hardest part, think again. Transitioning out of the Air Force brings shifts that can be subtle at first, then insistently loud—especially when your metrics for success go from mission ready check lists to much fuzzier measures like 'happiness' and 'enough sleep'.

Next, we transition from the practical steps discussed above to the emotional core: embracing the "Self-love" mindset shift.

Reconnecting with Civilian Pace and Priorities while Protecting Yourself

Having reconnected with civilian pace and prioritized self-protection, the next step is to apply that balanced mindset to your career. The Air Force trains for continuous improvement and readiness. That perfectionist instinct serves you well in aircraft maintenance bays, Intel cells, and flight decks— but in civilian life, that same drive can burn you out.

- Reframe daily goals: instead of "upgrade skills every quarter," aim for "keep skills functional and balanced with life."
- Practical step: pick one professional skill to maintain (e.g., a certification renewal or two hour weekly practice) and one personal routine that supports your well being (e.g., 20 minutes of physical activity or an evening walk).
- Reinforcement: tell your partner the plan and ask them to check in monthly—small public commitments help reinforce self-love.
- Name any limits you need (no work after 8 p.m., two social

events per week) and communicate those boundaries to your new civilian network so others can support them.

Civilian time moves at variable speeds. Some days are sprints, some are puzzle pieces you don't fit into until later.

Step 1: Create a weekly priority map

- Label three non negotiable (family dinner, job search task, time for hobbies) and slot them visibly on a shared calendar.

Air Force Transition Reflection

- What three items, if consistently protected, would give your week structure and meaning?
- Write a brief reflection in your personal journal to celebrate new sources of pride as you transition.
- Consider recording these reflections in a private journal, a shared document, or a digital note taking app.
- Include in that reflection who in your circle you can ask for accountability and which boundaries you'll enforce to protect those priorities.

Building on the structure you've mapped out in your weekly priority plan, it's time to find new pride markers. Service gave you obvious pride markers; now you may need new ones.

Avenues for new pride markers:

- Mentoring a young professional
- Mastering a craft (woodworking, photography, etc.)
- Completing a community project

By mentoring, you reinforce your own leadership and teaching abilities while creating a lasting impact on someone else's career. Mastering a craft offers a tangible sense of progress and mastery that can reignite passion. Community projects connect you to others, fostering a shared sense of purpose.

For couples: share one proud moment from civilian life each week at dinner. Keep short notes of wins—big or tiny—in your personal journal and review them monthly to boost confidence. Where possible, invite others into these activities to strengthen community bonds and create reciprocal support.

Bridging the Technology and Innovation Gap while Maintaining Balance

Building on the idea of bridging the technology and innovation gap, the following steps translate Air Force technical skills into civilian language:

- Replace jargon: instead of "we performed systems integration," write "led cross team technical projects."
- Actionable step: build a one page skills résumé that translates jargon into measurable outcomes. For example, a military role of "systems integration" could become "coordinated cross functional teams to integrate software and hardware, resulting in a 20% reduction in deployment time."
- Seek a mentor in your desired field and schedule two informational interviews per month.
- Build a new network: join a veterans' meet up, volunteer, or start a hobby group.
- Relationship Building Strategy: invite a civilian friend to a low pressure activity—coffee or a short hike—then follow up with a specific plan for a second meet up.
- Balance outreach with boundaries: limit networking time each week so relationship building doesn't overwhelm your self care practices.

Rebuilding Community

Having laid the groundwork for a resilient community, we now turn to cultivating self-love, recognizing that the health of the individual and the community are deeply intertwined. Cultivating Self-love

In the broader discussion of self care, an Air Force example illustrates how a structured routine can support resilience during transition. The routine includes:

- A five minute gratitude note to start the day
- A weekly journal entry titled "what I did well"
- A quarterly self check covering medical, mental, and social goals

When sharing these reflections, use soft landing phrases that begin with an intent statement such as "I want to be clear about…"—this provides space for feelings. A brief role play with a partner can help practice these conversations and reflect on how they felt. These tools illustrate how disciplined habits from the Air Force translate into civilian self care practices. After establishing these habits, pause to reflect: How has this routine contributed to your overall well being, and what changes have you noticed in your mood, energy, and sense of purpose?

Following the cultivation of self-love, we now explore how to adapt communication styles. This section focuses on aligning communication with self care practices.

In the broader communication discussion, an Air Force transition illustrates how adapting tone—such as using soft landing phrases—can help maintain relationships and support mental resilience.

Air Force transition — combine military style self care with softer civilian communication. Practice soft landing phrases such as:

- Acknowledging effort: "I appreciate the effort you made today."
- Seeking clarity: "Let's revisit that plan together."

- Offering support: "How can I support you?"
- Military context: "I'm grateful for the support and training I received."
- Civilian context: "Could you share your thoughts on this project?"
- Cross role context: "I appreciate the insights you've shared; I'll consider them moving forward."
- Feedback context: "Thank you for the feedback; it's valuable for my growth."

These phrases help smooth the transition by blending structured self care with approachable dialogue.

In the wider context of self care and communication, an Air Force transition exemplifies how to blend disciplined self care routines with softer civilian communication.

Self-care: adopt a military-grade plan: a five-minute morning gratitude note, weekly "what I did well" journalling, and a quarterly self-check (medical, mental, social goals).

Communication: directness is efficient, but civilian social cues are softer. Practice "soft-landing" phrases: lead with intent ("I want to be clear about…"), then give space for feelings. Communication Adaptation Prompt: role-play with your partner one brief conversation using a softer opener and reflect on the outcome.

In the wider context of self care and communication, an Air Force transition exemplifies how to blend disciplined self care routines with softer civilian communication. The routine involves a five minute morning gratitude note, weekly "what I did well" journalling, and a quarterly self check covering medical, mental, and social goals. While directness is efficient in military contexts, civilian social cues favour a gentler approach, so practice "soft landing" phrases such as "I want to be clear about…," then give space for feelings. These habits preserve strengths while redefining success, connection, and self care. They are particularly helpful for veterans because they replace the regimented schedule of service with a consistent, intentional structure that supports mental resilience, maintains a sense of purpose, and facilitates a smooth transition to civilian life. To practice the communication adaptation, role play a brief conversation with your partner using a softer opener and reflect on the outcome.

Marines-specific transition realities

Understanding and Adapting the "Semper Fi" Mindset

Having explored the core principles of the "Semper Fi" mindset in the previous section, you can now apply them to everyday life. If you grew up under a "Semper Fi" banner — or lived it day-to-day — that loyalty and commitment are hardwired. That's a strength and a resource for resilience. It can also make civilian life feel odd: personal choices weigh differently, social cues are softer, and performance metrics are invisible. The next pages offer concrete ways to honor that loyalty while shifting habits to support healthy masculinity and long term resilience during transition.

For instance, Sergeant First Class (ret.) James Lee left the Marines after 18 years and returned to his hometown, where he started a construction business. By applying the same discipline, clear communication, and unwavering reliability that defined his Marine service, he built a reputation for quality and trust. The transition was smoother because he could rely on his own internal compass, and the business thrived, giving him purpose and community support.

In the broader discussion of mindset adaptation and healthy masculinity during transition, an Air Force veteran's experience with the "Semper Fi" mindset illustrates how core values can be reinterpreted for civilian life. It shows how loyalty and discipline can coexist with emotional intelligence and softer communication, strengthening resilience while preserving integrity.

Having explored the core principles of the "Semper Fi" mindset in the previous section, you can now apply them to everyday life. If you grew up under a "Semper Fi" banner — or lived it day today — that loyalty and commitment are hardwired. That's a strength and a resource for resilience. It can also make civilian life feel odd: personal choices weigh differently, social cues are softer, and performance metrics are invisible. The next pages offer concrete ways to honour that loyalty while shifting habits to support healthy masculinity and long term resilience during transition.

Communication: directness is efficient, but civilian social cues are softer. Practice "soft-landing" phrases: lead with intent ("I want to be clear about…"), then give space for feelings. Communication Adaptation Prompt: role-play with your partner one brief conversation using a softer opener and reflect on the outcome.

From Military to Civilian Life: Decision Making and Autonomy

The discipline of making clear choices under pressure becomes a powerful tool for independent decision making in civilian settings. By translating the Semper Fi principle of responsibility into everyday autonomy—choosing a job, a career path, or even a leisure activity—veterans reinforce their sense of self efficacy while remaining true to the warrior's commitment to duty. This practice simultaneously nurtures healthy masculinity, which values personal agency, and emotional connection, which thrives on mutual respect for each other's decisions.

Framing autonomy as part of healthy masculinity helps reduce the friction of transition: making deliberate choices builds confidence, and small, repeated acts of agency strengthen psychological resilience.

Having explored how to reconcile the warrior ethos with emotional connection, we now turn to practical ways to exercise autonomy in civilian settings. The key is to maintain the Semper Fi focus on purpose while allowing room for personal choice, thereby fostering a healthier form of masculinity that balances mission driven action with emotional awareness. By framing autonomy as part of healthy masculinity, the shift from military to civilian life is reframe as an extension of disciplined decision making rather than a departure from it; this alignment reduces friction by validating personal choice as a natural expression of strength and responsibility.

In the Corps, orders, SOPs, and tight teams made decisions predictable. Out here, the play book is lighter and you're expected to write parts of it yourself. Practical moves: - Start small: practice making one autonomous decision each day — from which networking event to attend to what project to volunteer for — and note the outcome. - Set a 30 days initiative: pick a personal or professional goal, break it into weekly tasks, and check progress every Sunday like a stop of AAR. These habits reinforce adaptive decision-making and support a resilient, balanced sense of masculinity in civilian settings.

- Start small: practice making one autonomous decision each day— from which networking event to attend to what project to volunteer for— and note the outcome. Then ask yourself: what did you learn? Each small decision reinforces the Semper Fi value of responsibility, while simultaneously allowing space for personal agency, a core component of healthy masculinity.

Having begun with daily autonomous decisions, the next step is a structured 30 days plan to maintain momentum in a mentally demanding civilian routine.

- Set a 30 days initiative: pick a personal or professional goal, break it into weekly tasks, and check progress every Sunday like a stop of AAR.

Reconciling the Warrior Ethos with Emotional Connection

Reconciling these elements is central to healthy masculinity: keeping the warrior's discipline while intentionally practicing emotional connection strengthens resilience and relationships during transition.

- The 2 minute Share: with a partner, set a timer and each person spends two minutes saying one thing that went well and one thing that felt hard that week. No fixing allowed — only listening. Marines use this brief exchange to reconcile the warrior ethos with emotional connection, turning training moments into moments of reflection. This practice embodies the Semper Fi principle of mutual accountability while encouraging honest emotional expression. If a participant runs out of words or a pause feels awkward, the partner may gently indicate a short pause, allowing the speaker to regroup or simply signal that listening is still active. This keeps the exchange comfortable and maintains the rhythm of the exercise.

This ritual aligns with the general communication strategies explored elsewhere in the book and supports resilient, emotionally literate masculinity.

- The 2 minute Share: with a partner, set a timer and each person spends two minutes saying one thing that went well and one thing that felt hard that week. No fixing allowed — only listening. Marines use this brief exchange to reconcile the warrior ethos with emotional connection, turning training moments into moments of reflection. Repeating the exercise reinforces the link between disciplined action and emotional openness, a cornerstone of healthy masculinity. For instance, a project manager might say, "I successfully led the sprint meeting, but I struggled to keep the team focused on deadlines," turning a routine status update into an opportunity for growth.

Adapting to a Mentally Demanding Civilian Routine

The mental rigors of civilian work mirror the strategic thinking of military training. Applying Semper Fi's focus on preparedness and continuous improvement supports mental resilience, enabling veterans to maintain healthy masculinity by balancing ambition with self compassion and by inviting emotional connection into everyday challenges.

Transitioning to a mentally demanding civilian routine calls for new strategies: prioritize recovery, build predictable micro-routines, and practice mental skills (planning, re framing, boundary-setting) that preserve resilience and model healthy masculinity in daily life.

Building on the new avenues for brotherhood and social support explored earlier, civvy life can be more mentally grinding than physically intense. New stress tools: These tools are built on the Semper Fi commitment to teamwork and shared purpose, and they are designed to cultivate emotional resilience within a framework of healthy masculinity—recognizing that true strength also comes from vulnerability and mutual support. For instance, one veteran, Tom, used the "Mindful Breathing" tool by practicing a five minute breathing exercise each morning, which helped him reduce stress levels before heading to duty.

- Micro-reset ritual: three deep breaths, a quick neck roll, and a 60-second goals check before starting work or family time. Reflect: Did this reset help you focus? What did you notice about your energy afterward?

- Scheduled downtime: block two non-negotiable hours per week for a hobby that's about joy, not productivity. Reflect: How did this hobby time affect your mood? Did it recharge you?

Finding New Avenues for Brotherhood, Social Support, and Belonging — including online communities, mentorship programs, and local volunteering

Finding new avenues for brotherhood and social support is not merely about maintaining old rituals—it is a strategic act of identity exploration. By deliberately seeking out new venues, veterans create spaces where their military identity can evolve alongside civilian roles, while also weaving stronger community ties that reinforce belonging.

- Host a monthly "wingman" dinner with old unit mates, rotating hosts and themes such as work updates, parenting experiences, coping with triggers, or recent wins. Consider adding activities like a brief icebreaker (e.g., "Two Truths and a Lie"), a gratitude round, or a short goal setting exercise to deepen connection and make each dinner more impactful. Sharing these meals reinforces camaraderie, fuels identity exploration, and expands your support network.

- Join a veteran group and a civilian team sport or club within the next 90 days to strengthen Marine specific community building, and weave these gatherings into broader social support networks (300) and community building (909). These gatherings serve as platforms for exploring personal growth and embedding you deeper into the community. If you feel socially anxious, start by attending a single event, observe the group dynamics, and introduce yourself to one or two familiar faces before fully engaging. This gradual approach can help you ease into new social settings.

Applying Military Values to Civilian Life and Identity Exploration

Building on the discussion above about applying military values to civilian life and identity exploration, the values are portable. Match them with civilian aims by translating language, keeping in mind the identity exploration themes, and recognizing that this bridge strengthens both individual identity and community belonging.

- Discipline → Daily habits: pick one habit (sleep, finances, skill study) and use a 21day check sheet.
- Drive → Targeted ambition: set a career skill to reach in six months and map weekly progress.
- Service → Family impact: schedule monthly "mission planning" with your partner to align goals, finances, and parenting.
- Core advice: translate military values—discipline, drive, service—into civilian action by embedding them into daily routines, career objectives, and family collaboration.
- Discipline → Daily habits: pick one habit (sleep, finances, skill study) and use a 21day check sheet, grounding your evolving identity in consistent routine. This practice integrates your military discipline into civilian life, enhancing personal identity and communal cohesion. For veterans, a practical tool is the free Google Sheets Habit Tracker template or the habit tracking app Habitual, which adds gamification and community support.
- Drive → Targeted ambition: set a career skill to reach in six months and map weekly progress, aligning ambition with your identity goals.
- Drive → Targeted ambition: set a career skill to reach in six months and map weekly progress, aligning ambition with your identity goals. By pursuing this drive, you solidify your personal identity and contribute to the broader community. Reflect on how pursuing these ambitions contributes to your sense of identity as a veteran.
- Service → Family impact: schedule monthly "mission planning" with your partner to align goals, finances, and parenting,

reinforcing your role in family identity. This shared mission nurtures your identity while strengthening family bonds within the community. For example, you could review next month's budget, set a parenting goal such as reading together nightly, and choose a community activity to support each other.

- Core advice: translate military values—discipline, drive, service—into civilian action by embedding them into daily routines, career objectives, and family collaboration.

Prompts and Reflections (Identity Focus)

Use these prompts to explore how the expanded brotherhood networks and community building activities shape your identity and reinforce a sense of belonging.

Continuing from the identity focused prompts discussed earlier, this exercise deepens that exploration. Reintegration Reflection: As part of your core reflection work, identify three Marine Corps values that helped you most during service. Next to each value, write one concrete civilian goal where that value will directly support your transition (for example: Honour → ethical leadership in the workplace; Courage → enrol in a public speaking course; Commitment → complete a degree program). To make the exercise more engaging, start by recalling moments in service when you felt especially proud or aligned with your goals—those moments often point to the values that will be most relevant in civilian life. Treat this as a single consolidated reflection exercise to clarify how service earned strengths map to post military objectives, align with your evolving identity, and guide actionable planning and progress tracking.

Ranking Needs: On a scale of 1–5, rate your current need for brotherhood, autonomy, purpose, and emotional closeness. After rating, identify the two needs that require immediate attention and write one specific, time bound action for each (who will help, what you'll do, and when). This needs assessment consolidates similar ranking prompts into a focused planning tool—particularly useful in a Marines specific transition, where changes to daily structure and social bonds often shift priority needs. To move from identification to action, apply a SMART framework to each of the top two needs, ensuring each goal is Specific,

Measurable, Achievable, Relevant, and Time bound.

The "Love Tank" Check: With your partner, each write one thing that fills your tank and one that drains it. Swap lists, discuss briefly to understand each other's priorities, and agree on one item to address this week with a concrete action. For Marines transitioning to civilian life, explicitly note any service related triggers or supports that affect your tanks (for example, routines that provide stability or situations that cause stress) and choose one step to test for a week, then revisit together. Example: "What specific morning ritual helps you feel energized?" Or "Which interaction this week feels most draining?"

These steps let you keep the best of "Semper Fi" while learning to be open, self directed, and connected outside the unit. Small, repeated moves build a different kind of strength — one your partner, kids, and neighbours will notice.

Coast Guard-specific transition realities

Coast Guard sailors learn to navigate the sea by keeping a steady watch. A shore watch is a daily, structured check-in modeled on that maritime rhythm. Pick a consistent time each day, pause together for 5–10 minutes, review what's happening, and set intentions for the rest of the day. To keep the conversation collaborative, use the "Status Check" cue: a short phrase—such as "Status Check" or "Let's pause"—that signals a shift from directive to dialogue. When you say it, ask, "How do you want to handle this?" And listen fully. By turning the familiar watch into a shared ritual, you preserve the Coast Guard's sense of rhythm while creating a calm, partnership focused routine for home life.

Balancing the mission mindset with civilian integration begins with the shore watch routine. Schedule a brief check-in with your partner each day and use the "Status Check" cue to transform any directive into a collaborative conversation. This simple practice keeps communication clear and respectful as you transition from a military to a domestic context.

Think of the shore watch: a daily pause that mirrors the steady vigilance of a sea watch. When you step onto civilian ground, keep that same rhythm but soften the tone. Before giving a directive at home, pause and say, "How do you want to handle this?" Then invoke the "Status Check" cue to signal a shift into collaborative dialogue. Repeat this routine at a predictable time each day to maintain structure and mutual clarity in your partnership.

Bridging the sea duty mindset into partnered life ashore is easiest when you embed a shore watch habit. Agree with your partner on a regular check-in—an hour or two each week—where you review the week's events and set next steps. Use the "Status Check" phrase whenever the conversation starts to sound like an order, and slow down to discuss options together.

The Coast Guard trains people to act fast and keep others safe. That mission mindset is invaluable, but ashore civilians usually expect softer timing and softer talk. To bridge that gap, adopt deliberate routines that preserve clarity without defaulting to orders.

Practical steps

- Pause-and-ask: before giving a directive at home, take a beat and ask a question such as "How do you want to handle this?" That small change shifts interactions from orders to collaboration while keeping intentions clear.

Pause before giving a directive at home. Ask a simple question: "How do you want to handle this?" When you feel an order like tone creeping in, say "Status Check" to signal a calm pause. This mirrors the shore watch practice of regular check-ins and keeps couple conversations purposeful and respectful.

- Establish a "shore watch": create a simple routine or ritual to mark the transition from duty-mode to home-mode (a five- to fifteen-minute check-in, a brief debrief, or a walk together). Treat it like a watch change—hand off mission thinking and consciously adopt a civilian tempo.
- Communicate triggers: tell family and friends what kinds of situations make you go into rapid-response mode and identify calming cues they can use to help you shift gears.

These small, repeatable practices make it easier to retain the strengths of sea-duty training while building smoother, more collaborative relationships ashore.

Coast Guard life is built on watches, crew cohesion, and routine. On land those rhythms feel optional, and loneliness can creep in. Rebuild structure with anchors you can share: a weekly dinner, a Saturday walk, or a bedtime ritual. Apply the shore watch by scheduling a brief daily check-in and reinforcing it with the "Status Check" cue. After the check-in, reflect together: list three shipboard routines you miss and brainstorm how to recreate their emotional purpose—team time, predictability, clear roles—in your shared home life.

Honour your service by adopting a shared shore watch routine: set a regular time for reflective conversation. Use the "Status Check" cue to keep interactions respectful and collaborative as you settle into partnered life ashore. This simple, consistent practice preserves the teamwork and rhythm of the Coast Guard while strengthening your civilian relationship.

Coast Guard work often flies under public radar, so it helps to create a tangible reminder of impact. Build a "service shelf" of photos and mementos that you review together each week. Celebrate wins privately and consider volunteering with local maritime groups where your skills are valued. During each shore watch check-in, use the "Status Check" phrase to invite your partner to share a rescue or mission memory; retelling together cements value and builds mutual understanding. Pair this with regular self compassion pauses—acknowledge service, give each other credit, and allow space for pride and gratitude. Pause and ask, saying "How do you want to handle this?" After a directive, de-escalates potential conflict by giving your partner agency and preventing the emotional charge that can arise from feeling ordered.

Self compassion looks like granting yourself permission to rest and to grieve the sea, and inviting your loved one into that practice. Try a daily micro practice you share: name one thing you did well that day and one small kindness you'll give yourself tomorrow. Schedule this at the same time each day as part of your shore watch routine, and use the "Status Check" phrase to invite a supportive partner check-in. Concrete options—paced breathing, a short run, a creative task—help you feel capable outside formal duty. Prompt for reflection: How does this ritual help you shift from duty mode to home mode?

Adapting communication styles during reintegration starts with the shore watch mindset. Check in regularly with your partner and use the "Status Check" cue to transform directives into collaborative dialogue. Consider also creating a shared document or scheduling a dedicated conversation to explicitly communicate triggers—this helps both partners anticipate reactions and stay aligned. This practice smooths the shift from military to civilian interactions and strengthens the partnership's foundation.

Establish a “shore watch”: create a simple routine or ritual to mark the transition from duty-mode to home-mode (a five- to fifteen-minute check-in, a brief debrief, or a walk together). Treat it like a watch change—hand off mission thinking and consciously adopt a civilian tempo.

Communicate triggers: tell family and friends what kinds of situations make you go into rapid-response mode and identify calming cues they can use to help you shift gears.

Direct, assertive talk saved lives; softer phrasing builds buy-in at work and at home. Practice converting commands into invitations: “Secure the line” becomes “Could you check the line when you have a minute?” Other translations include: “Open the door” → “Could you open the door when you get a chance?” “Finish the report” → “Would you mind finishing the report by Friday?” “Check the data” → “Could you double check the data when you have a moment?” “Call the client” → “Would it be possible for you to call the client?” The ‘Love Tank’ Check: each week, ask your partner which communication style made them feel most heard, then try that approach for three days. These practices echo the communication strategies introduced earlier, ensuring that the style you use supports teamwork and personal relationships.

Communicate triggers: tell family and friends what kinds of situations make you go into rapid-response mode and identify calming cues they can use to help you shift gears.

Coast Guard transition: Skills from service—problem solving under pressure, seamanship, search planning—translate to civilian outlets. List five service skills, then next to each write two civilian roles or hobbies where those skills apply. This list is a practical map for rebuilding purpose.

Finding New Forms of Purpose and Identity

A practical starting point is to list five service skills, then write two civilian roles or hobbies where those skills apply. For example, if one of your skills is project management, you might phrase it in a civilian context like this: “Managed a cross functional team to deliver a project on time and under budget, coordinating logistics and stakeholder communication."

Begin by asking yourself: What core values guide your decisions? What activities light up your enthusiasm? Write down at least three answers. Then, list how each value or passion could shape a new role, hobby, or volunteer opportunity. Reflect weekly on whether these choices bring a sense of meaning and alignment with your evolving identity.

Coast Guard transition: Skills from service—problem solving under pressure, seamanship, search planning—translate to civilian outlets. List five service skills, then next to each write two civilian roles or hobbies where those skills apply. This list is a practical map for rebuilding purpose, helping you see how your expertise can support new goals.

Understanding the USSF Transition Experience

The Space Force blends cutting edge technology with a culture of rapid iteration. When you translate that mindset to your home life, the same principles—clear metrics, continuous feedback, and small, celebratory wins—apply to building intimacy after deployment. In the next sections we will explore concrete rituals that mirror the Space Force's operating model, helping you and your partner stay aligned while you both transition into civilian roles.

The transition from active duty to civilian life reshapes your sense of self and community. Pay attention to the emotional stages—loss of routine, search for belonging, redefinition of purpose. Use reflective practices, such as journalling or support groups, to process feelings and to anchor your identity in new experiences. When creating reintegration rituals with your partner, intentionally pair those reflective practices with shared routines (daily check-ins, a weekly debrief, or a short shared project) so your individual processing becomes part of rebuilding connection. Remember that your service skills are not lost; they can be the foundation for a renewed purpose in civilian life and for cooperative routines that support both partners.

Okay, Space Force veterans: you served in the newest branch with a seriously technical mission and a start-up like vibe. That mix of innovation, geeky pride, and mission focus creates a transition path that looks different from any other. This section zeroes in on what makes that path unique and gives specific steps for translating technical chops and military rhythms into a civilian life that actually fits. Translate those rhythms into reintegration rituals with your partner—shared weekend experiments, agreed communication check lists, or a joint planning ritual—to preserve mission focus while rebuilding home life. Depending on your interests or schedule, you could try a morning walk that doubles as a "daily brief," a weekly 30 minute "debrief" over dinner to review the week, a rotating chore chart that assigns tasks for the week, a 5 minute check-in ritual before bed, or a shared hobby project that you work on together on the weekends. These varied rituals keep the rhythm of teamwork alive while fitting into different time slots.

Rhythms and Predictability: Building Relationship Cadences

Rhythms in the Space Force are not only about mission training; they are a framework for predictability that keeps teams cohesive. Apply the same cadence to your relationship: set a weekly "debrief" where you review shared goals, celebrate small wins, and adjust plans—just as a unit reviews after a sortie. This structured ritual gives you both confidence that your partnership will evolve with the same systematic, data driven approach the Space Force uses daily.

Space Force's culture encourages rapid iteration and cross disciplinary collaboration. Teams experiment with new software, hardware, and tactics in sandbox environments, turning constraints into opportunity. Leaders reward creative solutions with recognition and resources, embedding experimentation in daily work. Veterans bring this mindset into civilian roles, and they can also bring it into their relationships: create small, low risk experiments with your partner (pilot a new evening routine for two weeks, iterate on chores distribution, or test a shared hobby) and use rapid feedback to refine what strengthens the household. After each experiment, schedule a brief weekly debrief with your partner. Use guiding questions such as:

- What worked well and why?
- What didn't meet expectations and why?
- What adjustments can we make for the next trial?
- How does this change affect our daily rhythm and stress levels?

Innovate Together: Relationship Hackathons

In the Space Force, experimentation is routine—hackathons, rapid prototypes, and feedback loops drive progress. Bring that same spirit into your partnership by hosting monthly "relationship hackathons." Pick a challenge (e.g., communication habits, household chores, intimacy routines), prototype a few solutions, run them for a week, then hold a short retro to decide what to keep. The result is a continuous improvement cycle that mirrors the Space Force's culture while deepening connection.

Technical expertise: highlight concrete achievements, quantified results, and certifications to demonstrate mastery. The innovative "relationship hackathons" foster collaboration and rapid problem solving. In these events, participants conduct a retrospective—a structured review of what worked, what didn't, and actionable lessons—to refine future engagement strategies.

Family reconnection: use this transition to strengthen ties—schedule regular calls, involve loved ones in project milestones, and celebrate successes together.

Personal Autonomy and Shared Direction

Without orders, you become your own commander. Use the Space Force's planning process: draft a weekly plan with three high impact tasks, block time, and review on Sunday with your partner. Pair the "Love Tank" check—rate your partner's emotional fill—and adjust daily actions. Treat this planning and check-in ritual as a joint command post that keeps relational health front of mind, just like a Space Force flight deck keeps the mission on target.

Personal autonomy is a hallmark of Space Force service. You learn to make decisions in ambiguous environments, manage resources, and set goals. In civilian life, these skills translate into entrepreneurship, project leadership, or self directed learning. When you value autonomy, also build intentional rituals with your partner that protect individual time while maintaining connection—clear weekly planning sessions, agreed solo-project blocks, and joint goal reviews let autonomy and partnership coexist.

Weekly Planning Ritual: The Relationship Flight Deck

Even the most well charted flight plan can encounter turbulence. To stay on course when unexpected changes arise—sudden weather, an engine hiccup, or a last-minute passenger request—plan for flexibility.

Reserve buffer windows in the schedule, create a contingency "baggage" list, and set up a quick check review at the end of each day to assess what went wrong and what can be adjusted. By treating disruptions as part of the routine, the crew learns to pivot without losing momentum or morale.

Set a Sunday planning session where you map the week's personal and joint objectives, then review each evening how they performed. After each review, ask the Love Tank question: "On a scale of 1–10, how full is your partner's tank?" Use the answer to adjust the next day's support or quality time. This systematic, data driven ritual echoes the Space Force's mission ready culture, ensuring both of you stay aligned and supported throughout the transition.

Integrating a New Identity

The transition demands a redefinition of identity beyond the uniform. Reflect on how your values, mission focus, and technical expertise intersect. Use storytelling to communicate your new role, aligning your military narrative with civilian career goals. Make identity work a shared exercise with your partner: practice telling your story together, create a short co crafted elevator pitch about the next chapter, and use regular rituals (a monthly reflection or a shared journal) to track how the new identity is taking shape for both of you.

Reclaiming Identity Through Innovation

Transitioning out of the uniform means redefining your core mission. Treat your identity work as a Space Force mission: set clear objectives (who you want to be), gather data (self reflection prompts), test hypotheses (try new roles), and iterate until the outcome feels authentic. By framing identity recovery as a continuous improvement process, you and your partner can support each other in building a shared, evolving sense of self beyond the uniform.

New-identity homework: write three strengths the Space Force helped you build and three civilian roles where they apply (e.g., systems thinking → project manager; secure commas → cybersecurity analyst).

Share lists with your partner and pick one civilian role to research together this month.

Reintegration Reflection: What challenges have you faced during this transition, and how can you leverage your strengths to navigate them?

Reintegration Reflection

Reflect on the foundational themes—loss of mission, structure, and identity—before exploring branch specific nuances.

What technical skill could you explain in plain English to a non military friend this week? What is one small habit to bring home that would make family life easier? Pick one and try it—then check in after two weeks.

Common civilian-veteran experiences across branches

Placement note: Move this section near the discussion on building a new daily routine post-service.

Loss of Mission and Structure

This is a foundational theme that appears across services and helps frame the common challenges of transition: the gap left when mission and routine disappear.

One of the most jarring shocks after leaving Space Force is the sudden absence of a clear mission day-to-day. This loss of mission and routine is a common, cross-branch experience and forms part of the core framework for understanding transition challenges. That sense of purpose and the schedule that came with it—briefings, check lists, timeliness—vanishes almost overnight. For many, this feels less like freedom and more like being adrift on a very calm, very empty ocean.

The Military-Mindset

You were trained to get things done: objectives set, roles clear, accountability visible. That mindset served you and your teammates well. When the mission stops, familiar reactions may arise—restless energy in the evenings, an urge to make rigid plans for every hour, or guilt about downtime. Those responses are normal. A common civilian veteran challenge is finding purpose after the command structure is gone. A practical way to reapply the military habit of clear goals without the weight of a command directive is a "missionlite" weekly plan. Pick 2–3 priorities (health, skills, social) and give each a simple, measurable task—run three times, apply to two jobs, call one buddy. Small targets create structure and give you a sense of progress while leaving room for flexibility. Treat this missionlite approach as an early, foundational tool to rebuild structure without recreating command pressure.

Reclaiming Individual Identity

Reclaiming identity is a foundational task that pairs with regaining structure; approach it as an early, practical exercise that applies across branches.

Common Civilian Veteran Experiences

This section offers a simple, foundational exercise to begin reclaiming identity. Without uniform and rank as shorthand, it's time to piece together who you are outside those labels. Try a personal inventory exercise: list three technical skills, three soft skills, and three things that make you laugh or feel competent. Then ask your partner or a trusted friend to add one item to each list. Comparing lists often highlights strengths people overlook in themselves.

Placement note: Move this section near the discussion on building a new daily routine post-service.

Finding purpose isn't a one night operation. It takes trial and error. Concrete options that support resilience, leadership identity, and community service connections:

- Further education: enrol in a night course tied to a civilian role you're curious about. (Supports resilience, leadership identity, and community service connections.)
- Project-based work: pick a three month contract to test a field (analytic, satellite ops, cybersecurity). (Supports resilience, leadership identity, and community service connections.)
- Volunteer shift: mentor a high school robotics team or teach basic coding at a community centre. (Supports resilience, leadership identity, and community service connections.)

Reintegration Reflection: Which of these three (study, short contract, volunteer) feels least risky to try this quarter? What would a first step look like this week? These reflections align with resilience, leadership identity, and community service connections.

Navigating Civilian Life

This discussion is grounded in resilience and leadership identity, and it highlights how community service can aid reintegration.

Practical civilian tasks can feel like a novel. Break them down with check lists and deadlines. Example: housing overhaul—Week 1: list must-haves; Week 2: schedule viewings; Week 3: apply. If paperwork is overwhelming, use a trusted non-profit or veteran service officer as a copilot.

Navigating Civilian Life

Practical civilian tasks can feel like a novel—long, unfamiliar, and full of unknowns. Break projects into small, concrete steps with check lists and deadlines so each phase is clear and achievable. Example: housing overhaul— Such projects also reinforce resilience and leadership identity, while opening opportunities for community service.

Week 1: list must-haves and deal-breakers;

Week 2: schedule viewings and take notes on each place;

Week 3: submit applications and follow up.

If paperwork is overwhelming, use a trusted non-profit, veteran service officer, or caseworker as a co-pilot to help interpret forms, track deadlines, and advocate when needed. The same checklist-and-deadline method—prioritize tasks, set one-step-at-a-time goals, use calendars or reminder app, and lean on peers or professionals—works equally well for employment searches, benefits claims, medical appointments, and other common civilian-veteran experiences. Small, scheduled actions turn an intimidating process into manageable progress.

Veterans often find civilian life feels slower. When you miss the intensity, intentionally create micro missions—like a weekend hackathon, a multi day hike with a buddy, or an intense workout block three mornings a week—to bring back the familiar rhythm without a military schedule. These micro missions echo resilience, leadership identity, and strengthen community service ties.

Building a New Life with a Partner

Building partnerships can deepen resilience and leadership identity and often involve community service connections.

Couples: use the Love Tank Check. Rate emotional, logistical, and social tanks from 0–10. Discuss one action each can take to bump a tank by at least two points this week. Single vets: apply the same check with a close friend or mentor.

Ranking Needs (Personal List)

- Security: finances, housing, healthcare
- Purpose: work, projects, community
- Connection: partner, friends, fellow vets

Which need is lowest for you right now? Pick one small action to move it up one notch this month.

Accepting that this phase takes time removes some pressure. Use structure intentionally—small missions, weekly check lists, and partner conversations—to rebuild purpose and daily flow. The tools are simple; consistent use makes them effective.

Inter-branch partner dynamics

Honoring the Diversity of Military Experiences

Recognizing that each branch brings its own rhythms, rules, and quirks is the first step toward smoother collaboration. When partners share the lived realities of different service cultures, they can anticipate how routines—such as meal planning, parenting, or financial decisions—will shift. Emphasize the shared goals of your relationship while honoring each partner's distinct background.

For a structured approach to decoding and translating the specific terminology that emerges in conversations, see "Translating military terms and acronyms."

When you and your partner—or your friends and neighbours—are building civilian veteran friendship networks, honouring the diversity of service experiences helps civilians offer relevant support and reduces misunderstandings. Acknowledging different branch cultures makes it easier for non military friends to appreciate routine changes, rituals, and timing that affect everyday life.

Not all service looks the same—even when everyone's wearing a uniform. Each branch has its own rhythms, rules, and quirks, and those differences show up in home life, in how partners cope with time apart, and in what each person expects from routine and support. If one or both of you served, recognizing these distinctions can reduce friction and create practical advantages for the relationship. Shifting focus from "branch identity" to the shared identity you build together helps you meet those differences with empathy. Ask each other to explain acronyms, schedules, or expectations—simple clarifications bridge the communication gaps that arise when two military cultures collide.

For a structured approach to decoding and translating the specific terminology that emerges in conversations, see "Translating military terms and acronyms."

When you're cultivating civilian veteran friendships, take time to translate those rhythms for civilian friends. Brief, concrete explanations about schedules, common rituals, or typical stressors give civilians the tools to offer practical help—childcare, meal support, or a flexible visit—at the right times.

Branch Specific Challenges and Opportunities

Navy and Coast Guard partners often deal with long stretches at sea: birthdays, holidays, and household chores get scheduled around a ship's timetable. Army and Marine Corps partners might face more frequent relocations and shorter, repetitive deployments—think a lot of packing and quick emotional goodbyes. Air Force and Space Force schedules can be more predictable, but frequent permanent change of station orders still mean saying "see you later" to friends and local supports. Recognizing that each branch's rhythm is only one piece of the partnership lets you adapt your routines and plan for the inevitable shifts, while keeping the focus on the couple's shared goals rather than on a single service label.

For a structured approach to decoding and translating the specific terminology that emerges in conversations, see "Translating military terms and acronyms."

Navy and Coast Guard partners often deal with long stretches at sea: birthdays, holidays, and household chores get scheduled around a ship's timetable. Army and Marine Corps partners might face more frequent relocations and shorter, repetitive deployments—think a lot of packing and quick emotional goodbyes. Air Force and Space Force schedules can be more predictable, but frequent permanent change of station orders still mean saying "see you later" to friends and local supports. Recognizing that each branch's rhythm is only one piece of the partnership lets you adapt your routines and plan for the inevitable shifts, while keeping the focus on the couple's shared goals rather than on a single service label.

For a structured approach to decoding and translating the specific terminology that emerges in conversations, see "Translating military terms and acronyms."

These practical rhythms also shape how you form civilian relationships: explaining a ship's timetable or a PCS cycle to neighbours helps them offer specific support (meal trains during deployment, helping with a last-minute move) and strengthens your civilian veteran network.

Practical prompt: Reintegration Reflection – Use the PCG (deployment play books) to guide your reflection on the challenges and opportunities that arise for inter branch partners. As you discuss, pause to explain any jargon or acronyms, and frame the conversation around the relationship you are building together. Plan the support needed during transitions, keeping both practical logistics and the emotional shift from branch centric identity to shared partnership in mind.

For a structured approach to decoding and translating the specific terminology that emerges in conversations, see "Translating military terms and acronyms."

Consider inviting a trusted civilian friend or a veteran peer to parts of this reflection or to a debrief afterward. Sharing selected parts of your play book can help civilians better understand how to support you and can begin or deepen a civilian veteran friendship.

- One partner writes three concrete ways deployments/moves changed daily life (meals, parenting, finances). Note which of those changes it would help civilian friends to know about so they can offer targeted support.

For a structured approach to decoding and translating the specific terminology that emerges in conversations, see "Translating military terms and acronyms."

- The other partner lists three things they wished they understood beforehand—especially things that, if shared with civilian or military friends earlier, would have helped those friends provide better support.

Share lists, then pick one item to problem solve together this week, using clear language and asking each other to translate any military terms that surface. Optionally invite a trusted civilian friend or veteran mentor to join the problem solving session to practice how they can help and to strengthen your civilian veteran network.

Bridging Communication Gaps

The simplest bridge is to translate jargon deliberately. When a partner mentions an acronym or protocol, pause and ask for a quick version. For example, if a Marine says "we had an OPORD," a concise reply could be, "Quick version—what was the mission goal and who did what?" This turns jargon into a story you can both hold, helping the relationship shift from a focus on individual branch identities to a shared narrative.

For a structured approach to decoding and translating the specific terminology that emerges in conversations, see "Translating military terms and acronyms."

To bridge communication gaps between branches, translate jargon deliberately. When an acronym or protocol is mentioned, pause and ask for a quick version. For example, if a Marine says "we had an OPORD," a concise reply could be, "Quick version—what was the mission goal and who did what?" This turns jargon into a story you can both hold, helping the relationship shift from a focus on individual branch identities to a shared narrative.

For a structured approach to decoding and translating the specific terminology that emerges in conversations, see "Translating military terms and acronyms."

Teach that same habit to civilian friends in your support network: a short, plain language translation of common terms helps civilians feel competent and confident when they want to help, and it makes your civilian veteran friendships more resilient and practical.

Prompt: The "Explain It Like I'm Home" Check

Each partner tells a five minute story about a typical workday, using no jargon, and the listener summarizes the story in one sentence and asks one follow up question.

For a structured approach to decoding and translating the specific terminology that emerges in conversations, see "Translating military terms and acronyms."

Each partner tells a five minute story about a typical workday, using no jargon. The listener summarizes the story in one sentence and asks one follow up question. This exercise turns unfamiliar terminology into shared understanding and strengthens the partnership's communication foundation.

For a structured approach to decoding and translating the specific terminology that emerges in conversations, see "Translating military terms and acronyms."

Swap roles.

Moving Past Branch Identity

Inter branch partner dynamics: Building civilian friendships can deepen a partnership beyond military ties. Branch pride runs deep, and it can be healthy. But a strong partnership also needs common ground outside service affiliation. Schedule one recurring non military date—rock climbing, a cooking class, community volunteering—something that builds a shared identity separate from unit badges and rank. Practical prompt: Ranking Needs

- Individually rank three non service values (family time, stability, adventure).
- Compare lists and pick one shared value to act on this month.

Practical Strategies for Mutual Understanding

- Schedule regular check-ins: set a 20 minute weekly slot to talk about feelings and plans without fixing everything.
- Share stories: keep a "deployment diary" to swap when time allows.
- Ask questions: replace assumptions with curiosity—"What was the hardest part?" Beats "You're fine."
- Celebrate wins: mark promotions, training graduations, or simply surviving a tough month with a small ritual.
- Seek support: if patterns repeat and create tension, bring in a counsellor who understands military life.

These strategies echo the general relationship building advice found in broader resources.

The "Love Tank" Check

Weekly: each partner names one thing that filled their tank and one that drained it. Then act on one small item that helps fill the tank before the next check.

These approaches honour where you came from while building something that works for both of you now. Small, specific practices—translation of jargon, scheduled check-ins, and shared non-military activities—create steadiness when the service calendar throws another curve ball.

Identity shift: from uniform to civilian

Embracing the shift from a life defined by uniform and command to one shaped by everyday choices is a big deal — and we're going to get practical about it. This section offers ways to grieve the loss, test out a civilian sense of self, and use concrete tools to move forward together with your partner. Use short journaling practices as you work through this material: keep a private daily log for two weeks noting one moment you missed the old routine, one moment you appreciated something new, and one question about who you want to become. Pair that personal journal with a shared weekly check-in with your partner where you read one entry aloud and listen without trying to fix anything. The grieving process acknowledges the loss of routine while opening space for new possibilities; journaling helps you notice patterns and measure progress. These journaling techniques build on the principles outlined in "Journaling for Self Discovery and Growth."

When your identity shifts from military to civilian life, give space to the fact that the uniform and structure provided a sense of community, purpose, and clear direction. It's normal to feel disoriented when those signposts go away. Try this short ritual: on a piece of paper, write three things you miss about your old routine and three things you don't. Then transfer that list into your journal and, over the next week, add one sentence each day about how each item shows up in your life now. Share the list with your partner during a quiet evening—no fixing, just listening. Naming and feeling that loss often softens it; tracking it in a journal lets you see shifts in feeling over time. This journalling process is grounded in the framework of "Journalling for Self Discovery and Growth."

Reintegration Reflection

This subsection expands the title into a practical exercise. Begin by asking yourself: what routines gave me a sense of purpose while in uniform, and what new routines could recreate that purpose in civilian life? Write down at least three old routines and three potential new ones.

Choose one small habit to start this week—perhaps a morning walk or a 10 minute gratitude note. After 10 minutes of free writing, circle the insight you'll act on over the next seven days. This reflective journalling aligns with the methods described in "Journalling for Self Discovery and Growth."

Reflect on what you miss and what you gain as you transition, using this moment to honour the structure you once relied on while embracing your evolving identity. Journal prompts to guide this reflection:

- What routines gave me a sense of purpose?
- What new routines could recreate parts of that purpose?
- What is one small habit I can start this week to test a new direction?

Spend 10 minutes writing freely, then circle one insight to act on in the next seven days. This exercise echoes the journalling strategies presented in "Journalling for Self Discovery and Growth."

Exploring Your Civilian Self — Try Before You Commit

Treat this transition like sampling stations at a fair: you don't have to buy a whole booth, but you can taste a variety of flavours. Pick a hobby you left behind—guitar, running, woodworking—and set a 30 days trial: attend one class or meet up per week. Or enrol in a weekend course unrelated to service—sushi making, improve, or a small business basics workshop. Keep a simple sampling journal entry after each session: date, activity, mood before, mood after, one insight, and a 1–10 "would do again" score. These low stakes trials let you see what sticks, mourn the loss of old routines, and discover new passions. The journalling element is consistent with the guidance in "Journalling for Self Discovery and Growth."

Treat this exploration as a gentle experiment with your new identity, allowing you to test civilian interests without full commitment. Use a short experiment journal: before each trial, write your intention; after each session, note what surprised you, what felt easy or hard, and whether you'd like to repeat it. Reviewing these notes after 30 days reveals patterns that guide next steps.

- What routines did the uniform give me that I miss most?
- Which of those routines can I recreate in civilian life (daily workouts, team check-ins, clear goals)?

Think of this period like sampling stations at a fair, not buying the whole booth. Take one hobby you left behind (guitar, running clubs, woodworking) and set a 30 days trial: one class or one meet up per week. Or sign up for a weekend course in something utterly unrelated to service — sushi making, improve, or a small business basics workshop. Keep a simple sampling journal entry after each session: date, activity, mood before, mood after, one insight, and a 1–10 "would do again" score. These low stakes trials let you see what sticks and give you a chance to mourn the loss of your old routine while discovering new passions.

Concrete Self-love Practices

- For men: Schedule a weekly "no pressure" hour to do something non competitive—sketching, stretching, or a podcast you don't have to analyse. Keep it consistent for six weeks.
- For women: Set a recurring meeting with a mentor or friend of interest to talk about goals, not chores—thirty minutes, coffee shop or call.
- For both: Try a 5 minute grounding exercise: breathe in for 4, out for 6, repeat 6 times before bed to reduce ramped up tension from habit.

These self-love practices dovetail with the reflective journalling framework discussed in "Journalling for Self Discovery and Growth."

These practices align with the self-love and resilience insights discussed earlier in the book. Add a brief journalling step to each practice to deepen awareness and track change.

- For men: schedule a weekly "no pressure" hour to do something non competitive — sketching, stretching, or a podcast you don't have to analyse. Before and after the hour, jot two lines in your journal about how you felt entering the hour and what changed by the end. Keep it consistent for six weeks.

- For women: set a recurring meeting with a mentor or friend of interest to talk about goals, not chores — thirty minutes, coffee shop or call. After each meeting, write one takeaway and one action step in your journal so conversations convert into momentum.

- For both: try 5 minute grounding: breathe in for 4, out for 6, repeat 6 times before bed to reduce ramped up tension from habit. Follow the grounding with a one sentence mood check in your journal to notice trends over time.

- For men: schedule a weekly "no pressure" hour to do something non competitive — sketching, stretching, or a podcast you don't have to analyse. Keep it consistent for six weeks.

These actions can be logged in a brief journal entry each week, noting mood before and after, to reinforce the self-love process described in "Journalling for Self Discovery and Growth."

Journalling prompt: before the hour write one expectation, after the hour write one sensation and one thought you want to remember. Over six weeks, note shifts in pressure to perform.

- For women: set a recurring meeting with a mentor or friend of interest to talk about goals, not chores — thirty minutes, coffee shop or call.

Document each conversation in your journal, reflecting on what you gained and how it aligns with your evolving civilian identity, as advised in "Journalling for Self Discovery and Growth."

Journalling prompt: after each meeting, list one concrete step you want to try and one resource or contact you'll follow up with. Review these entries monthly to track progress.

- For both: try 5 minute grounding: breathe in for 4, out for 6, repeat 6 times before bed to reduce ramped up tension from habit.

After each session, jot down your relaxation level on a scale of 1-10 in your journal, linking the practice to the reflective methods of "Journalling for Self Discovery and Growth."

Journalling prompt: immediately after grounding, write a online mood rating and one image or word that captures how your body feels. Use these markers to notice when tension returns and which practices help.

Identifying Transferable Skills — Make Them Speak Civilian

As you identify transferable skills, rely on the exercises earlier in the book that helped you name and map them. Here, focus on translating the language: swap military-specific terms for clear civilian equivalents, and give concrete examples of results (what you achieved, how you solved problems, who benefited). Use a focused journalling exercise: take one military task per entry and rewrite it in civilian terms, then add a short result statement and a metric if possible.

Example journal conversion template:

- Military line: Led a platoon in high tempo operations.
- Civilian phrasing: Managed a 30person team in high pressure environments, coordinating schedules and logistics to meet mission deadlines.
- Result: Reduced task completion time by 20% and maintained team readiness; stakeholders reported improved reliability.

Framing skills this way reduces the grief over structure by showing how your strengths create value in civilian roles, and tracking these translations in your journal builds a portfolio of clear, civilian facing examples you can use in applications and interviews.

Identify the core skill you want to highlight—such as leading a squad—and reframe it in civilian terms. Write a one paragraph explanation that avoids jargon, e.g. "led a squad" becomes "managed a team of X people to meet tight deadlines, achieving Y result." Use this concise summary in job applications or when explaining your background to new friends. Practice by swapping summaries and refining each other's sentences.

Navigating Civilian Roles and Expectations with Your Partner

This brief section complements the material on post service relationships by offering practical, partner-focused steps you can use together. It's not a repeat of earlier coverage; it's a hands-on bridge that turns insights into shared actions you can try at home.

Talk openly about expectations. Use the "Ranking Needs" prompt: each partner lists their top five needs—structure, quiet time, social contact, predictable income, new learning—then compare. Where the lists align, plan together; where they differ, negotiate small experiments for two months and review. This process helps both partners navigate the shift from military to civilian identities and maintain mutual support.

Military life taught you to check equipment; now check emotional tanks. Once a week ask: "On a scale of 1–10, where's your tank?" Follow up with one action to top it up: a walk, a chore taken, or 20 minutes of focused conversation.

Understanding Civilian Challenges — Real Talk

Keep this section focused on clear, practical expectations so you and your partner can plan together. It highlights the differences you'll face without repeating earlier analyses; think of it as the pragmatic companion to the book's broader discussion of post service transitions.

Expect less public recognition and more ambiguous schedules. Translate that into tactics: build your own structure (calendar blocks for job searching, physical fitness, and social time), and appoint one accountability buddy — civilian or veteran — to check in weekly.

This framework helps you navigate civilian challenges by giving clear boundaries and steady support.

Reconnecting with Past Interests — A Roadmap

Pick two interests: one familiar, one brand new. Schedule them on your calendar for six weeks. Journal one sentence after each session: what felt good, what felt awkward. Use these notes in partner conversations to map a social life that works for both of you.

Closing reminder: this is incremental work. Keep the prompts and reflections visible — taped to the fridge or saved on your phone — and review them every month. Small experiments plus honest conversation will help you and your partner craft a civilian life that fits who you are now.

Benefits and entitlements by branch

Place this material with the financial literacy and benefits navigation resources for service members transitioning to civilian life.

Branch-Specific Benefits: Getting Clear About What's on the Table

You've worked hard; now it helps to know exactly what each branch has in the benefits toolbox. Different services package similar entitlements in slightly different ways, and the paperwork routes vary too. Below you'll find the most commonly used benefits, clear examples, and quick actions you can take.

Educational Benefits: Using Your GI Bill and Alternatives

The Post9/11 GI Bill can cover up to 100 % of instate public tuition for eligible veterans; MGIBAD provides up to 36 months of support for education programs. If you have at least 36 months of post9/11 service, you could receive full tuition at a state university plus a monthly housing allowance. Request your Certificate of Eligibility (COE) to confirm your exact eligibility on the VA site, compare tuition coverage, housing allowance, and transferability rules, and get the necessary letters of service from your personnel office. If you're married and considering transferring benefits to a spouse or child, talk it through now.

Housing Benefits: VA Home Loans Made Practical

VA home loans often offer lower interest rates and little or no down payment. Surviving spouses sometimes qualify for special no down payment options. Example: a veteran with sufficient service and a COE may avoid private mortgage insurance and use the VA funding fee (or an exemption) to save thousands. Action step: Meet with a Approved lender and bring your DD214, COE, and recent bank statements. Ask about county limits and whether the lender requires residual income proof.

Healthcare Access: Tricare and CHAMPVA Basics

If you're leaving active duty, Tricare plans—Prime, Select, and Tricare For Life for Medicare eligible vets—differ by cost and network flexibility. Surviving dependence can sometimes use CHAMPVA for medical and pharmacy benefits. Quick check: list current prescriptions and providers. Call Tricare or CHAMPVA to confirm coverage transfers and time line so there's no gap in care.

Place this paragraph with the financial literacy and benefits navigation resources for transition planning.

You've worked hard; now it helps to know exactly what each branch has in the benefits toolbox. Different services package similar entitlements in slightly different ways, and the paperwork routes vary too. Below are the most commonly used benefits, with clear examples and quick actions you can take to confirm eligibility and start claims or enrolments early in your transition planning.

Place this section with the financial literacy and benefits navigation resources for transition planning.

Educational Benefits: Using Your GI Bill and Alternatives

This section gives an early, practical summary of education benefits—what's available, how to confirm eligibility, and immediate steps to enrol or transfer benefits.

Place this material with the financial literacy and benefits navigation resources for transition planning.

Educational benefits: The Post9/11 GI Bill can cover up to 100% of instate public tuition for eligible veterans; MGIBAD provides up to 36 months of support for education programs. If you have at least 36 months of Post9/11 service, you could receive full tuition at a state university plus a monthly housing allowance. Request your Certificate of Eligibility (COE) on the VA site to confirm exact eligibility, then compare tuition coverage, housing allowance, and transferability rules.

Get the necessary letters of service from your personnel office. If you're married and considering transferring benefits to a spouse or child, discuss transferability now so you meet any service or timing requirements.

Place this summary with the financial literacy and benefits navigation resources for transition planning.

Housing Benefits: VA Home Loans Made Practical

This practical summary explains how to use VA home loans, who qualifies, and the immediate documents and questions to take to a lender.

Place this guidance with the financial literacy and benefits navigation resources for transition planning.

Surviving spouses sometimes qualify for special no down payment options. Example: a veteran with sufficient service and a COE may avoid private mortgage insurance and use the VA funding fee (or an exemption) to save thousands. Action step: Meet with a Approved lender and bring your DD214, COE, and recent bank statements. Ask about county limits, whether the lender requires residual income proof, and any available fee exemptions for which you may qualify.

Place this note with the financial literacy and benefits navigation resources for transition planning.

VA home loans often offer lower interest rates and little or no down payment. Surviving spouses may qualify for special no down payment options. A veteran with sufficient service and a Certificate of Eligibility (COE) can often avoid private mortgage insurance; the VA funding fee applies unless you qualify for an exemption. Confirm specifics with a Approved lender early in your housing search.

Action step: Meet with a VA-approved lender and bring your DD-214, COE, and recent bank statements. Ask about county limits and whether the lender requires residual income proof.

Place this overview with the financial literacy and benefits navigation resources for transition planning.

Healthcare Access: Tricare and CHAMPVA Basics

This concise healthcare overview is designed to be reviewed early in transition planning so you can prevent gaps in care and coordinate benefits for yourself and dependence.

Place this guidance with the financial literacy and benefits navigation resources for transition planning.

If you're leaving active duty, Tricare plans—Prime, Select, and Tricare For Life for Medicare eligible vets—differ by cost and network flexibility. Surviving dependence can sometimes use CHAMPVA for medical and pharmacy benefits. Quick check: list current prescriptions and providers. Call Tricare or CHAMPVA to confirm coverage transfers, enrolment steps, and timeliness so there's no gap in care.

Place this action step with the financial literacy and benefits navigation resources for transition planning.

Healthcare access: If you're leaving active duty, Tricare plans (Prime, Select, and Tricare For Life for Medicare eligible vets) differ by cost and network flexibility. Surviving dependence can sometimes use CHAMPVA for medical and pharmacy benefits. Action step: create a list of prescriptions and current providers, then contact the appropriate plan now to confirm enrolment rules and avoid lapses in coverage.

Quick check:

- List current prescriptions and providers.
- Call Tricare or CHAMPVA to confirm coverage transfers, enrolment steps, pharmacy network access, and effective dates so there's no gap in care.

Retirement pay formulas depend on rank and years served; the amount you choose for your Survivor Benefit Plan (SBP) directly determines the monthly payments received by your loved ones after you pass away. Plan carefully during the retirement paperwork window, and consider running a simple "What if?" Scenario with your partner to estimate the monthly support you'll need if one spouse dies.

Transition services are essential for preparing for life after the military. Each branch offers a Transition Assistance Program (TAP) – for example, TAP for the Army – that covers resume writing, interview techniques, and connections to employers. These programs often include local job fairs and mentor matching opportunities. Action step: enrol in your branch's transition classes early, collect workshop certificates, and schedule mock interviews with a TAP counsellor.

Disability compensation claims and appeals can be complex. Keep a dedicated folder with medical records, incident reports, and buddy statements. If your claim is denied, book a Veterans Service Organization (VSO) consult within 30 days to review the decision and prepare an appeal.

Reintegration reflection helps prioritize benefits and streamline paperwork. Ask yourself: "Which benefit will I prioritize first (education, home loan, healthcare, retirement/SBP, or disability) and who will be my point person for paperwork and deadlines?"

This consolidated "Benefits and Transition Services" section provides a comprehensive overview of retirement pay, SBP, disability compensation, and transition support to help you plan for a smooth post service life.

Before signing big forms, talk finances and future safety nets with your partner. Short, honest conversations now avoid awkward surprises later.

By breaking benefits into manageable steps—learn the specific rules for your branch, gather key documents, and use transition services—you'll trade uncertainty for action. Little wins in paperwork add up to big peace of mind.

Relocation and family readiness patterns

Branch Specific Transition Nuances – this section examines how relocation patterns and family readiness vary by branch, and how the accompanying service related stressors impact family readiness. These dynamics illustrate the link between branch specific challenges and the broader concepts of stress management and trigger normalization.

Understanding how each branch shapes moves helps you plan practical steps before the next permanent change of station. Below are common stress points for families in each service, concrete ways to shore up readiness, and short prompts you and your partner can use together.

Air Force: frequent moves and remote duty – the Air Force's high mobility schedule and remote assignments create unique stressors that test family readiness. Understanding these patterns helps families prepare for the emotional and logistical challenges that accompany each transition.

Air Force families often change bases every two to three years and may face assignments where one partner is isolated from local support. Practical steps to mitigate the resulting stress include:

- Self care tool kit: Pack a "first month" box with familiar items for kids and adults—favourite snacks, classroom supplies, a bedside lamp—to reduce the first week scramble. This practice helps stabilize emotional responses and lowers the likelihood of trigger based stress.
- Spouse work plan: Use My CAA funds for a short, portable credential (e.g., project management, medical coding) that travels with you. A clear career plan reduces uncertainty and supports family resilience during relocation.
- When facing remote duty, set a weekly check-in ritual (video call + 30 minute "no logistics" zone) to keep emotional connection steady. This ritual helps normalize emotional triggers and prevents

stress build-up.

These steps help families manage the stressors associated with frequent moves and remote duty.

- Self care tool kit: Pack a "first month" box with familiar items for kids and adults—favourite snacks, classroom supplies, a bedside lamp—to reduce the first week scramble. This practice helps stabilize emotional responses and lowers the likelihood of trigger based stress.
- Spouse work plan: Use My CAA funds for a short, portable credential (e.g., project management, medical coding) that travels with you. A clear career plan reduces uncertainty and supports family resilience during relocation.
- When facing remote duty, set a weekly check-in ritual (video call + 30 minute "no logistics" zone) to keep emotional connection steady. This ritual helps normalize emotional triggers and prevents stress build-up.

Reintegration Reflection: What three items would you include in your "first month" box that help you feel at home? Selecting grounding items can mitigate stress and reinforce a sense of belonging after relocation.

Army: unit bonds as family backbone – the Army's strong unit cohesion often serves as the primary support network. While this can be comforting, reliance on the unit for resources may intensify stress when families are in new environments.

Army units often function like extended support networks. That cohesion helps during deployments but can create dependence on the unit for resources. When a family moves, this dependence can magnify the stress of adjusting to a new community and finding local support.

- Actionable habit: Within 60 days of arrival in your new town, map two non unit contacts (neighbour, school counsellor) and use the FRG to get updates. Build a small, personal support plan—babysitter names, nearby grocery pickup, and a trusted mechanic. Identifying independent contacts early helps reduce stress and enhances family readiness.

Branch Specific Transition Nuances

Navy — port calls and long stretches at sea

Navy life often means long deployments and extended single parenting periods. Prioritize household continuity so routines and responsibilities keep running while one partner is away.

- Practical fix: create a shared household binder (digital and paper) with routines, medication lists, bill pay instructions, and kid schedules. Teach at least one teenager how to handle basics.

- Spouse-to-spouse: join a Navy spouse group and ask for "deployment play books" — short, battle-tested guides from other families.

- The "Love Tank" Check: During deployment, send one small, predictable message daily (photo, 10-second audio) to keep emotional reserves from draining.

Marine Corps — frequent moves and short notice orders

Marines often face a fast cadence and short notice relocations. Keep records and use available family services to ease transitions.

- Keep a "school record" folder updated with immunizations and transcripts for smoother transfers.

- Use Semper Families resources for counselling and respite when the schedule gets intense.

- After every move decision, practice a 5 minute debrief with your partner—what's working, what's overwhelming—so small frustrations don't build.

Coast Guard — scattered postings and geographic isolation

Coast Guard assignments can place families in remote or coastal locations with limited services; proactive community scouting reduces risk.

- Before a move, identify the nearest clinic, grocery, and an emergency contact within a 30 minute radius.
- Build local networks early: introduce yourself to neighbours, unit spouses, and base liaisons to locate informal supports and resources.

Cross branch checklist (practical, quick actions)

- Maintain both digital and paper copies of critical documents (Ids, medical, school records).
- Create a simple, shared calendar for appointments, child pickup, and bill deadlines.
- Compile a short, family "deployment/move play book" with key contacts, routines, and fallback plans; share it with caregivers and trusted neighbours.
- Schedule regular check-ins (daily or weekly) to monitor household operations and emotional well being.
- Support network: tap the Coast Guard Foundation's programs for travel grants and education help when distance complicates family needs.

Short checklist for every family

(Place this compact checklist at the end of the relocation and family readiness patterns section or within the broader relocation advice so readers have an actionable takeaway to use immediately.)

- One "first month" box packed and labelled. (Include toiletries, basic kitchen tools, phone chargers, a few outfits, basic cleaning supplies, and any essential documents you'll need on arrival.)

- Digital household binder accessible to both partners. (Store passwords, insurance and identification scans, moving documents, medical records, and an editable task list in a shared cloud folder or app.)

- Two non-unit contacts in new community. (Identify at least two people or services outside your household—neighbours, local colleagues, or community organizations—you can reach out to for help, advice, or practical support.)

- One portable skill or certification for the spouse. (Choose a short course, license, or credential that is transportable and increases employability across locations.)

- Weekly emotional check-in ritual. (Set aside 15–30 minutes each week to share feelings, concerns, and small wins to keep communication steady during transition.)

Use this as a closing exercise after relocation planning so the family leaves the conversation with one clear, completed action. (See the practical checklist at the end of the "Relocation and housing transitions" section for step by step guidance.)

Fitness culture and civilian life alignment

Self care, boundaries, and social support networks are the scaffolding that transforms the regimented fitness culture of the military into a personal love practice. By setting clear limits on time, effort, and emotional energy—just as a training schedule sets limits on reps and rest—you give yourself space to nurture the body and the spirit. When you pair that discipline with the support of peers, family, and veteran communities, the routine becomes less about duty and more about intentional self love, allowing you to honor your limits while celebrating your progress.

Understanding the Unique Fitness Culture of Military Service

The rigorous physical culture that shaped service members extends beyond the uniform; it instilled a mindset that thrives on structure, measurable goals, and mutual accountability. By understanding this mindset, you can better adapt those principles to civilian life and personal resilience, using them to support self-care, set healthy boundaries, and connect with supportive communities.

The daily commitment to physical training becomes a ritual of self respect. Establishing boundaries—such as a "no phone" gym window—protects the practice from external distractions, mirroring how a commander protects his unit. This safeguard ensures the activity remains a pure act of self care. When you share this disciplined space with a supportive network, each workout reinforces the message: your health matters, and your worth is reflected in the consistency you bring to your own body.

If you've worn boots long enough, you know physical readiness was more than a box to check — it was a daily program. That routine trained muscle and mind: early ruck runs, PT docks, standards that didn't argue. When service members leave the uniform behind, that discipline can either be a secret weapon or a source of friction as life loosens up. By translating those habits into personal targets—clear, measurable goals—and embedding them into daily routines, you maintain the momentum while also caring for recovery and sleep, setting boundaries, and leaning on social supports where needed.

Adapting military discipline to self-love means converting the mindset of "mission first" into "self first" without losing structure. When you schedule cardio or strength sessions as non-negotiable appointments, you honour the body like a unit respects its chain of command. This disciplined schedule feeds the self-love loop—every completed workout signals mastery, which strengthens the emotional foundation that supports boundaries and fosters healthy relationships with others.

Contrasting Military and Civilian Fitness Expectations

In the military, fitness is a collective, command driven endeavour, whereas civilian fitness is often individualized and driven by personal motivation. Understanding these contrasting expectations is key to a smooth transition and helps you align your training with the new context while prioritizing self-care, setting appropriate boundaries, and finding the right social supports.

Physical well-being and self-love share a reciprocal relationship: as you train, you learn the power of bodily awareness; as you practice self-love, you motivate the body to honour that awareness. Establishing a training routine that respects recovery—much like a mission debrief—creates a safe zone for reflection, allowing you to set boundaries that protect your mental bandwidth while simultaneously feeding a supportive network that celebrates each milestone.

Bridging the Gap: Transitioning to Civilian Fitness

Use the same principles that kept you fit in uniform—discipline, accountability, and measurable metrics—but apply them to a civilian context, treating workouts like scheduled appointments and tracking progress like mission reports. This approach preserves structure while allowing flexibility for personal growth, recovery, and the boundary-setting needed to balance fitness with other life demands; consider also how community or peer support can provide accountability.

Military fitness asks, “Can you do the job under stress?” Civilian fitness often asks, “Do you feel good doing this?” Neither approach is superior—each serves a distinct purpose. Veterans may miss the structure and peer pressure that pushed them to personal records; civilians may not understand why a Saturday at 0600 matters. Aligning the two cultures involves setting personal targets—specific, measurable goals that satisfy the military emphasis on performance while meeting the civilian desire for positive experience. The rules may have changed, but the value of fitness remains.

In the same way a soldier follows a drill to maintain readiness, a veteran can follow a fitness regimen to maintain readiness for emotional resilience. Each session reinforces the principle that self care is a discipline, not a luxury. When this discipline is practiced within a circle of supportive peers, boundaries are respected, and self-love becomes a shared, reinforcing practice that nurtures both body and community.

Bridging the Gap: Transitioning to Civilian Fitness (continued)

Recognize that the absence of a formal chain of command means you must become your own commander, setting the pace and adjusting the plan as life evolves. This autonomy reinforces the habit of intentional routine building but also requires you to consciously set boundaries, protect recovery time, and cultivate a support network that offers accountability and encouragement.

Military fitness asks, “Can you do the job under stress?” Civilian fitness more often asks, “Do you feel good doing this?” Neither is better — they’re different. Veterans may miss the structure and peer pressure that pushed them to PRs; civilians may not understand why a Saturday at 0600 matters. Recognize the gap: the rules changed, not the value of fitness.

To align fitness culture after transition, create a personal system that blends military-style accountability with civilian flexibility. Use “personal targets” as your anchor: clear, measurable goals tied to purpose (health markers, time-based runs, strength milestones, or simply consistency). Then build the scaffolding you need:

A regimented training schedule sets a predictable rhythm that supports boundary setting: you know when to push and when to pause. This rhythm is the same cadence that allows you to engage with friends, family, and veteran groups without overextending. By framing fitness as an expression of self-love, you invite others to witness and celebrate the discipline, reinforcing the network that sustains your well being.

- Schedule: Block regular sessions on your calendar like appointments. Treat them as non-negotiable to recreate the routine you valued, and consider time for stretching or mobility work as part of your daily routine; include explicit recovery time to honour personal boundaries.

The link between fitness culture and self-love is most evident when you recognize that each rep is a reaffirmation of your worth. Structured exercise demands accountability; self-love demands acceptance. When you hold both in balance, you create a resilient system where boundaries protect your energy, the social network provides encouragement, and the disciplined routine turns physical effort into a tangible act of caring for yourself.

- Accountability: Find a civilian workout group, training partner, or an online community that matches your intensity and goals, and use it as a peer support system for both fitness and self care, prioritizing groups that respect your boundaries and broader well being.

By translating the precision of military training into daily self care habits, you embed a sense of purpose into your wellness routine. Setting boundaries around time, effort, and emotional engagement turns the gym into a sanctuary. The supportive community—whether fellow veterans or close friends—acts as a morale boosting squad that celebrates each disciplined step, reinforcing the mutual reinforcement of fitness culture and self-love.

- Metrics: Translate military metrics into civilian friendly targets—e.g., instead of only aiming for a service specific test score, pursue a 5K time, a bodyweight milestone, or reliable sleep and recovery metrics that align with good self-care practices.

- Adaptability: Prioritize time-efficient workouts (HIIT, short strength circuits) when life gets busy, and allow sessions focused on enjoyment so fitness remains sustainable.
- Rituals: Keep small rituals (pre workout routine, warm-up sequence, gear) to preserve the culture and focus you miss.
- Mark a 10 minute "reset" slot after each task to check in with your body and set a boundary before the next activity.
- Share one ritual with your partner or friend so you both benefit from shared focus and mutual accountability.

This ties concrete routine steps to the broader themes of self care, boundary setting, and building a supportive network.

The aim is not to recreate the past exactly but to respect what worked — discipline, measurable progress, and camaraderie — while fitting them into civilian life.

The structured approach to training—sets, reps, and progression—mirrors the process of setting healthy boundaries. By treating each workout as a commitment to oneself, you cultivate an internal dialogue that prioritizes self care. Sharing this commitment with a support network reinforces the behaviour, turning disciplined fitness into an act of love that honours both personal limits and communal encouragement.

Concrete moves to create routine without commanding orders:

These concrete moves help you create a routine that feels intentional rather than commanded, integrating the habits of discipline with the flexibility of civilian life while emphasizing self-care, boundary-setting, and building social support.

Integrating military discipline into fitness routines transforms them from mere workouts into rituals of self affection. When you allocate specific time for stretching, breathing, and recovery, you create a space where the body speaks, and your mind listens. This deliberate listening strengthens the bond between the disciplined body and the loving self, and the surrounding social network validates that connection.

- Set personal targets: pick one measurable goal (e.g., three 30 minute sessions weekly, a 5K in 12 weeks). Put it on your calendar like a drill and track it alongside recovery markers such as sleep hours and hydration, and coordinate those targets with boundaries and supports that protect your recovery.

- Community that clicks: join a vets' running group, a Cross Fit box with military friendly coaches, or an online crew that posts weekly check-ins to provide accountability and belonging.

- Invite a teammate to set a weekly boundary, such as "no phone during workouts," to reinforce healthy habits.

- Create a shared calendar with reminders for group meet ups and personal boundaries so everyone stays aligned.

This builds social support while honouring the need for clear limits in every interaction.

- Try something new: martial arts, cycling clubs, or weekend kayak trips give purpose and fresh novelty.

- Self-care built in: schedule a weekly mobility session or a guided meditation app for mental recovery.

Quick Action Prompt — Reintegration Reflection

Take five minutes to reflect on which routines from service supported your well-being and which you want to keep as acts of self-care. Identify one small, tangible habit to adopt this week (for example: consistent wake time, a daily 10-minute walk, or five minutes of journalling) and name one person who will check in with you about it.

Adapting Military Discipline to Self-Love and Physical Well-Being

Channel your training into compassionate self-care: use structure to protect sleep, nutrition, movement, and recovery rather than punish yourself. Treat routines as supportive tools—consistent wake times, meal windows, and short workout slots can be anchors that promote both physical health and emotional balance.

- Establish a consistent daily routine (e.g., 6 am wake, 6:15–6:45 PT, 12 pm quick walk, 18–30 Min review).
- Break tasks into short, focused blocks; use the 5 minute rule to keep momentum.
- End each day with a 5 minute reflection: what worked, what needs adjustment.

Fitness Beyond Physical Exertion

See fitness as a holistic practice that includes mental and emotional care, not only physical output. Rest, recovery, social support, and enjoyable movement are all part of staying well.

Use your military discipline—structured wake times, meal windows, and workout slots—to build a simple, flexible schedule that centres self care. Track progress with a notebook or an app and name an accountability partner—spouse, buddy, or coach—to check in twice a week. Prioritize rest days and adjust the plan with kindness to avoid burnout. This approach turns disciplined routine into a holistic health and wellness strategy that supports body and mind.

Add a daily boundary line: "I will not respond to work emails after 7 pm" to ensure recovery time is protected.

Physical training is medicine for mood and focus. Add mental fitness practices as acts of self-love: five minutes of breath work after a run, brief journalling about wins, or therapy sessions for processing service transitions. Emotional check-ins with your partner can be short but meaningful, and small, consistent practices build resilience over time.

Set a boundary for each training session—such as "I will not check my phone for 30 minutes after the workout"—to protect the space for recovery and mental reset.

Shared Fitness Activities for Couples

Turn fitness into couple strengthening time:

- Create a shared fitness calendar that includes family, work, and self care windows.
- Allocate a "flex day" each week for spontaneous activity or rest, respecting both partners' boundaries.
- Celebrate joint milestones with a small ritual—like a favourite snack or a photo—to reinforce the shared journey and keep the bond alive.
- Try a beginner partner yoga class once a week.
- Follow up with a 10 minute gratitude circle: each partner shares one thing they appreciated about the other's effort.
- Keep a simple journal entry titled "Session Reflections" to note boundaries, feelings, and progress, linking to real world examples of successful strategies.
- Plan a hilly two-hour hike with a picnic — one partner navigates the route, the other packs snacks.
- Join a casual sports league together and keep score light.

The "Love Tank" Check – Adapted for Physical Well Being

Once a month, each partner rates their "love tank" (0–10) and lists one physical activity they want to do together next month. This rating reflects how physically connected you feel, while the activity plan keeps you both moving toward shared health goals.

Prioritizing Physical Well-being for Resilience

Regular movement boosts mood, sharpens focus, and helps relationships by lowering stress reactivity. Small, consistent habits — a shared walk after dinner, a Saturday climb session, a 15-minute mobility routine — add up. Start with one habit, keep it simple, and build from there.

Reflection Prompt — Ranking Needs

Prioritize your physical well being over the next 90 days by ranking the four key fitness dimensions: strength, stamina, mobility, and stress relief.

- Rank them in order of importance.
- Choose the top two.
- Schedule one focused activity per week that targets each of those top two areas.

Make sure your plan is realistic and fits your current schedule.

Bringing military grit into civilian life doesn't require copying old orders. Use the structure, keep the camaraderie, and choose activities that make you and your partner healthier and closer — one scheduled workout, one shared hike, one short check-in at a time.

Case studies: diverse branch experiences

Illuminating Diverse Journeys: Case Studies Across Branches

Transitions look different depending on the uniform you wore. Below are compact case studies that highlight common post-service adjustments for each branch, with practical tips partners can use to offer support and concrete prompts for veterans to process what's shifted.

Army Veterans: From Field Ops to Office Clocks

Army life often means unpredictable days, heavy physical demands, and constant movement. Switching to a 9-to-5 desk routine can feel like being handed a slow-motion script.

[Relocate to the branch-specific transition nuances section.]

- Practical tip for partners: Offer to help create a "mission brief" for the week — a shared calendar with workout blocks, downtime, and job-search tasks so the structure feels familiar.
- Self care example: For a male vet who thrived on team PT, try a Saturday blast—join a community boot camp or volunteer for a neighbourhood clean-up that uses those physical skills.
- Reintegration Reflection: What parts of your field routine are most missed? List three elements (e.g., camaraderie, physical challenge, clear goals) and one civilian habit that could replace each. (This prompt is part of the Reintegration Reflection tool, which is collected in the book's Tools section for easy reference
- Marine Corps Veterans: Moving from Tight-knit Packs to Solo Decisions
- Marines frequently describe a deep unit bond that makes solo

civilian life feel strangely quiet and raw.

- Concrete support for partners: Schedule weekly "check-in" walks where no problem solving is allowed—just listening and shared silence if that's what's needed.

- Personal practice: Try a short daily ritual that re-centers identity—10 minutes of breath work before work, or a simple strength routine that maintains a sense of competence.

- The "Love Tank" Check (partner dialogue): When you feel disconnected, what refills your tank—shared tasks, direct praise, or physical touch? Rank three and compare answers.

Navy Veterans: Relearning Day-Night Rhythms After Long Deployments

- Life at sea rewrites body clocks and family rhythms. Shore life asks for different timing and intimacy skills.

- Action step: Reintroduce regular mealtimes and light cues (open curtains in the morning, dim lights at night) to restore a natural cycle.

- Job-match idea: Translate seamanship into civilian roles—logistics, project coordination, or maritime training jobs are tangible fits.

- Reintegration Reflection: What sensory triggers (sounds, smells) still pull you back to the ship? How can your partner help create safe boundaries around those triggers?

Air Force Veterans: Shifting from High-Tech Tempo to Slower Civilian Pace

- High-stakes, technical roles can leave vets missing the adrenaline of fast ops.

- Career move: Target civilian employers that value technical certifications; list three skills and a civilian job that uses them.

- Stress tactic: Use short, focused decompression routines—5-

minute grounding after a high-pressure meeting.

- Partner prompt: Ask, "When did work feel most meaningful?" Use that answer to map post-service purpose.

Coast Guard Veterans: Balancing Community Service with Personal Life

Coast Guard service often blends rescue duty with community ties.

- Practical habit: Volunteer together in low-stress community roles to maintain the service impulse without burnout.
- Reflection: Which rescue stories carry over into current anxieties? Share one with your partner and note what support felt helpful.

Space Force Veterans: Finding Identity in a New Branch

Space Force vets face the novelty of a brand-new service identity.

- Identity tip: Keep a skills journal—technical specialties and problem-solving examples that translate to civilian tech roles.
- Partner activity: Attend a public tech talk together to normalize the transition to new communities.

Each case points to one clear aim: make supports specific. Use the prompts above in partner talks and personal journals to move from shared observation to small, doable changes—because practical shifts build steady, lasting resilience.

Resilience and Self-Love: Strength Beyond Service

Self-Love for Male Veterans

Vulnerability as strength: redefining manhood post-service

Practicing self-compassion: When guilt or shame shows up, try the "Minute Buffer." Stop for 60 seconds, breathe, name the feeling, and say one kind sentence to yourself ("I did the best I could with what I knew"). Repeat one more time.

This minute-buffer exercise is an example of the Reintegration Reflection, designed to help you pause, acknowledge your feelings, and move forward with self compassion. After completing the buffer, you may log the reflection in your Love Tank to track emotional resources.

Minute Buffer: Use a daily check-in with a partner or friend—30 seconds each—where you say one feeling and one need. No advice given, just listening.

This quick 30second check-in is an intentional practice within the Reintegration Reflection framework, encouraging honest sharing without advice. You can record the insights in your Love Tank to see how open communication replenishes your emotional reservoir.

Redefining self-worth: Make a list of roles you value besides titles—neighbour, coach, dad, gardener—and rate them. Which gives you the most quiet pride? Which needs attention?

This role ranking exercise is a core activity of the Love Tank Check, letting you quantify how much each identity contributes to your inner reservoir of pride. Note the scores in your Love Tank to track growth over time.

Invite a civilian friend to a low pressure activity (coffee, a hike) and try one conversational pivot that matters: after small talk, ask, "What's been the heaviest thing for you this month?" Use a Minute Buffer, pause, and listen.

Inviting a civilian friend and asking a deep question is a concrete example of the Love Tank Check, probing the quality of your relational connections. Record the conversation in your Love Tank to see how connection fuels your emotional strength.

Reintegration Reflection: After a challenging interaction, take 5 minutes to journal what feelings surfaced, what coping strategies were used, and what you learned about yourself. This helps cement growth and prepares you for the next day.

Below, we unpack a fresh definition of strength that aligns with the tools of Reintegration Reflection and Love Tank Check.

Strength can be the willingness to be open enough to repair, to say "I don't know" or "I need company," or to accept help without shame. The shift takes practice. Below are quick prompts to get started.

You can use the Reintegration Reflection to record how each phrase resonates with your personal narrative, and the Love Tank Check to gauge the strength you draw from acknowledging vulnerability.

Reintegration Reflection

Take a few quiet minutes to answer these questions after returning to everyday life:

- What felt familiar, and what surprised me?
- Where did I feel supported, and where did I feel isolated?
- What small routines helped me settle, and which need rebuilding?
- Who do I want to reconnect with, and what first step will I take?
- What boundaries or supports will help me accept help without shame?

This section contains prompts you can use to examine your mask and other coping patterns.

When do you put the mask on automatically?

What does the mask protect you from, and what does it cut you off from?

- When do you put the mask on automatically?
- What does the mask protect you from, and what does it cut you off from?

Use the following prompts to assess your emotional reservoir and how well you're replenishing it.

- With your partner: each names one thing that fills and one thing that drains your "tank" this week.

"No defence mechanisms: ten minutes total."

Ranking Needs

- List five needs, rank them, and share one rank with a partner to see if their perception matches yours.

These are not soft exercises; they are training drills that use honesty and tenderness as equipment.

Guided self-compassion practices

Reintegration Reflection (prompt) – part of the daily Love Tank Check, tying self compassion to routine practice.

- Where did I use toughness as a shield today?

This prompt is a self compassion exercise that feeds into the daily Love Tank Check, helping you recognize moments where strength could be softened.

- What would I say to a fellow veteran saying the same thing?

Use this reflection as a self compassion prompt that feeds into the Love Tank Check, encouraging supportive language toward yourself.

Write one sentence answers. Keep them visible on the fridge or phone.

These brief responses become the daily Love Tank Check entries, ensuring self compassion practices stay front of mind.

Connecting with Shared Humanity and Extending Compassion

This practice expands your Love Tank, as empathy toward others reinforces your own emotional reserve.

Practical ways to connect:

- You've been part of units that ran on mutual support; similar systems exist after service. Reach out with small, clear offers: "Want to grab coffee Saturday at 9:00 am?" Or "Can I call you for 20 minutes to vent?" Brief, direct invitations reduce awkwardness and build trust.
- Join a group tied to an interest (running club, woodworking class) and bring a buddy the first time so conversation isn't a

blind date.

- If you're a military couple, adapt communication: schedule a weekly 20-minute "shifts review" where each person gets uninterrupted time to speak about stressors and wins. Use a timer; it keeps things fair.

Including such outreach in your daily Love Tank Check reminds you that extending compassion to others also nurtures your own self compassion.

Practical ways to connect:

These actions are incorporated into the daily Love Tank Check, aligning self compassion with everyday relational habits.

This strategy, when noted in the Love Tank Check, reinforces the connection between shared interests and emotional support.

Adding this to your Love Tank Check ensures mutual self compassion and equitable dialogue.

Putting It Into Practice: Daily Checklist

- Self-care item (15–60 minutes): pick one—walk, hobby, nap.
- Reframe one negative self talk and rewrite it.
- Connection move: message one person, or accept an invite.
- Kindness act toward yourself: say one genuine compliment in the mirror.

The "Love Tank" Check (couples prompt)

Each partner rates emotional energy from 0–10. Share one thing that would add two points for you this week. Small asks often win bigger returns.

Final thought: your service trained you to follow plans and habits. Use that strength now to build habits of kindness. You're not erasing the past; you're giving it the respect it deserves by treating the person who carried it with care.

Healthy masculinity and resilience during transition

Practice prompt: The "Small Vulnerability" exercise. Share one minor worry—such as a financial niggle or a sleep problem—with a trusted friend or partner. Watch the response. Most often you'll find support, not judgment. Note what felt different when you were honest, and consider how this small act of emotional honesty is a building block for re-framing masculinity during transition. This exercise demonstrates the new masculine skill of emotional honesty.

Re framing Masculinity: A Path to Personal Growth. This approach does not discard the discipline, responsibility, and physical courage that served you, but expands the toolbox to include emotional honesty, willingness to ask for help, and steady presence that listens. By deliberately practicing these skills in reflection exercises like the Small Vulnerability prompt, you can begin to weave them into everyday interactions, reinforcing healthy masculinity during transition.

This is not about rejecting the parts of masculine identity that served you—discipline, responsibility, physical courage. It's about adding new options to the toolbox: emotional honesty, asking for help, and steadiness of presence that includes listening. Use these options in your reflection and ranking exercises to see how they strengthen civilian connections.

Quick partner exercise: The "Love Tank" Check. This simple activity helps partners articulate how they honour each other's military experience and emotional needs, supporting the reframe masculine qualities of listening and support.

Identify how honoring these examples supports the re framed masculinity.

- Each partner names one example from military life they want honoured (a ritual, phrase, habit).

Identify how honoring these examples supports re framed masculinity.

- Each partner names one way they want emotional support (checking in text, a Sunday phone call, a quiet hour together).
- Score current satisfaction from 1–5 and pick one small change to try this week.

Score current satisfaction from 1–5 and pick one small change to try this week.

Ranking Needs: List three emotional needs (e.g., validation, downtime, practical help). Which one feels lowest on your list right now? Use this ranking to pinpoint which aspects of masculinity you need to nurture further and how to apply them in civilian life.

Closing thought: Redefining healthy masculinity is a slow practice, like learning a new formation. It takes repetition, honest feedback, and small wins. Try one new habit this week—share a worry, ask for a hand, or listen without trying to fix—and see what changes in how you relate to others and to yourself.

Addressing stigma around seeking help

Breaking Down Barriers: Re-framing Vulnerability and Seeking Help

This discussion precedes the section on rituals of self care and solitary restoration, helping to lay the groundwork for personal healing practices.

This chapter connects directly with rituals of self care and solitary restoration. It reframe help seeking as essential maintenance—an ongoing, practical act of care rather than a sign of weakness or failure.

Placement: Move this section near the material on rituals of self care and solitary restoration.

If you grew up in or spent years inside the military, you've probably heard the line: "Suck it up, get back to it." That instruction can be useful in a firelight or during an all-night convoy, but it can also follow you home and make it harder to admit when you're struggling. The same structure that teaches mission focus sometimes discourages admitting pain. That contradiction is what we need to name, call out, and change. By confronting this mindset, we pave the way for meaningful self care rituals.

Remember, seeking help is a form of essential maintenance, echoing the self care rituals of solitude and restoration discussed elsewhere.

Placement: Move this section near the material on rituals of self care and solitary restoration.

Challenging the "Man Up" Mentality

This heading introduces a practical challenge to a common cultural message and links directly to self care rituals that support emotional restoration.

Placement: Move this section near the material on rituals of self care and solitary restoration.

"Man up" is shorthand for a set of expectations: don't cry, don't show fear, and don't ask for help. For many men who served, that messaging was reinforced by leaders, peers, and the training schedule. Start by noticing when you use that phrase on yourself or others. Try this micro task: the next time you hear someone say, "Man up," replace it in your head with, "Let's figure this out together." See how it shifts your posture. Preparing for this shift sets the stage for later self care rituals.

By treating help seeking like essential maintenance, you align this challenge with the self care rituals that support recovery and resilience.

Placement: Move this section near the material on rituals of self care and solitary restoration.

Re-framing Seeking Help as Strength

This heading prepares the reader to see therapy and support as structured practices—like other self care rituals—that build readiness and endurance.

Placement: Move this section near the material on rituals of self care and solitary restoration.

Think about how you train for a deployment: drills, physical fitness, briefings. Therapy and counselling are training for the emotional side of life. Booking an appointment, showing up, and doing the work takes planning and commitment—skills you already have. Concrete reframe: Treat the first session like a mission brief: list objectives, give the clinician context, and set measurable goals. The "readiness check" analogy is strong. Call asking for help a "readiness check" for your life—no shame, just maintenance. These practices dovetail into self care rituals.

- Treat the first session like a mission brief: list objectives, give the clinician context, and set measurable goals.

- Call asking for help a “readiness check” for your life—no shame, just maintenance.

Just as we plan missions, we also plan self care; seeking therapy is another essential maintenance routine that complements solitary restoration rituals.

Placement: Move this section near the material on rituals of self care and solitary restoration.

- Treat the first session like a mission brief: list objectives, give the clinician context, and set measurable goals.
- Call asking for help a “readiness check” for your life—no shame, just maintenance.
- Treat seeking help as essential maintenance, aligning with the self care framework and solitary restoration practices.
- Call asking for help a “readiness check” for your life—no shame, just maintenance.
- Treat seeking help as essential maintenance, aligning with the self care framework and solitary restoration practices.

Placement: Move this section near the material on rituals of self care and solitary restoration.

This readiness check is a core part of the self care maintenance routine and pairs naturally with solitary restoration rituals that sustain long-term resilience.

Placement: Move this section near the material on rituals of self care and solitary restoration.

The Impact of Military Traumas and Assignments

This heading introduces how specific assignments shape patterns that affect help seeking and solitary restoration practices.

Placement: Move this section near the material on rituals of self care and solitary restoration.

Certain assignments—combat tours, reckon, working in mortuary affairs, or repeated high stress duty—leave specific patterns: hyper vigilance, numbing, distrust. Those patterns make opening up feel risky. Acknowledge the logic: in operational terms, vulnerability could have cost a mission. That survival logic persists. Naming that helps you see why asking for help feels dangerous and makes it easier to take the next cautious step. Understanding these patterns strengthens the foundation for self care rituals.

Viewing help seeking as essential maintenance can ease the fear built by operational logic and can be integrated with solitary restoration rituals that rebuild safety and trust.

Placement: Move this section near the material on rituals of self care and solitary restoration.

Normalizing Conversations about Mental and Emotional Health

Normalize means making talk about feelings as routine as talking about a PT test. Start small:

- Squad-level: add a two-minute "how's your head" check during a group hangout.
- Home: a weekly check-in where each person names one win and one struggle.

Share a short story once a month about a challenge and what helped. When someone says, "I had trouble sleeping after deployment," respond with, "Thanks for telling me—what helped you?" That response models curiosity instead of judgment.

Identifying Trusted Allies and Support Systems

Trusted allies aren't always therapists. They're the people who will listen without immediate fixes. Create a list:

- Three civilian friends who make you feel human, not judged.
- Two fellow veterans who get the jargon and the odd triggers.
- One family member who can check in reliably.

Practice this script for calling an ally: 'Hey—real quick. Can I run something by you? I need a sounding board, not advice.' Short, direct, low pressure.

Reintegration Reflection

- Rank your top three barriers to asking for help (e.g., fear of judgment, career impact, not knowing where to go).
- For the top barrier, name one small action you can take this week to chip it away.

Moving Forward

The shift from "handle it alone" to "ask for what you need" doesn't happen overnight. It's a series of small, tactical choices that build stamina for emotional health. Think of it as mission planning—identify allies, set the objective, and run the ops. If you treat emotional care the same as operational readiness, asking for help becomes another way of staying effective and keeping the people who matter in your life safe.

Body image and fitness without obsession

Rethinking Strength: A Holistic Approach to Health and Well being

We've talked about how asking for help and showing vulnerability actually fits into operational readiness. Now let's flip the script on another military default: the single minded focus on physical appearance and "being fit" as the only measure of strength. A healthy service member — and a healthy veteran — is not just a lean silhouette on PT day. Strength includes emotional grit, mental focus, and sustainable physical care. This view echoes the self love prompts that appear elsewhere in the book, reminding us that value comes from function, not numbers.

Challenging Unrealistic Ideals

Boot camp and unit culture often come with unspoken standards: how you look in a PT shirt, how fast you run, how you stack up on social media. Those comparisons can morph into internal critics that shame you during off ramp days or after a deployment when life isn't built around daily PT schedules. If you notice constant negative self talk about your body, that's a red flag. Try this quick check, a prompt that parallels the self-love exercises found in other parts of the book:

- Reintegration Reflection: List three things your body did for you during service (carried gear, moved you through tough conditions, protected others). Read them out loud.

This reflection mirrors other self-love prompts that ask you to recognize your body's worth beyond appearance.

That exercise helps anchor value in function rather than in measurements.

Redefining Strength

Here's a practical, less flashy definition of strength, a definition that aligns with the self-love prompts that encourage recognizing internal assets:

- Mental toughness: getting up and asking for help when your head's a mess; following through on treatment.
- Emotional intelligence: spotting your triggers and saying, "I'm on edge today" instead of snapping.
- Physical well-being: movement and fuel that let you keep showing up for work, family, and life.

Try Ranking Needs: On a scale of 1–5, rate each of those three areas for yourself. Pick the lowest score and write one small thing you can do this week to nudge it up.

Cultivating Mindful Awareness

Mindful awareness isn't woo; it's useful. It's the practice of tuning in to hunger, rest needs, stress levels, and what movement actually feels good — not what you think you should do because of an expectation.

- Develop a healthier relationship with food: swap "I blew it" thinking for "I refuelled." Make one meal this week focused on nourishment: protein + veg + carb you enjoy.
- Find joy in movement: if ruck marches feel like punishment now, try hiking with a partner, bicycling with your kid, or a 20-minute kettle bell circuit that doesn't leave you hating yourself.
- Prioritize self-care: schedule two 15-minute recovery blocks this week — one for stretching and one for deep breathing.

Practicing Self-Compassion

Fitness and health will fluctuate. That's normal. When setbacks happen, try this micro-practice:

- The "Three-Kind" Pause: When you notice self-criticism, name it ("I'm beating myself up"), offer a kind counter-statement ("I did what I could today"), and state one next step ("Tomorrow I'll try a 10-minute walk").

Celebrate small wins. If you ran one extra minute, that's progress. If you had a better night's sleep, that's progress. Track those wins so they become evidence you can rely on.

The 'Love Tank' Check (for partners)

Physical changes can affect intimacy and connection. Partners, ask weekly, 'How full is your tank?' Be specific—touch, words, errands handled, or alone time.

Physical changes can affect intimacy and connection. Partners: ask weekly, "How full is your tank?" And be specific — is it touch, words, errands handled, time alone? Use answers to plan actions that support both physical care and emotional closeness.

Quick Wrap-Up Prompt

Pick one area from Mental toughness, Emotional intelligence, or Physical well-being. Write one tiny habit you can repeat for two weeks. Meet with your partner or a friend and report back — accountability beats anonymous guilt every time.

Journaling for self-discovery and growth

Embracing Journaling as a Tool for Post-Service Identity

These journaling practices echo the resilience and leadership identity themes explored earlier and align with the shared goals and identity concepts. They also help you notice and name boundaries and shifts in self-worth that show up in relationships after service, giving you language and examples to set healthier limits and claim your value.

You left the uniform, but you didn't leave everything that made you who you are. Still, that shift can feel like stepping off a cliff with a map scribbled on a napkin. Writing is one of the best maps you can make for yourself—cheap, portable, and judgment-free. Below are practical ways to use a notebook or app to process the transition and build a new sense of self.

These prompts connect with resilience and leadership identity themes discussed earlier, and help you reflect on shared goals. Use them also to explore how your boundaries and sense of self-worth have changed: who you let in, how you ask for support, and what you need to feel respected in relationships.

This section aligns with the resilience and leadership identity themes and the shared goals and identity concepts. Include focused reflection on how your career shaped expectations around boundaries and self-worth—how you were treated, the roles you assumed, and the ways those experiences influence your relationships now.

Aligning with your career and transition goals, this exercise invites you to a focused 15–20 minute sit down—pen in hand, no distractions—using specific prompts to get you rolling.

The exercises echo the resilience and leadership identity themes and reinforce shared goals and identity. Add prompts that explicitly ask about boundaries and self-worth in relationships (for example, "When did I feel respected or dismissed?" Or "Where do I need clearer limits?") So your reflections translate into concrete relational changes.

Reintegration Reflection

Consider how these moments relate to resilience and leadership identity and shared goals, and how they shaped your boundaries and sense of self-worth.

Here we integrate the resilience and leadership identity insights and the shared goals and identity framework. Also use this space to track how you are re-establishing boundaries and rebuilding self-worth in family, friendships, and new civilian roles—note what feels respectful and what requires adjustment.

- What were two moments in service that changed how you see the world? Describe them in detail: sounds, smells, what you were thinking.

Reflect on how each challenge connects to resilience and leadership identity and shared goals, and note any effects on your boundaries or self-worth.

- List three challenges you faced during transition. For each, write how you handled it and what worked, even if it was small (calling a buddy, handing in paperwork early, taking a walk). Then add: did this help you set a boundary or protect your self-worth? How?

Example: "When I left active duty, my biggest daily win was getting back into a regular sleep schedule. It felt tiny, but it helped my mood."

This example illustrates resilience and leadership identity and how small wins support shared goals. Notice, too, how small wins can restore a sense of self-worth and make it easier to enforce simple boundaries (like keeping a bedtime or saying no to extra obligations).

Documenting Strengths, Coping Tools, and Connections

This section reflects resilience and leadership identity themes and supports shared goals and identity. Use it to inventory strengths and the coping tools you use to set boundaries, sustain relationships, and reinforce your self-worth.

Use journalling to inventory the tools you brought from service and determine how they can be applied in civilian life.

The inventory aligns with resilience and leadership identity and enhances shared goals and identity. As you list tools, specifically note which help you establish healthy boundaries, which bolster your confidence, and how they can be used in relationships and civilian work.

Ranking Needs

Skills I Used in Service vs. How That Helps Now

Skill I Used in Service | How That Helps Now |

Leadership – running a community team | Managing projects and motivating co-workers in a corporate setting |

Stress Management – staying calm in high stakes missions | Handling tight deadlines and high pressure client meetings |

Strategic Planning – developing mission plans | Crafting business strategies and long term goals |

Communication – briefing teammates | Presenting ideas clearly to stakeholders |

Adaptability – operating in fluid environments | Pivoting quickly when market conditions change |

Prompt: Name three coping mechanisms you developed under pressure. How could you adapt each one to a civilian habit? For example, if you used ritual (pre-mission checks), create a morning checklist for job applications or family time.

Moments of Belonging

Write about a person, a crew, or a unit that gave you belonging.

- How do you keep that sense alive?
- Phone calls, annual meet ups, or a text thread can bridge the gap.
- If contact faded, use the journal to draft a message you might send.
- Re-establishing these ties strengthens your civilian identity and nurtures self compassion.

Methods for Jour3naling That Actually Stick

Free writing: Set a timer for 10 minutes and spill whatever comes out.

This quick burst captures raw thoughts, helping you notice patterns of strength and areas for growth—key to both civilian skill mapping and self kindness.

Prompt Based Journaling

Use one question per entry from this chapter.

Examples:

- "What military skill helped me solve a workplace challenge?"
- "How does this experience reinforce my self value?"

Each prompt guides you toward connecting past competencies with present aspirations and nurturing self-love.

Try a two-minute nightly entry: "What went well today?" And "What do I need tomorrow?" It's quick, builds self-awareness, and won't feel like another task on the to-do list.

Cultivating Self-Kindness on the Page

This is where the journal stops being a log and starts being a friend.

The "Self-Compassion Check"

- Write a short letter to yourself after a mistake. Begin, "Dear [Your Rank/Nickname], I'm with you on this…" Then list three things you did right, even if the outcome wasn't perfect.

Prompt: List one imperfection you can accept today and one small act of kindness you'll do for yourself (cook a meal you enjoy, call a supportive teammate, take a rest).

Partnering Up: Journaling for Military Couples

Share an entry once a week and read it aloud to each other. Use these excerpts as conversation starters—what surprised you, what you'd like more of. For couples where one or both partners served, adapt a short "Love Tank Check": each writes what fills their tank (time together, chores done, physical touch) and one thing that empties it. Compare lists, then pick one small change to try that week.

Final Prompt to Start Today

- Write one page answering: "Who am I when I'm not on duty?" Focus on actions and values—what you enjoy, what you protect, and what you want more of. Keep that page; revisit it monthly to see how your answer changes.

Journalling isn't a cure-all, but it's a tool that gives you a clearer picture of self and a way to practice kindness toward it. Grab a pen and try the first prompt now—no pressure, no rank, just you and the page.

Boundaries and self-worth in relationships

Establishing Clear Boundaries for a Strong Sense of Self-Worth

You learned to follow orders, keep watch, and respect the chain of command. Now it's time to learn one of the less discussed but equally important skills: how to set boundaries that protect your energy, time, and sense of self. Think of boundaries as the perimeter you set around your well being—clear, visible, and defended without apology. Saying what you need doesn't mean you have to be harsh. Respectful assertiveness is firm and direct, delivered with civility. For veterans who are used to crisp language, this is familiar territory—just aimed inward this time. Try this script: "I can't take on extra shifts right now—I'm prioritizing medical appointments and family time." Short, specific, and not begging for approval.

These boundaries are part of a larger self care framework that includes nurturing relationships and maintaining a reliable support system. Suggested placement: with the material on rituals of self care and solitary restoration, where boundary-setting can be paired with daily practices that replenish energy and reinforce identity.

By setting clear limits, you also protect your time for family and medical appointments, which are key components of self care. Suggested placement: with rituals of self care and solitary restoration so you can practice these scripts during quiet, intentional moments.

Reflecting on how you set boundaries helps you integrate self care into everyday life. Suggested placement: with the sections on rituals of self care and solitary restoration to link reflection with concrete restorative practices.

Where in your day are you automatically saying "yes"?

- Consider how these yes responses affect your well being.

Suggested placement: include these prompts in your rituals of self care and solitary restoration as short journalling or mindfulness cues.

- List three situations you'd like to respond to differently, and write a one sentence boundary for each.

Suggested placement: use this exercise as part of your rituals of self care and solitary restoration to make boundary-setting a regular reflective habit.

Educating Others and Setting Limits

When you clearly state limits, you teach people how to treat you. That matters in civilian friendships, workplaces, and even family gatherings. Teaching others about your limits reinforces the supportive network that underlies healthy self care. Example: if a former teammate still expects the late night calls you used to make while deployed, tell them, "I'm off phones after 9 p.m.—I'm recharging." If a civilian friend pressures you about attending every social event, try, "I appreciate the invite, but I'll pass this time." Suggested placement: alongside rituals of self care and solitary restoration so you can rehearse and reinforce these messages in calm, restorative settings.

Practical script bank:

Use these scripts as tools to strengthen your self care routine. Suggested placement: with the material on rituals of self care and solitary restoration so you can practice them during solo restoration moments.

- Clear limits are essential for creating healthy habits. Below is a practical script to help set them:
- To family: "I want to be present at dinner; let's keep phones away for the first 30 minutes."
- Suggested placement: include this script bank within the section on rituals of self care and solitary restoration to make using these

scripts a regular, solitary practice.

- To a co-worker: "I can help with this, but I'll need until Friday to finish it."

Boundaries as Self-Care

Setting limits is not selfish; it's basic maintenance. If you're in the vehicle of life, boundaries are the brakes and the GPS. Prioritizing sleep, medical appointments, therapy sessions, or family time are all boundary moves. Some veterans who handle care taking expectations might set a boundary like: "I can do grocery runs on weekends, but weekday mornings are for my health appointments." Others who feel pressure to always provide could try: "I'll contribute emotionally by talking through this on Sundays when I can be fully present."

Ranking Needs:

- Rank the top five needs (sleep, work, family time, appointments, socializing).

- Pick one need to protect this week with a boundary and note how you'll state it.

The Foundation of Healthy Partnerships

Healthy pairings respect each person's limits. Couples can set a weekly check-in where each partner lists one thing they need kept sacred—no questions asked. For military couples, adapting communication is key: replace mission brief tone with curiosity. Try, "When you say X, I hear Y—what did you mean?" This avoids assumptions and keeps trust intact.

The 'Love Tank' Check:

- Each partner lists two actions that make them feel valued.

Learning to say no without guilt is huge. Practice with quick, guilt free lines: "No thanks," "Not this time," or "I'm not available." No long explanation required. If you feel obliged to justify, use a short buffer: "No, I can't—thanks for understanding." If you do feel guilty, jot down why and question whether that guilt belongs to you or to someone else's expectation.

Final Exercise:

- This week, say no to one request that drains you. Write down how you said it and how it felt.
- Afterward, note any change in your energy or mood.

Boundaries protect who you are as much as anything you carried in uniform. They let you show up as someone who knows their worth—and who won't apologize for guarding it.

Rituals of self-care and solitary restoration

Prioritizing Activities Outside of Service Identity

You don't need to quit everything military associated to be whole. Instead, build mini identities that sit next to your service identity. Pick a hobby that has measurable progress (guitar, woodworking, running) and track it with a simple log: date, 15–45 minutes spent, one small accomplishment.

By carving out these mini identities, you practice self care and set healthy boundaries between your service life and civilian pursuits.

- Start a personal project with clear milestones: "Finish five watercolour postcards by month's end" or "Cook three new recipes this month."

Ranking Needs

Ranking your needs is a tool for self care and boundary setting, helping you recognize what you have been neglecting.

Prompt: Rank the following for you right now — Physical activity, Creative time, Social connection, Quiet reflection. Put an "X" beside the one you've been ignoring.

Action: Block at least one 60–90 minute slot this week to prioritize that ignored need.

Prioritizing this ignored need is an act of self care and boundary setting.

Physical activity outside the regiment supports self care and signals a boundary between duty and personal well being.

Physical movement doesn't have to be a gym ritual. Ideas that actually stick:

Each idea serves as a gentle reminder that self care is not just a hobby—it's a boundary that protects your mental health.

- Tactical walk: 25–40 minute brisk walk with no phone (or with voice memos to capture thoughts).
- Couple's stretch: 10 minutes of partner-assisted mobility work after dinner (good for connection and bodies).
- Month of micro-hikes: aim for one local green space visit per week; start with 20–40 minutes and add one new route each month.

Scheduling Dedicated Time for Personal Pursuits

Put personal pursuits on the calendar like any other appointment. Examples:

- Sunday morning "me slot" for two hours — no work, no kid duty, no guilt.
- Midweek 30-minute slot labelled "creative work" that repeats on your phone calendar.

The "Love Tank" Check

Prompt for couples: Each evening, say one sentence about what filled your tank today and one sentence about what drained it. No debating. Just listening.

Action: Once a week, use those notes to plan one small activity that fills both tanks.

Self-compassion isn't talk; it's practice. Try this:

- Three-kind-phrases: When you mess up, say silently: "I did the best I could with what I had. I can try again. I deserve care."
- Gentle check-in: When stress spikes, pause for a 90-second body

scan and name one thing that's okay right now.

Closing prompt: Commit to one ritual for the next 21 days. After three weeks, write a short note about what shifted — more energy, less irritation, clearer priorities — and share it with a friend, partner, or therapist. Small, consistent habits do the steady work of helping you reclaim a self that's whole, practical, and human.

Mentoring, peer support, and community building

- This week: locate a local veteran group and RSVP to an upcoming event. By attending, you create a mentorship opportunity and contribute to community service, reinforcing each other.
- Monthly habit: bring a new person for coffee or invite them to a casual activity—walk, softball, or a skills swap. By sharing a skill or listening to another's experience, you practice mentorship while strengthening community service.

The Power of Community Building

Community building is more than expanding contacts; it is a structured form of mentorship and service that creates shared purpose.

Finding Strength in Collective Resilience

By engaging in group problem-solving and shared accountability, you create a mentorship ecosystem that also delivers community service. These projects illustrate the community service connections framework introduced earlier. For creative ways to connect, see 'Creative Outlets as Pathways for Healing and Identity Work'.

Hearing someone else tell how they recovered from a rough patch is underrated medicine. By joining a peer accountability pair—meeting twice a month to set goals and report progress—you practice mentorship while pooling resources and building community service. Small wins add up and the group will help you see progress when you're stuck. These projects illustrate the community service connections framework introduced earlier. For creative ways to connect, see 'Creative Outlets as Pathways for Healing and Identity Work'.

Amplifying Your Healing through Shared Experiences

By sharing stories and skills in a group setting, you reinforce both mentorship and community service. These projects illustrate the community service connections framework introduced earlier. For creative ways to connect, see 'Creative Outlets as Pathways for Healing and Identity Work'.

When you share your story—coaching a newer vet, speaking at a community night, or writing a short blog post—you shift from receiver to contributor. By mentoring someone and contributing to a community event, you strengthen both mentorship and community service. That shift boosts confidence and gives meaning to what you lived through. Start by mentoring one person for six sessions, or sign up to co-host an information night at a local veterans' centre. These projects illustrate the community service connections framework introduced earlier. For creative ways to connect, see 'Creative Outlets as Pathways for Healing and Identity Work'.

Discovering Your Post Service Identity

Exploring new roles—taking a class, trying a hobby, or volunteering—provides both mentorship opportunities and community service. These projects illustrate the community service connections framework introduced earlier. For creative ways to connect, see 'Creative Outlets as Pathways for Healing and Identity Work'.

You don't have to pick one label. Sample new roles like a menu: take a class, test a hobby, volunteer in different settings. By experimenting and mentoring others in these activities, you create a cycle of learning and community service. Make a simple experiment plan—try three new activities in three months, then rank what fit. Reflection prompt: Ranking Needs—list what each activity met (skill, purpose, social, creative). Use the results to shape where you focus next. These projects illustrate the community service connections framework introduced earlier. For creative ways to connect, see 'Creative Outlets as Pathways for Healing and Identity Work'.

Quick wrap up: pick one mentorship contact, one peer event, and one community project to try in the next 30 days.

Creative outlets for healing and identity exploration

Color map: On a sheet, use colors to mark places in your day that feel safe, tense, or joyful.

By visualizing where you feel safe versus tense, you begin to recognize the spaces where your authentic self thrives, turning the map into a tool for identity exploration and self discovery.

Texture box: Glue fabric, sandpaper, and foil to a board — the tactile contrast helps you name feelings without a speech.

The physical textures mirror the layers of your personality, making it easier to identify and accept parts of yourself that you might otherwise keep silent.

Try a shared project: create a two-panel piece where each partner paints one side, then discuss the emotions you see.

Collaborating on this artwork forces you to negotiate roles and narratives, revealing how your shared history shapes individual identities.

Music: Catharsis and Connection

Music becomes a mirror for your internal dialogues, offering a soundtrack to your evolving identity and a bridge to deeper self understanding.

Music can be a pressure valve. Try this:

As you release tension through melody, you also peel back layers of the self, uncovering strengths and memories that inform your sense of self.

- Create three play lists: “When I Need Calm,” “When I Need Energy,” and “When I Want to Remember.” Notice which songs bring tears, anger, or relief.

Each play list functions as a narrative chapter, letting you chart your journey from calm to energy to memory—an evolving map that sharpens identity exploration.

- Group jam: find a community music night or take a basic guitar class for veterans. Playing together builds immediate social ties.

Playing together not only builds community but also lets you experiment with new roles, reinforcing a sense of self beyond the uniform.

Performance Arts: Trying on New Roles

Through acting or improve, you inhabit different persona, enabling a deeper interrogation of your core values and identity.

Acting or improve can be surprisingly therapeutic:

By stepping into another character, you expose hidden emotions and beliefs, creating a safe space for self discovery.

- Role swap exercise: With your partner, pick a scene (ordering coffee, a job interview) and act it as your service persona, then as your current self. Discuss differences in language and posture.

By switching between service and civilian scripts, you confront and integrate disparate aspects of your identity, fostering self discovery.

- Community theater: Small roles give a confidence boost and let you practice being someone else safely.

Crafting and Building: Tangible Progress

Hands-on projects are great for focus and pride:

- Start a simple build: a birdhouse, a toolbox, or a raised garden bed. Set milestones and celebrate each completed step.

- Skill boost: sign up for a weekend carpentry or welding class at a local VA centre or community college.

Photography: Capturing Perspective

Use a camera to document post-service life:

- 30-day photo project: one image per day of something that represents "home." Review the set to see how your view shifts.
- Storyboard your week: three photos that tell how you felt — share with a friend or partner.

Movement and Embodiment: Mind-Body Connection

Physical expression helps process stored tension:

- Tactical breathing + movement: after a three-count breathing set, do five minutes of walking with focused body scans.
- Somatic prompt: "Where do I feel this emotion?" Move that body part slowly for two minutes.

For couples: try partner yoga or a basic martial arts class to build trust and non verbal communication.

Reflection Prompts to Try Tonight

- Ranking Needs: List your top three needs this week (safety, connection, competence). Which creative activity addresses one of them?
- The "Love Tank" Check: Name one small creative task your partner could do that would make you feel seen this week.

Pick one outlet, give it three honest tries, and note how it shifts what you feel or how you talk about yourself. Small creative steps add up — and they often lead to conversations that matter.

Learning new skills for an updated self

Embracing New Skills: A Journey of Self-Discovery and Growth

You left a structured role with specific tasks and training; now you have the rare chance to pick new skills that fit the person you are becoming. Think of this phase as trying on uniforms you never knew existed—some will fit, some will sit in the closet, and a few will surprise you by feeling right. The point is to try, adjust, and keep what works, while noting how each new skill uncovers a deeper sense of self and fuels personal growth. Celebrate each milestone, no matter how small, because every completed lesson, project, or demonstration is a victory that reinforces your evolving identity.

Identifying Interests that Spark Curiosity

Start small and be specific. Make a short list of things that pull your attention when you have downtime. Use these prompts:

Examples: If you find yourself browsing car forums, sketch out a beginner mechanic course; if podcasts on true crime keep you up, try a short workshop on audio production. The idea is to match curiosity with a low-cost trial—one class, a weekend meet up, or a volunteering shift—so that each small attempt becomes a micro victory that confirms your growing expertise and self-confidence.

Exploring New Hobbies and Vocations

Once you pick an interest, map a concrete three step plan: learn, practice, apply. Each step is an opportunity to discover how the skill shapes your identity, builds competence, and offers tangible achievements to celebrate.

Once you pick an interest, map a concrete three step plan: learn, practice, apply. Each step is an opportunity to discover how the skill shapes your identity, builds competence, and offers tangible achievements to celebrate.

- Learn: Sign up for a basic class or online module (e.g., HTML fundamentals; soldering basics; community theater audition prep). Each lesson adds a new layer of knowledge, reinforcing your evolving identity.

- Practice: Commit to two weekly sessions—one focused, one playful. For coding, build a one page personal site; for woodworking, make a simple shelf. Consistent practice turns skill into habit, turning each completed session into a small victory that fuels confidence.

- Apply: Use the skill in a social setting—lead a community group project, teach a short session at a veteran meet up, or sell a small craft at a fair. Applying what you've learned publicly celebrates mastery and invites feedback, closing the loop of growth.

Specific role examples for veterans: lead a neighbourhood civic team (use your leadership skills for civilian projects), get certified in a technical trade (HVAC, welding), or join a writers' circle to turn service stories into publishable essays.

Practicing Patience and Celebrating Small Victories

Real skill growth needs patience. Try this short ritual: after each practice session, write down one thing you did better than before and one tiny goal for the next session. Celebrate by telling your partner or posting a progress photo—publicly or privately, accountability builds momentum.

The Small Wins Checklist:

- Completed first lesson or shift. Check.

- Stuck through a frustrating hour. Check.

- Shared progress with someone. Check.

Embracing Skill Acquisition as a Continuous Process

Make a habit of monthly reviews. Ask:, What surprised me? What felt meaningful? Which doors opened? Keep adapting. Learning doesn't stop when a certificate arrives; it's a steady commitment to showing up, staying curious, and making room for fresh purpose.

Partner Prompt: Sit down with your significant other and pick one new skill each of you will try for 30 days. Compare notes weekly and use the "Love Tank" Check to give encouragement—small praise, specific feedback, a shared reward. Doing this turns skill-building into a team mission worth pursuing.

Impact of self-love on romantic relationships

The "Love Tank" Check

This brief check serves as a daily reminder that honoring your own worth strengthens both your self love and the quality of your romantic relationship. When you recognize the value you bring, you create space for healthy boundaries and deeper connection with your partner.

- Partner asks: "How's your tank today?" Answer honestly with one line about an internal source of value (skills, character, small wins).
- Practice: Do this once a week to prevent codependents and strengthen mutual respect. By regularly affirming your own strengths, you reinforce the foundation of self-love that allows both you and your partner to set and honour healthy boundaries.

Vulnerability Starts with Self Acceptance

True openness is easier when you accept who you are.

Try a 5-minute nightly practice with your partner: each person names one insecurity and one strength. Use neutral tone rules — no fixing, no judgments, just listening. That small ritual teaches both of you that being known doesn't mean being judged. Because self acceptance means you value your own needs, you can set boundaries that reflect that value, and the boundary setting itself reinforces your self-love.

Example prompts:

- "When I left service, I worried about losing purpose. One strength I still have is discipline."
- "I get anxious in crowds. A strength is that I plan ahead to manage it."

Modeling Healthy Boundaries Through Self Care

Boundaries show respect for your needs and teach your partner how to respect them too. Start with a simple boundary: "I need 30 minutes after work to decompressing." Say it calmly, not as a demand. Follow through — if you skip the decompress time, the boundary loses weight. When you practice self acceptance first, setting boundaries feels less like punishment and more like affirming your self-love, which in turn nurtures a healthier romantic partnership.

Ranking Needs

Ranking your needs helps you prioritize tasks effectively. For example:

- Need: Finish the quarterly report
- Rank: 1
- Deadline: 15th March

By assigning ranks, you can focus on high priority items first and manage your workload more efficiently.

How Partnership Changes When Self-Love Is Strong

When both partners carry internal validation and self compassion, the relationship shifts from dependence to a balanced partnership. You still lean on each other, but you don't collapse into one another to find identity; instead, intimacy deepens—no longer needy—and trust grows because each person shows up whole.

Partner Dialogue Exercise

This Partner Dialogue exercise has been consolidated into the section Foundations, Prompts, and Practical Tools to avoid duplication.

These practices are simple, repeatable, and military-friendly: measurable, routine-based, and mission-oriented. The mission now is quieter arguments, clearer needs, and a partnership that rests on two people who value themselves first, and each other second.

Tips from male veterans who embraced self-love

- Mental: ten minutes of guided breathing or a short podcast on a non-military topic.

Self-care for couples: trade tasks so each person has one guaranteed hour per week to do a chosen practice—no interruptions, no guilt.

The Power of Camaraderie

This principle supports the self-love framework by reinforcing belonging and mutual respect.

Camaraderie isn't just for formations and missions; it's how men heal and stay connected.

Example: start a monthly "project night" with other vets—fix a lawn mower, cook a big meal, train together for a 5K. The work creates natural openings for honest talk and mutual support. The hand son projects serve as a practical application of the foundational prompts, encouraging reflection through action.

Rethinking Success

If you've been defining success by rank, pay grade, or medals, give yourself permission to widen the scorecard. Try a "Ranking Needs" prompt with your partner: list five things that make you feel valued (e.g., teaching, mentoring, time outdoors, quiet, money stability). Rank them 1–5 independently, then compare. You might find that emotional presence or a creative hobby ranks higher than an extra promotion. Use this Ranking Needs prompt alongside foundational exercises to broaden your definition of worth beyond external metrics.

Rediscovering Personal Joy

Joy is not frivolous. It's a compass. Pick one activity you loved before service or one curiosity you never tried. Block it in the calendar—no apologizing. If you're stuck, test two low stakes options: a weekend watercolour class or a half day fishing trip. Report back to your partner on what surprised you. Scheduling these activities reinforces the self-love practice of honouring personal interests.

Integrating Past Experiences

Healing involves naming what happened and deciding what it will mean now. Integration doesn't erase memories; it places them in a life where you have more choices. Integration honours memories while opening space for new choices, a concept echoed in self-love practices.

Reintegration Reflection (prompt): Write for five minutes about a hard memory and then write one sentence about what you want that memory to teach you today. Share, if comfortable, with a trusted friend or partner and discuss any support steps that would help—therapy, peer group, or a mentor. The Reintegration Reflection prompt is designed to work hand-in-hand with the foundational tools, helping you translate memories into growth.

Final pairing exercise: The "Love Tank" Check—each partner lists one way they feel most emotionally filled and one thing that drains them. Compare lists and pick one action from each list to try this week.

Change like this isn't instant. It's steady practice—putting small, brave habits in place that create more honest connections with partners, friends, and yourself.

Self-Love for Female Veterans

Resilience and leadership identity—and expanding through transition

- Leadership and team management: Running shift rotations → leading a project team.
- Communication and public speaking: Briefing a patrol → presenting quarterly results.
- Problem-solving and adaptability: Adjusting plans on the fly → troubleshooting supply-chain hiccups.
- Time management and organization: Preparing gear lists → managing deadlines and calendars.
- Strategic planning and execution: Mission planning → launching a small business or non-profit program.

Action item: Create a one-page "Skill Snapshot" that maps military tasks to civilian outcomes. Bring this to interviews, networking meetups, or when talking with a partner about next steps.

Challenges of Relinquishing Command

It's normal to feel off-balance when authority is less obvious. That frustration can show up as impatience, withdrawal, or wanting to fix everything. Acknowledge the shift without making it a character trait.

Conversation prompt for couples: The 'Role Check'

Use this short exercise as part of your regular couple communication and identity work. It helps surface how military leadership shows up in your relationship and supports conversations about what to carry forward and what to leave behind.

- Partner A describes one moment they felt in charge in service, merging the heading and bullet to avoid duplicate Ids; include what felt meaningful and what felt burdensome.

- Partner B shares a time they saw that leadership style help or clash in civilian life, noting the outcomes and any adjustments that followed.
- Discuss what parts of "command" each of you wants to keep, and which parts you're ready to set down. Name specific behaviours to preserve and practical steps or support needed to let other behaviours go.

Re-framing Your Self-Perception

You're more than rank or ribbons. Say that out loud: "I am a leader, problem solver, and contributor." Practice it. Re framing is not denial. It's expanding your identity. Try small identity experiments—volunteer to lead a local initiative, take a class, or coach youth sports—to test and grow your civilian self-image. This is especially important for female veterans, whose resilience and leadership may be overlooked; re framing helps translate those strengths into new, respected civilian roles.

Exercising Leadership in Civilian Life

Leadership gets new canvases. Here are concrete next steps you can try alone or with your partner:

Volunteer: Run a neighbourhood safety walk or lead a veterans' meet up — consider co leading with your partner or inviting others to build community and practice collaborative leadership.

- Education: Take a certificate course in project management or public speaking; consider joining a class or workshop with others to practice skills and build civilian credentials.
- Start a venture: Use mission planning skills to draft a simple business model for a side gig.
- Mentor: Offer monthly coffee chats with younger vets or students.

Reflection prompt: Ranking Needs

- Rank three ways you'd like to lead now (community, professional, family).
- Pick one and write a 30-day plan with two measurable goals.

Ending note: Your resilience and leadership did not retire with your uniform; they only need new uniforms—new settings, new roles, new vocabulary. Test them, adjust, and trust that what you carried into service still carries you out into the next chapter.

Care giving dynamics and setting boundaries

Self-awareness keeps you from burning out, and keeps care giving effective.

- Recognize signs of burnout: increased irritability, insomnia, withdrawal from social activities, or constant physical tension. If you notice these, run the "Reintegration Reflection": list three stress signs and three immediate fixes (call a friend, swap duties, book a respite care session).

- Communicate effectively: Use short, direct statements that work in civilian settings. Try the "Love Tank" Check with your partner: each of you names one thing that fills your tank and one thing that drains it. Then negotiate one change for the week.

Cultivating Sustainable Balance

Balance isn't a static state; it's a set of ongoing choices.

- Re-evaluating priorities: Weekly, use the "Ranking Needs" prompt (consolidated in the 'Foundations, Prompts, and Practical Tools' section)—rank top five activities (care tasks, work, sleep, social time, self-care) and adjust time allocation.

- Seeking support: Join a local veteran caregiver group or an online forum. Swap resources, ask for shifts, and borrow coping strategies that actually work.

- Practicing self-compassion: Say out loud, "I am doing what I can today." Repeat it when guilt creeps in.

Quick Reflection Prompts

- Reintegration Reflection: What one care giving task could I outsource this month?

- Ranking Needs: Rank your top five needs for this week; which two will you protect? (This prompt is consolidated in the

'Foundations, Prompts, and Practical Tools' section.)

- The "Love Tank" Check: One fill, one drain—share and commit to one tweak. (This prompt is consolidated in the 'Foundations, Prompts, and Practical Tools' section.)

Being intentional doesn't mean doing everything yourself. It means choosing how you expend your energy so you can keep showing up—clear-headed and human—for the people who need you most.

Body image empowerment and self-acceptance

Catch – Name – Reframe.

Catch: Notice the thought ("I look awful").

Name: Label it ("That's a comparison thought").

Reframe: Offer a kinder truth ("My body kept me alive and carried me through hard work").

Practice this aloud during mundane tasks—showering, driving—so it becomes a reflex.

Prioritizing Health: Nourish, Move, Rest

Swap dieting scripts for vitality goals. Choose three small actions: add a protein at breakfast, walk fifteen extra minutes three times a week, and go to bed thirty minutes earlier. Track them on a simple checklist; wins build confidence.

Re-framing Scars and Changes

Scars and shifts in shape tell stories. Try writing a brief caption for each notable change — two sentences Max — focusing on what happened and what you learned. Share one with a trusted fellow veteran or partner to practice owning the narrative.

Cultivating Appreciation and Self-Compassion

Self-compassion can sound soft, but it's practical. When self-criticism hits, offer yourself the same advice you'd give a battle buddy. Say: "You did what you needed to do. Rest now."

The "Love Tank" Check (for couples): Each week, partners answer—

what did I do to fill your tank this week? One physical, one emotional gesture. Small actions that honour bodies—massage, cooking a favourite meal, or praising a visible effort—count.

Connecting with Supportive Communities

Find fellow female veterans' groups, online forums, or local meet-ups where body stories are treated with respect. Share a small victory—maybe you tried a yoga class or let someone see a scar—and invite feedback that centres function and resilience, not looks.

Final prompt: Rank Needs—list three body-related needs (safety, rest, praise). Rank them by urgency and pick one to address this week with a small, specific action.

Breaking free from narrow beauty rules doesn't happen overnight, but with steady, practical steps and a few honest conversations, your body can once again feel like the reliable partner it has always been.

Navigating biases and representation in society

- What single skill from service do I underplay that I can showcase this week?

Building Supportive Communities

Isolation sneaks up fast. The fix is twofold: first, find people who get it; second, create situations that make connection easy.

Isolation sneaks up fast. The fix is twofold: find people who get it, and create situations that make connection easy.

Action steps:

Join a local female-veteran meet up or a mixed veteran peer group that schedules a monthly coffee, hike, or skill-swapping night. Small recurring events reduce the social friction of showing up.

- Try "pair-and-share" at community events: pair with one person for 10 minutes to swap short service stories, then rotate. That quick structure keeps conversation from stalling.
- Online groups: pick one platform and one group that feels respectful; limit time to avoid scrolling fatigue. Post one question a week — people respond to specifics, like, "How did you handle the first civilian job review?"

The "Support Net" Check

- Who are three people I can call when I'm doubting myself?
- Which two groups could I try this month and how will I show up?

Educating Others and Advocating for Change

You don't have to be on a stage to shape perception. Everyday actions matter.

How to act:

- Share an honest story with a friend or co-worker about a specific moment in service that taught you something unexpected. Short, concrete anecdotes change assumptions faster than lectures.

- When you see misleading portrayals in media or conversation, point out one factual correction calmly, then offer a brief alternative image — "Actually, many women served in X role; they did Y."

- Support local or national policies that protect veteran benefits and access to care. Attend one town-hall or sign one petition and forward it to your network.

- Short, concrete anecdotes change assumptions faster than lectures.

Practicing Self-Compassion

Pressure to educate or advocate can drain you. Keep a personal care plan that's realistic.

Examples:

- Mindful five: pause three times a day for five breaths, noting one physical sensation and one strength.

- Self-care slot: block 45 minutes weekly for something purely for you — a run, a craft, a phone call with a friend.

- Professional backup: if old stressors resurface, contact a counsellor familiar with military culture for a short check-in.

The "Love Tank" Check (for couples)

- Love Tank Check (for couples): What fills my tank this week? (Affection, help with chores, shared silence)

- Love Tank Check (for couples): What's one small ask I can make to my partner that honours my veteran experience?

Love Tank Check (for couples): By calling out biases, updating the story you tell about yourself, building clear social supports, teaching others through specific stories, and protecting your emotional reserves, you'll create a stronger, more believable identity — one that matches the skills and courage you already carry.

Mentorship and community building for women veterans

Action step: Make a list of three mentorship programs near you that offer virtual options. Reach out with a one-paragraph intro about your background and a specific ask (e.g., "Can we meet for one hour to discuss translating my MOS into civilian job titles?"). Short, direct requests get better results than vague ones.

Celebrating Unique Strengths and Experiences

Every woman veteran brings her own mix of skills and stories. A strong group is one that names those strengths out loud—skills, leadership style, care giving experience, technical know-how. Celebrating those differences builds trust and pride, not competition.

Reflection prompt: Reintegration Reflection — list three strengths you used in the military and one civilian context where each would be valuable. Share one item from your list with a peer or mentor this week.

Creating and Maintaining Your Circle

Circles don't appear overnight. Commit to small habits: attend one meeting or event each month, send a check-in text to a fellow veteran every two weeks, and offer help when you can—a babysitting swap, ride to an appointment, resume feedback. These low-effort investments compound into a dependable network.

The 'Love Tank' Check (adapted for peer care): Once a month, rate the mutual support in your circle from 1–10. If it's under an 8, pick one actionable change (e.g., host a pot luck, set up a peer-mentor hour, or start a shared resource document).

Final nudge: start now. Pick one mentorship program, one online group, and one activity to join. Small moves create the circle that keeps you steady—and gives you places to bring both the hard days and the good ones.

Self-advocacy in healthcare, benefits, and employment

Relocate this content near the portion of the book that discusses vulnerability and emotional strength for women veterans.

Assert Your Right to Healthcare: Own the Conversation—A Guide for Female Veterans

You gave a lot to your service — now it's okay to insist that the system give you clear, respectful care in return. As a female veteran, you carry unique experiences and needs, so it's essential to voice those clearly. Think of it like briefing a new team: if you miss key details, the mission can go sideways. Below are practical steps to make sure your appointments actually move the needle.

Understanding Your Medical History — Simple, Clear, Actionable (for Female Veterans)

Start with a one-page "medical brief" you can hand to any provider. Include:

- Active diagnoses and when they were made.
- Current medications (dose + how you take them).
- Past surgeries or hospitalizations with dates.
- Any service-related incidents or exposures that could matter, such as deployment injuries, PTSD, or gender specific health concerns.

Tip: Keep a paper copy in your wallet and a digital photo on your phone. Update it after major visits or when new treatments begin.

Communicating with Providers — Say It Like You Mean It (for Female Veterans)

You gave a lot to your service … You're the subject matter expert on your body. Short, direct statements work best:

- "My pain started after [event]. It limits me this way."
- "I tried X treatment; these were the results."
- "I want to understand alternative options before deciding."

If a doctor uses jargon you don't follow, ask for plain terms. If they rush you, say: "I need five minutes to make sure I understand this." No badge required to be assertive.

Tips for the Appointment (Prep + In-Person)

- Be prepared: jot three must-ask questions beforehand (symptom cause, treatment options, side effects).
- Be clear: describe current symptoms in short, measurable terms — intensity, frequency, triggers.
- Be assertive: if you feel dismissed, ask for another clinician or a patient advocate.
- Be an active participant: repeat back the plan to confirm you and the provider are on the same page.

Quick Script Practice

Practice with a partner or friend: "I want to make a plan that fits my life. Can we review options and time line?" Say it once. Say it twice. It gets easier.

Navigating the System with Confidence

Bring a support person when you can — a partner, a comrade, or a friend who will back you up and take notes. Keep a running log of appointments, test results, and who said what. If a recommendation doesn't sit right, ask for a second opinion; that's standard practice, not an insult.

Practicing Assertiveness — Small Drills, Big Payoff

- The Five-Minute Prep: Before an appointment, write your top concern, desired outcome, and one boundary (e.g., "I will not accept opioids without discussing alternatives").
- The "Pause and Confirm": After a plan is proposed, pause, then say, "Can you explain why this is best for me?"

These drills train you to be clear without being combative.

Additional Considerations — Practical Checkpoints

- Keep appointment notes in a notebook or app.
- Bring someone for moral support and extra ears.
- If unsure, get a second opinion and compare recommendations.

Reintegration Reflection

What one health detail would you put at the top of your one-page medical brief? Rank its importance and write down the words you'll use to tell a provider.

The 'Medical Mission' Check

Was the visit: helpful / unclear / dismissive? What one question will you ask next time to get closer to helpful?

You served with clarity and purpose. Use that same clarity now when you ask for care. Make appointments count, speak plainly, and hold firm to what you need.

Journaling for self-discovery and growth

Relocated to the section on partnering with male allies and inclusive communities to consolidate guidance on journaling and community support.

Relocated to the section on partnering with male allies and inclusive communities. Original journalling guidance has been integrated there to align personal reflection with community-based reintegration strategies.

Relocated to the section on partnering with male allies and inclusive communities to align reflection practices with community reintegration supports.

Relocated to the section on partnering with male allies and inclusive communities, where this suggested journalling routine is presented alongside community and allyship strategies.

Prompts and related exercises have been moved and consolidated with the practical tools and the section on partnering with male allies and inclusive communities for consistent use and cross referencing.

- Reintegration Reflection: This prompt has been consolidated with the section on partnering with male allies and inclusive communities for consistent use and cross referencing.
- The Support Scroll: This prompt has been consolidated with the section on partnering with male allies and inclusive communities for consistent use and cross referencing.

Relocated to the section on partnering with male allies and inclusive communities to integrate identity exploration with community and allyship resources.

Relocated to the section on partnering with male allies and inclusive communities so the work of mapping what stays and what changes appears alongside community-based reintegration supports.

Try this exercise: (The full exercise and worksheet have been moved to the section on partnering with male allies and inclusive communities for consistent use; see the book's practical tools for the complete materials.)

- Strengths Inventory: Write five skills you used in service—discipline, quick decision-making, caring for others—and next to each, list one civilian context where that skill is valuable. Example: "Logistics planning → managing family moves, budgeting, or work projects."

- Growth Focus: Pick one non-military skill you want to build (cooking a basic meal, public speaking, small-business bookkeeping). Write three concrete steps and a reasonable time line.

Documenting Your Path to Self-Acceptance

Small wins matter. Capture them so they don't disappear under heavier days.

Daily micro-prompts:

- One Small Win: What went better today than yesterday? No win is too small.

- Self-Compassion Note: Write one sentence you'd say to a close buddy going through the same thing. Now say it to yourself, out loud.

Articulating Aspirations and Future Goals

Want a practical way to plan life after service? Break goals into bite-sized actions and social supports.

The "Vision & Steps" template:

- Envision your ideal week (work hours, family time, hobbies). Be specific: mornings, evenings, weekend activities.

- Set three achievable goals for the next six months (learn a skill, reconnect with an old friend, attend a community group). For each goal list two clear next steps and someone who can hold you accountable.

Partner and Group Practices

Journalling can be private or shared. For couples: try The "Love Tank" Check — each partner writes one paragraph about a need that wasn't met this week and one small thing the other could do to restore connection. Read them aloud together without defending; listen.

For veteran groups: pass a prompt at the start of a meet-up (e.g., "A choice I'm proud of") and spend five minutes writing, then five minutes sharing. Short, focused, and honest beats long monologues.

Final Prompt to Carry Forward

Once a month, pick a page to re-read aloud to yourself or with a trusted person. Track changes in tone and content—those shifts are signs of growth, even on tough days. Journalling won't fix everything overnight, but it gives structure to your processing and lets you chart real progress.

Vulnerability and emotional strength

- Partner A: State one need in 15 seconds (example: "I need help with dinner twice this week so I can rest.")
- Partner B: Reflect back what you heard, then ask one clarifying question.

Practicing this for five minutes twice a week builds clarity and reduces resentment.

Expressing Needs and Feelings Openly

Clear requests beat vague hints. Replace "You never help me" with "I need 30 minutes this evening to decompress; can you take the kids for a walk?" Concrete asks increase the odds of getting support. For male and female veterans, this might look different: a male vet might ask a buddy to join a weekend workout as an outlet; a female vet might request a quiet hour to work on a certification while her partner handles a household task. Both are acts of self-care.

Ranking Needs

- List your top five needs right now (sleep, time alone, social contact, purpose-driven work, therapy).
- Rank them and pick the top two to address this week with a specific plan.

Seeking Support and Fostering Resilience

Asking for help is a tactic, not a trait. Connect with a peer group, a therapist who knows military life, or a faith community. Share one small problem and accept one small offer of help. Over time, these exchanges build a network that responds quicker than trying to manage everything solo.

Re-framing Vulnerability as Bravery

Finally, try this mental shift: keep a log of three moments each week when you showed up honestly. No matter how small—saying "I'm overwhelmed," admitting a mistake at work, or asking for directions—mark it as a win. Brave is not being flawless; brave is choosing to be seen, again and again.

Partnering with male allies and inclusive communities

Find groups that celebrate veteran strength and make space for female-specific issues. Try one new community per month—an in-person meeting, a Facebook group, or a themed workshop—and give it three tries before deciding if it fits. Specific groups to consider include Women Veterans Alliance, Female Veterans United, and The Military Woman's Coalition.

Quick practice: Join a group chat, introduce yourself, and ask for one small thing: a recommendation for a local therapist, a tip for job fairs, or a favourite veteran-friendly coffee shop.

Strategic Use of Support from Male Allies

Think of some men in your network as bridges: they can introduce you to new professional contacts, advocate for veteran programs, or back a policy ask. Be explicit about what you want. For example, ask a supportive male colleague to co-present at a community forum or to mentor a younger vet during a hiring drive.

Nurturing Authentic Connections

Quality trumps quantity. Invest in relationships that let you be real. Simple habits build depth: weekly check-ins, celebrating wins, and shared rituals like a monthly walk. Practice these skills:

- Vulnerability: share one small failure and one hope.
- Active listening: mirror what you heard before responding.
- Empathy: name feelings you see before offering advice.

The 'Love Tank' Check — with a partner or close friend, list three ways each of you feels supported and one thing you want more of. Swap lists and pick one item to act on this week.

Resilience-Building Initiatives and Safe Spaces

Plug into programs tailored to women who served, in the military—VA Women's Health Services, the Women's Veterans Alliance Resilience Program, and the USO's Women's Initiative are places to find mentorship, training, and peer groups. When starting a support circle, set clear boundaries: how often you meet, confidentiality rules, and what kinds of help members can request.

Collaboration for Mutual Growth

Team up with allies on a project—host a panel, run a skills clinic, or organize a donation drive. Working side-by-side builds trust faster than small talk ever will.

Closing prompt: Ranking Needs — list your top three needs right now (emotional, practical, professional). Which community or ally can meet each one? Pick one action to take this week and schedule it now.

Career reinvention and education

Practical step: Pick one subject you enjoy and take a single class. If it sticks, map a two-year plan: classes, certifications, volunteer hours. If not, you've gained a new contact or a story.

Cultivate a Support Network

Your team should include mentors, fellow vets who've walked this route, and professional groups tied to the field you want. Reach out for an informational interview—15 minutes is often enough—and treat each conversation like a reckon mission: learn, record, thank.

Networking script: "I'm transitioning from the military into X. I'd value 15 minutes to ask how you entered the field and what skills mattered most." Simple, direct, respectful—works every time.

Practice Profound Self-Compassion

Reinvention can bruise confidence. Allow space to feel off-balance. Be as kind to yourself as you would be to your squad mate after a tough operation.

Self-care prompts: Journal one frustration and one small win each week. Set micro-goals—apply to two positions, complete one module—and celebrate them.

Celebrate Every Milestone

Mark progress visibly. Share wins with your partner, a mentor, or a vet buddy. A small ritual—favourite meal after completing a certificate, a weekend hike for landing an interview—builds momentum and reminds you that progress is happening.

Reintegration Reflection

What mission objective are you setting for the next six months? List three transferable skills you will highlight, one class you will try, and one person you will ask for advice this week.

Parenting roles and balance after service

Specific self-care actions for veterans:

For those who use physical training to decompress, schedule three weekly runs or gym sessions—treat them like duty time.

- For women who find social support grounding: arrange one weekly coffee with a friend, or a veterans' peer group meeting.
- For anyone: set a "quiet 20 minute block" after dinner where phones are in another room and you do breathing or read.

Prioritizing Self-Care (The Practical Checklist)

- Schedule self-care: block it in a calendar and protect it.
- Ask for help: call on family, friends, or hire a babysitter for a predictable slot each week.
- Take breaks: micro-breaks of five minutes can reset you during a long day.
- Practice mindfulness: two-minute breathing or a simple grounding check (feet on floor, five deep breaths).

Openly Discussing Expectations Around Childcare

Have a no-accusation meeting where each person states needs in the format: "I need X because Y." Example: "I need to have dinner on the table by 6:00 p.m. twice a week because it helps us feel we had family time." Listen, then repeat back what you heard. That simple step keeps misunderstandings small.

The "Love Tank" Check

- Partner A: Name one childcare task where you want more help.
- Partner B: Name one way you feel appreciated this week.

Swap answers and pick one small change to implement this week.

Mutual Support in Parenting

Teamwork means gratitude and swaps. Try a "trade day" once a month: swap bedtime routines or solo parent a weekend day so the other can rest without interruptions. Keep a running list of "quick wins" to thank each other—a sticky note, a text, or a five-minute back rub work wonders.

Final Prompt for Partners

Schedule a 30-minute planning session this weekend: create the two-week schedule, list three non-negotiable self-care slots, and agree on a monthly check-in to tweak the plan. Small routines build trust, calm, and the breathing room necessary for both parenting and rebuilding civilian life.

Stories of female veterans: lessons and hope

- The Self-Love Minute: each morning, say one appreciative sentence about yourself (e.g., "I handled that briefing well yesterday"). Say it out loud, write it on a sticky note, or tell a supportive friend.
- Mirror Task: spend five minutes listing three strengths you used in service and one way you'll use them this week at home.

These tiny habits compound. Many women credit them with restoring confidence during long transitions.

Empowering Takeaways and Reflection Prompts

Reintegration Reflection: Which two service skills can you translate into civilian parenting or job roles? Write them down and share with your partner.

Ranking Needs: List your top three support needs (healthcare, child care, community) and circle one to action this month.

The 'Love Tank' Check: Once a week, ask your partner, "What filled your tank this week? What drained it?" Use answers to schedule two small supportive acts.

A Path Forward

Telling and sharing these stories creates practical road maps: small scripts, shared check lists, and daily rituals. They make healing visible, specific, and repeatable—so other women can borrow what worked and adapt it for their own lives.

Daily self-love routines for women veterans

Cultivating Intentional Daily Self-Care Practices

(Note: These practical routines are designed to be woven into the broader self-care and self-love guidance for women veterans so they connect with existing goals, triggers, and supports.)

Self-care isn't a one-off spa day or a motivational poster — it's the small, daily choices that add up. For veterans and military couples, those choices often need to work around shift schedules, medical appointments, kids, or the odd twenty four hour alert. Below are straightforward, doable practices that honor the physical, emotional, and mental parts of you. These practices are intended to be integrated into the main self care and self love framework for women veterans so they connect with other strategies, resources, and support plans.

Prioritizing Quiet Reflection and Mindfulness

(Note: Use these micro-practices as part of the broader self-care/self-love routine so they reinforce other coping strategies and supports.)

Try this: sit somewhere steady, close your eyes, inhale for four, hold two, exhale for six. Repeat five times. If sitting still feels impossible, use a "walk and breathe" version — three slow laps around the block focusing on footfalls and breath. For couples, do a one minute check-in before bed: each person names one feeling and one need. Reintegration Reflection: What time of day can you reliably carve out two minutes? What will you do with them?

When placed within a broader self-care plan, these brief practices can be linked to triggers, sleep routines, and support options to make them easier to maintain.

Nurturing Physical Well being through Mindful Movement

(Note: Present these movement options alongside broader self-care guidance so they align with medical needs, rehabilitation plans, and personal goals for women veterans.)

Move in ways that respect injuries, deployments, and real-life aches. Options: a ten-minute beginner yoga flow (find a veteran-specific class or You Tube video), a 20-minute dance party in the kitchen, or weighted band strength work in your garage. For male and female veterans with joint pain, chair-based mobility drills can be powerful — shoulder rolls, ankle circles, hip lifts. The point is presence: notice your breath, the tension in a muscle, and the relief afterward. Ranking Needs: Which three movements leave you feeling more like yourself?

Embed these movement choices in the larger self-care plan so they coordinate with medical guidance, physical therapy recommendations, and daily responsibilities.

(Note: Frame self-kindness practices within the broader self-love guidance to normalize them and tie them to concrete resources and relationship supports.)

Link these self-kindness actions to the broader self-care/self-love framework so they reinforce routines, supports, and achievable goals.

(Note: Integrate emotional naming and expression practices into the wider self-care plan so they are supported by trusted listeners, clinicians, and creative outlets already identified in your care plan.)

Feelings that get pushed down tend to come out sideways. Practice naming emotions: “I’m angry about X,” or “I’m tired and overwhelmed.” Use a private journal, a trusted friend, or a clinician to process. Creative outlets help too — a 15 minute sketch session, voice memos where you speak freely, or writing a letter you don’t send. For couples, try a 10 minute “feelings only” talk: no fixing, just listening.

These emotional expression practices work best when they are part of a larger self-care and support plan that identifies safe people, professional resources, and regular creative or reflective opportunities.

Setting Boundaries and Seeking Support

Setting clear boundaries and asking for support are closely related steps in protecting your time, energy, and well being. Below are practical, focused strategies that combine both topics so the guidance is usable right away.

- Clarify what you need. Identify specific behaviours, times, or tasks that drain you and define a concrete boundary (for example: "I will not answer work emails after 7 p.m." or "I need 24 hours' notice before hosting visitors").

- Communicate plainly and calmly. Use "I" statements: "I need…" or "I can't…" followed by the boundary and, when helpful, a brief reason. Be concise and respectful.

- Offer alternatives when possible. If saying no to a request, propose another option: "I can't take that on today, but I can help on Friday" or "I'm unavailable evenings, can we schedule for morning?"

- Set consequences and follow through. Decide in advance what you will do if the boundary is crossed (e.g., end the conversation, decline future requests) and apply it consistently so your boundaries are taken seriously.

- Manage guilt and push back. Expect discomfort when first setting limits. Remind yourself that boundaries protect relationships by making expectations clear. Rehearse short responses to common objections.

- Seek support intentionally. Identify friends, family, mentors, or professionals who respect your boundaries and can offer practical help or emotional backup. Be explicit when asking for support: "Can you watch the kids Saturday morning so I can rest?" Or "Can we check in weekly about my workload?"

- Use community and professional resources. Support groups, counselling, employee assistance programs, and trusted peers can provide advice, accountability, or relief when setting boundaries feels overwhelming.

- Create systems to reinforce boundaries. Use calendar blocks, auto responders, shared family agreements, or delegated task lists to reduce ad hoc requests that test your limits.

- Review and adjust. Periodically evaluate whether your boundaries and support network are working. Adjust boundaries or seek different supports as circumstances change.

Combining clear boundaries with a reliable support network makes limits sustainable and reduces stress while preserving relationships.

Boundaries keep your energy usable. Say no to invites that drain you and yes to small comforts that refill you. Examples: turn off notifications during dinner, block a Sunday morning for yourself, or agree with your partner on a code word that signals needing quiet. Reach out when you need it — a buddy call, a VA resource, or a peer group can be lifelines.

Reconnection and Bridges: Relationships Across Worlds

Relationship-Building Strategies with Military Partners

The return home from service can feel like stepping onto a new planet, even with the familiar presence of your partner beside you. The shared experiences of separation, deployments, and the constant demands of military life can create an unspoken distance. This section offers a guide to bridging that gap, focusing on the foundational skills that rebuild intimacy and understanding. We'll explore how to create a space for genuine dialogue, where feelings can be shared without judgment and where active listening allows you to truly hear each other. You'll learn practical ways to identify what makes conversations difficult and how to express your own needs respectfully. We will also examine how the unique expressions of love languages, especially within the context of military service, can be intentionally applied to strengthen your bond. Furthermore, we'll look at establishing routines for communication, debriefing after deployments, and planning for the future, all designed to help you reconnect and thrive as a couple. These practices emphasize intentional communication and align with the principles of emotional safety, sacred space, and active listening.

Intentional communication foundations

You come home from a long shift, a deployment, or a training rotation, and the couch knows you personally. Your partner is there, but lately the distance between you feels like it started during those long separations and never quite shrank. This is not about blame. It's about making a choice to start talking—really talking—in ways that pull two people back into one team. Creating a sacred space for dialogue and practicing active listening supports this choice and builds emotional safety.

Cultivating Open and Honest Dialogue: The Bedrock of Reconnection

By intentionally cultivating dialogue within a sacred space and engaging in active listening, couples can rebuild intimacy and trust.

Reconnecting with your partner takes deliberate effort and a willingness to speak plainly. In busy households—PT at dawn, commuting, childcare, medical appointments—talk can drift into short updates instead of meaningful conversation. Yet open, honest dialogue can rebuild closeness fast if you set a few basics in place. Establishing intentional communication, grounded in emotional safety, and fostering active listening are key to this process.

Establishing a Safe and Sacred Space

A sacred space for conversation nurtures emotional safety and encourages active listening.

Pick a spot and time where you both can turn off distractions—e.g., the car's back seat after picking up the kids, a quiet hour after lights out, or Sunday morning over coffee. Make eye contact, put phones face down, and say, 'I want to talk about something important—are you ready?' That brief check-in signals respect and safety. When both feel secure, difficult topics shift from ambushes to teamwork, and active listening naturally reinforces trust.

The Art of Active Listening

Active listening, practiced within a sacred space, ensures emotional safety and deepens connection.

Active listening looks simple on paper but takes practice. Try this drill: one partner speaks for three minutes about something that matters; the other only listens and then paraphrases what they heard for one minute—no rebuttal, no "but." If you're a veteran used to quick fixes, this slow motion exchange will feel odd at first, but it prevents misunderstandings and cools defensiveness. This drill supports emotional safety and exemplifies active listening, reinforcing the sacred space of communication.

Acknowledging and Validating Perspectives

By establishing a sacred space and practicing active listening, validation becomes even more powerful and emotionally safe.

You don't have to agree with your partner's view to acknowledge their feelings. If your partner says, "I felt abandoned when you were gone," try: "I hear that you felt abandoned, and that hurt you." That sentence names their experience without implying fault. Validation looks like: listening, naming feelings, and reflecting them back. It builds trust and keeps conversations from escalating into old fights.

Collaboratively Identifying Communication Triggers

Make a shared trigger list. Example entries: "talking about finances during tax season," "comments about weight after deployments," or "sudden criticism when I'm tired." Sit down with a notepad and identify triggers—yours and theirs—and label what each trigger usually leads to (shutting down, arguing, sarcasm). Then create small rules: like pausing the conversation after five minutes of rising tone, or using a safe word to take a cooling break.

Striving for Empathy and Understanding

Ask open-ended questions: "What was the hardest part for you today?" "What would help you feel safer right now?" Try perspective swaps: each partner explains the other's point of view for one minute. This is less about correctness and more about stepping into one another's boots.

The Power of "I" Statements

When you need to bring up a need, say, "I feel overwhelmed when dishes pile up; I need help with mornings." That keeps the focus on your experience rather than pointing a finger. Veterans often communicate in direct language—use that clarity, but frame it in personal terms.

Regular Emotional Check-Ins

Schedule a short weekly check-in—ten minutes on Tuesday night. Use prompts: "The 'Love Tank' Check" where each rates their emotional tank from 0–10 and names one refill action. Or "Reintegration Reflection": after a period apart, share three things that changed for you and one thing you want to keep the same. These rituals prevent small gaps from widening.

Put these practices into daily life, and you'll find conversations shift from defensive skirmishes to planning sessions. Communication isn't a one-time fix; it's the routine maintenance that keeps your team ready for whatever comes next.

Love languages in service life

Understanding how the five love languages show up during active duty can make reconnection after service less awkward and more effective. Below are practical, branch-friendly takes on each language—what they look like in uniformed life and how to use them when time, distance, and duty complicate things.

Words of Affirmation: Recognizing and Validating Sacrifices

Service members hear radio checks and Sit Reps all day; what they may not hear enough of are simple human acknowledgements. Try these targeted moves:

- Tactical gratitude: write a short letter that names a specific sacrifice—missing birthdays, late-night training, or the mental load of planning for deployment. Drop it in a care package or leave it in a gear bag.
- Unit-aware praise: when friends or family thank someone for "their service," add detail: "Your steady leadership at last year's fund raiser meant our kids kept soccer practice running." Specifics matter.

Reintegration Reflection: List three sacrifices your partner made in the last year. How will you thank them this week in a way that names one action they took? Use this exercise together with a short "Ranking Needs" tool so gratitude and practical follow-through stay aligned.

Acts of Service: Acknowledging Unseen Tasks and Responsibilities

Placement note: Move this section to sit alongside deployment debrief routines.

Active-duty life comes with a lot of behind-the-scenes labour: paperwork, gear upkeep, family coordination during TDY. Acts of service hit hard when they're practical and visible.

- Concrete example: take the car for an inspection before a leave period, pre-pack a checklist for PCS moves, or handle childcare pick ups the week after a long exercise. These are gestures that reduce friction.

- For the transitioning veteran: offer to help rework resumes, sort medical records, or sit in on VA intake calls—these acts are love and logistics in one.

Ranking Needs: Which unseen task keeps you or your partner up at night? Rank three and pick the top one to fix this month.

- Concrete example: If vehicle maintenance is the unseen task causing stress, one partner takes responsibility this month to book the service, pay or confirm the appointment, and send the booking confirmation to the other — removing the mental load and preventing last-minute scrambling.

- For the transitioning veteran: Use acts of service to reduce cognitive burden—offer clear, specific help (e.g., "I'll schedule the oil change for Friday at 10 a.m."), follow through, and use simple tools like shared calendars or checklist notes. Keep communication direct and practical to avoid misinterpretation and to build trust.

When windows of time are small, quality beats quantity by a mile.

- Micro-dates: a 20-minute video call with a planned topic (funniest thing that day, one hard moment, a quick shared play list;) can feel as fulfilling as a longer but unfocused conversation.

- Pre-leave rituals: build a "leave checklist" that includes one intentional activity—cooking a favourite meal together, a five-mile hike, or a visit to a spot that holds good memories.

The "Love Tank" Check: On a scale of 1–10, how full does your partner's "time tank" feel after a typical week? What action can raise your partner's 'time tank' by two points?

Receiving Gifts: Cultivating Appreciation for Small Tokens

Gifts in military life often serve as anchors—items that tie a person to home.

- Thoughtful packages: include small practical items (socks with a note,), homemade treats that travel well, or a play list—printed photo for times when bandwidth is low.
- DIY gestures: a handmade charm on a zipper pull, a laminated photo, or a dog-tag with a private message can be deeply meaningful without costing much.

Partner Dialogue Prompt: Share one small thing that made you feel seen while apart. How can you reproduce that for each other?

Physical Touch: Navigating Intimacy and Connection

Touch can be complicated when duty, policy, or distance interferes, but there are workarounds that preserve closeness.

- When together: prioritize short, intentional touches–hand on the shoulder during a briefing, an five-second hug focused on breathing together for calm.

When apart: exchange textured items (a scarf, a baseball cap) that carry scents, send heartfelt texts describing a future embrace, or agree on a "reconnection ritual" for the first night home.

Action Plan for Intimacy: Pick one physical ritual to practice within 72 hours of reunion (e.g., a ten-minute "decompression hug" where both share three things they noticed that day).

Bringing it together: apply one language per week for five weeks and track small changes. These focused, practical moves honour military realities and create real pathways back to closeness after service.

Deployment debrief routines

Reconnecting with Purpose: The Power of Post-Deployment Debriefing

Complementing the pre-deployment care giving plans you put in place, a post-deployment debrief helps translate those plans back into everyday life. It reconnects purpose with practice, aligning expectations and emotional needs after time apart.

You made it home. The boots are off, the duffel is unpacked, and now comes the tricky part: stepping out of mission mode and back into "us" mode. A post-deployment debrief routine is not formal paperwork; it's a planned, compassionate practice that helps two people line up feelings, expectations, and needs after months apart. Tie this routine back to the pre-deployment care giving agreements so both partners can see what worked, what didn't, and what should change.

Creating a Safe Space for Honest Conversations

This sets the tone for reviewing how your pre-deployment care giving plans translated into reality and for deciding what needs adjustment.

Set aside time that feels like a reset button. Block a weekend morning or an evening with no screens and no interruptions. Choose a private spot—your kitchen table, a park bench, or the back of the camper—somewhere you both can sit without feeling rushed. Start by agreeing to ground rules: no blaming, no interrupting, and a limit on problem-solving for the first round—this is about sharing, not fixing. After the first sharing round, reserve time to revisit the pre-deployment care giving plan and note any updates or role changes needed.

Prompt: Reintegration Reflection

Use this prompt alongside your caregiving-plan checklist to compare experiences and expectations.

Take 10 minutes each to answer these aloud without rebuttal from your partner. After both have spoken, spend a few minutes comparing what you heard to your pre-deployment care giving agreements and identify one or two concrete adjustments.

Sharing Your Stories: Highlights, Challenges, and Emotional Landscapes

Sharing specific moments helps you test whether the care giving arrangements you planned held up, and it highlights where more support or clarification is needed.

This is where storytelling matters. One partner might talk about a small kindness that stayed with them; the other might mention the hardest day. Share specifics: a memory, a scent, or a moment that stuck. Use "I" statements—"I felt…"—so it stays personal and less accusatory. At the end of your stories, note any adjustments to your care giving plan prompted by what you heard.

Practical example: spend fifteen minutes each on "high point" and "low point" of the deployment. After each share, the listener repeats back what they heard: not to judge, but to validate that the story landed accurately.

Navigating Reintegration and Transition

Reintegration is often two steps forward, one back. You may find roles shifted—who cooks, who manages finances, how time is spent. Talk about what felt normal before and what needs to change now. Expect awkwardness. Expect laughter. Expect confusion. Those are signs you're adjusting.

Prompt: Ranking Needs

Each partner writes their top three needs right now (emotional support, help with kids, alone time, medical care, paperwork). Compare lists. Where they overlap, plan immediate supports. Where they differ, schedule follow-ups—small steps beat vague promises.

Identifying Areas of Need and Providing Support

Be specific when asking for help. Instead of "I need more support," try "Can you take the kids to soccer on Tuesday so I can go to the VA appointment?" Or, "Can we agree to one tech-free hour each night?" If professional help is necessary, treat it like any other check-up—book it, share the appointment times, and go together when possible.

Concrete self-care for veterans: a 20-minute morning walk to reset cortisol and clear thinking; a weekly peer coffee with another vet to exchange practical tips; a short breathing routine before bed to drop hyper vigilance.

Celebrating Resilience and Sacrifices

Close your debrief with gratitude. Name two things you admired about the other person during deployment—big or small. Consider a small ritual: a homecoming dinner where each person brings one story and one small gift that symbolizes what kept them going.

Prompt: The "Love Tank" Check

On a scale of 1–10, how full is your "love tank" today? Discuss what would move it up two points this week.

A thoughtful, regular debrief routine turns the awkwardness of return into intentional reconnection. It's not a cure-all, but it gives both of you structure, clarity, and permission to be messy while rebuilding. Keep it practical, keep it kind, and keep showing up.

Pre-deployment care giving plans

Collaboratively Establishing Pre-Deployment Care giving Plans

You've got the debrief routine down—now let's flip the calendar and prepare for departure. Putting a care giving plan in place before a deployment reduces stress during the weeks and months ahead, especially when kids are involved. Think of this section as your tactical checklist: clear roles, reliable contacts, and practical routines that keep household life moving while one person is away. Build these plans so they plug directly into your everyday rhythm and your agreed communication practices—that way care giving tasks are part of the routine and expectations are clear before distance makes course corrections harder.

Building a Support Network

Start by mapping out people who can step in without a drama bulletin. Make a short list: two family members, one neighbour, a close friend, and any local providers (babysitter, paediatrician, landlord). For each person, write one or two specific tasks you'd want them to cover—school drop-off two days a week, a weekend backup for date-night-cancelled emergencies, or a quick grocery run when you're running on fumes.

Action step: Host a 30-minute "mission brief" with each support person. Go over expectations, share schedules, and exchange contact info. Give them a simple responsibilities sheet so everyone knows who does what and when. During the brief, confirm how they'll receive routine updates (text, calendar invite, group chat) and agree on escalation steps for unexpected problems so communications fit your established patterns.

Communication Strategies

Distance is easier now than in past decades, but it still requires planning. Set up regular check-ins that match your family's energy—daily texts for a couple who prefers small, frequent updates; a twice-weekly video call for families who want longer conversations. Use one shared space for updates: a group chat, a private social thread, or a calendar everyone can access. Tie these check-ins to routine anchors (after dinner, Sunday planning) and agree on the tone and purpose of each check-in so communication supports connection without becoming a logistical burden.

Concrete idea: Schedule a weekly virtual family night—choose a theme (board games, watch-along movie, story time) and rotate who picks. For kids, send a "care package" with pre-written questions or prompts to read on calls, so conversations feel natural, not like interviews. Include a short list of daily, or weekly update prompts (school highlight, one worry, one win) so communication reinforces the household routine and helps maintain emotional closeness.

Managing Household Responsibilities and Finances

Split the to-dos and put systems in place so nothing slips through the cracks. Make a list of recurring chores and assign an owner for each: lawn care, mail handling, school approvals, and vet visits. For money, set up automatic bill payments and alerts. If the non-deploying partner needs account access, arrange it now and document passwords securely. Schedule periodic finance check-ins (monthly or quarterly) as part of your routine so both partners stay informed; agree on how financial updates will be communicated and who is responsible for each transaction or approval.

Tool tip: Create a single binder or digital folder with important documents—insurance cards, power-of-attorney forms, bank contact numbers—and a short "if-this-happens" guide. Run a dry fire drill: have the non-deploying partner practice paying a bill or calling a provider while the deploying partner watches and takes notes.

Emergency Contact Protocols

Decide who makes what calls if something urgent happens. Identify two primary emergency contacts plus one backup. Write out decision making authority for medical or legal situations and make sure copies of critical forms are stored where family members can reach them. These protocols reinforce the relationship building strategies that help maintain trust during separation.

Quick template to include in the binder: emergency contact names, relation, phone numbers, and what each person is authorized to act. Share the same info with kids in an age appropriate way so they know who to call. Including this template supports the relationship building strategies that keep communication clear and consistent while apart.

Preparing Children for Deployment

Help kids understand the time line. Create a countdown calendar with pictures and small rituals for important milestones. Let children pick ways to stay connected—letters, drawings, or a special pillow with notes inside. This approach aligns with the relationship building strategies that nurture a sense of security during separation.

Prompt for families: Reintegration Reflection—ask kids what they want to tell the deploying parent while they're away and mail those messages periodically. Encourage open talk about feelings and validate their worries without minimizing them. Reflective communication strengthens the relationship building strategies that sustain emotional bonds across distance.

Supporting the Non Deploying Partner

Acknowledge the load they'll carry and plan for emotional check-ins. Schedule short weekly calls specifically for feelings and logistics—no multitasking allowed. Encourage the non deploying partner to identify one self care practice (gym, coffee with a friend, a hobby) and block time for it. These actions reinforce the relationship building strategies that preserve the partner's well being during deployment.

Local resource tip: Find a support group or meet up for partners of deployed service members and share the meeting info in your binder. Connecting to support networks supports the relationship building strategies that help partners feel connected and understood.

Quick exercise: The "Love Tank" Check—each week, non deploying partner ranks needs (sleep, help with kids, emotional time) and shares the top two items. The deploying partner responds with what they can realistically support from distance. This exercise embodies the relationship building strategies that keep both partners aligned and supportive across distance.

Acknowledge the load they'll carry and plan for emotional check-ins. Schedule short weekly calls specifically for feelings and logistics—no multitasking allowed. Encourage the non deploying partner to identify one self care practice (gym, coffee with a friend, a hobby) and block time for it.

Local resource tip: Find a support group or meet up for partners of deployed service members and share the meeting info in your binder.

Quick exercise: The "Love Tank" Check—each week, non-deploying partner ranks needs (sleep, help with kids, emotional time) and shares the top two items. The deploying partner responds with what they can realistically support from distance.

A pre-deployment care giving plan isn't about controlling every possibility; it's about giving your family predictable handles to grab when life gets unpredictable. With clear roles, scheduled communications, backed-up finances, and a thoughtful plan for kids and the partner holding the fort, departures become less chaotic and come-backs less likely to trip you up.

Symbolic gestures and rituals

Incorporating Branch-Specific Symbols

If military service is part of the bond, use that shared language. Respectful, visible reminders can be comforting without being flashy:

Place each item in a special box or visible spot:

- A small flag
- A unit challenge coin
- A ceremonial uniform item

Symbolic Gestures for Separation and Reconnection

- Wearable options: a simple hat, patch, or bracelet you both agree on — civilian on the outside, meaningful on the inside.

Quick idea: designate a "mission patch" ritual. Each month the non-deploying partner writes a short note describing a moment that made them proud of the other, folds it into an envelope, and adds it to a box labelled with the unit or branch. Read together on return.

- What surprised me about being together again?
- What small habit from separation do we want to keep?
- What do we need to change to feel grounded as a team?

Tips for Creating Meaningful Rituals

- Start small: pick one symbol and one short ritual.
- Be intentional: choose things that mean something to both of you, not what looks good to others.
- Be consistent: repetition builds the meaning.
- Have fun: rituals should bring comfort and a few laughs.

The "Love Tank" Check

Weekly, ask each other: "On a scale of 1–10, how full is your love tank?" Follow up with one small thing each can do that week to raise it by one point.

These tiny, steady practices give you a shared script during separation and a predictable path back to each other at reunion. They don't fix everything, but they build more moments that matter.

Homecoming planning and customs

Prompt: The Countdown List

- Write three small surprises you'll each prepare.
- Share one hope for the first week back (sleeping in, catching a movie, relearning your morning routine together).

Aligning Reunion Expectations

Blunt talk before the reunion saves friction later. Discuss emotional needs and boundaries: does one person want lots of touch and talk right away, while the other needs quiet? Say it out loud and set realistic expectations—no Hollywood montage guarantees instant smoothness.

Try this quick exercise: The 'Expectation Check'

- Each partner names two expectations and one boundary for the first 72 hours.
- Rank those items together and agree on a fallback plan for when stress shows up (e.g., "If tempers flare, take a 20-minute reset and reconvene.").

Establishing New Rhythms

Reintegration is a rhythm reset. Create a new daily schedule together: who'll do morning coffee, evening check-ins, and weekend chores. Schedule regular date nights—even low-effort ones count (pizza and a board game, a short hike).

These suggestions align with the self care guidance provided earlier and the relationship guidance discussed later, creating a unified approach.

Example rhythm: Sunday family meeting for the week; Wednesday 30-minute "state of us" check; one weekend morning for whatever hobby you missed.

These suggestions align with the self care guidance provided earlier and the relationship guidance discussed later, creating a unified approach.

Balancing Individual Needs

These suggestions align with the self care guidance provided earlier and the relationship guidance discussed later, creating a unified approach.

Honouring personal space matters. Communicate clearly when you need solo time or focused connection. Keep doing the hobbies that keep you grounded—run, read, shoot, sew—and protect them.

These suggestions align with the self care guidance provided earlier and the relationship guidance discussed later, creating a unified approach.

Prompt: Ranking Needs

These suggestions align with the self care guidance provided earlier and the relationship guidance discussed later, creating a unified approach.

- Each person lists three activities that recharge them.
- Agree on when and how those activities will happen without guilt.

These suggestions align with the self care guidance provided earlier and the relationship guidance discussed later, creating a unified approach.

- Agree on when and how those activities will happen without guilt.

Gradual Reintegration into Civilian Life

These suggestions align with the self care guidance provided earlier and the relationship guidance discussed later, creating a unified approach.

Take it easy. Prioritize sleep and self care, accept help from friends and family, and get professional support if you need it—there's no shame in asking for backup. Rebuilding civilian routines takes time; small steps are wins.

These suggestions align with the self care guidance provided earlier and the relationship guidance discussed later, creating a unified approach.

Crafting Symbolic Reconnection Gestures

These suggestions align with the self care guidance provided earlier and the relationship guidance discussed later, creating a unified approach.

Create a ritual that marks "we're back." Write letters to each other during the first week, make a small art piece, or plant something in the yard to mark this new phase. These gestures become shorthand for commitment.

Celebrating Reintegration Milestones

Celebrate the return, the end of deployment, and small wins—first family dinner together, first uninterrupted sleep, first weekend outing. Acknowledge the resilience it took to get here.

Reaffirming Commitment Through Shared Experiences

Plan a short trip, try a new hobby together, or book a workshop. Shared experiences rebuild trust and closeness. Final prompt: pick one shared activity to do within the next month and one longer-term plan for the next six months. Put dates on them and treat them like important ops.

Reintegration Reflection

- What went well in our homecoming plan?
- What surprised us emotionally?
- What one small change will make our daily life smoother this month?

Short, practical, and done together—that's the trick. You already know how to plan a mission; use that skill to plan your homecoming.

Managing long separations

Proactive Connection Amidst Separation

Time apart tests even the most solid partnerships—think of it like PT for the heart: uncomfortable, necessary, and better with a plan. The next few pages give you clear tools for staying close when miles (and missions) keep you apart.

Scheduled, Dedicated Communication

Set a communication rhythm that both of you can live with. Call it a cadence if that helps—call it whatever gets you to pick up the phone. Specific examples:

- Daily 10-minute check-in: A short, predictable time to share wins, weather, or what went wrong with dinner. Keep it low-pressure but sacred.
- Weekly video chat: Make one night "face time night," with a simple agenda—share a photo album, read the same short article, or update a shared whiteboard of plans.
- Monthly virtual dinner date: Order take out to each other's locations or cook the same recipe, then eat together over video.

Quick prompt: Reintegration Reflection — what communication schedule feels realistic for both of you right now? Rank it 1–5 for feasibility.

Creative Technological Bridges

Use tech the way some units use equipment: smart, not flashy. Try these concrete ideas:

- Record a 2-minute video message of everyday life—walk through the backyard, show a silly face, read a passage from a book—and send it for off-shift viewing.
- Mail a care package that includes a handwritten note, a play list

QR code, and a small token (a patch, a coffee bag). Unboxing is an event.

- Sync a streaming service and press play at the same time. Text one-word play-by-plays if the connection drops; it adds a laugh.

Prompt: The "Love Tank" Check — what tech-based surprise would fill your partner's tank this month? One item, one week, one cost estimate.

Shared Routines and Rituals

Shared habits keep two lives moving in the same tempo. Examples that translate well when apart:

- Morning coffee ritual: Send a photo of your cup and one thing you're grateful for each morning.
- Synchronized workouts: Do the same 20-minute routine at 0700 and text a sweaty selfie afterward.
- Co-curated play list: Add songs for each other, then press shuffle during downtime.

Reflection: Ranking Needs — list three rituals you want to keep or start. Which one is highest priority and why?

Validating Emotional Impact

Separation breeds real feelings—loneliness, anger, boredom—and these deserve plain talk; create a non-judgemental zone: set a 15 minute weekly slot where emotions are named without fixing. Use phrases like, "I noticed I felt…," and respond with curiosity, not defence.

Quick exercise: Each writes one sentence describing the hardest thing about this separation. Swap and read aloud on your next call.

Intentional Reunion Planning

Plan one intentional reconnection per reunion: a short road trip, a workshop, or even a weekend of "no phones unless an emergency". Surprise elements work well - an unexpected hike, a photo book waiting at the door, but agree in advance on boundaries (crowded public events may be overwhelming after long separations).

Self-Care and Personal Growth

Both partners should fill their personal tanks. Suggestions tailored to veterans:

- For a veteran who responds well to structure: set a workout goal or sign up for a skills class.
- For a veteran who values social ties: plan a small support dinner with civilian friends who ask kind questions.
- Mindfulness micro-practices: five-minute breathing breaks after stressful messages.

Reflection prompt to share: What self-care activity did you try this week, and how did it help your connection?

Wrap-Up Prompt

Pick one communication rhythm, one tech surprise, and one self-care action to try this month. Check in together on progress in two weeks—short, honest, and with humour. Small, consistent moves beat grand gestures every time.

Non-sexual physical affection ideas

Reconnecting Through Gentle, Non-Sexual Physical Touch

After you've put routines, video dates, and meaningful reunions into motion, there's another tool that's low-tech, immediate, and often underrated: non-sexual physical touch. For veterans and military couples, touch can rebuild trust and a sense of safety in ways paperwork and plans can't. Think of it as small tactical moves that soften the perimeter — no fireworks required.

The Language of Touch (and How to Speak It)

Physical touch has its own grammar. It can be clear and brief, or slow and deliberate. Start with consent, a quick check-in like, "Can I put my hand on your shoulder for a minute?" Models the respect many of you practiced in service and sets up a safe space. The point is to use touch to say, "I see you," or "You're not alone," without turning every contact into a bid for sex.

Concrete Gestures That Actually Work

Here are specific actions you can try, with a few veteran-flavored scenarios:

- Prolonged hug after a long shift: One partner waits by the door; the other comes in, drops the bag, and the hug lasts longer than the three-second airport squeeze. Practice breathing together for 30 seconds. Reintegration Reflection: How did that hug change your mood?

- Hold hands during chores or while walking the dog: Keep thumbs linked. It's low-key but consistent. Try it during a grocery run and notice if conversation opens up.

- Pat on the back after a win: Debrief like you would after a mission. A hand on the shoulder and "Good job" acknowledges effort and competence.

- Rest a hand on a shoulder during a talk: This shows attentiveness without interrupting the speaker. The receiver can nod if it's welcome.

"Lingering embrace before sleep: Lie on your side and drape an arm over the other—no pressure to escape."

- Head scratches and shoulder rubs to relieve tension: Short, targeted touch for sore spots after physical training, yard work, or a rough day thinking about VA paperwork.

The Benefits in Plain Terms

Intentional non-sexual touch:

- Helps reset the nervous system after stress.
- Builds trust by signalling safety and presence.
- Encourages clearer communication; people who touch report feeling heard.

Ranking Needs: Which of these do you both want more of—comfort, presence, reassurance, physical closeness? Rank them 1–4 and compare.

Practice Prompts for Veterans and Their Partners

The "Love Tank" Check: Once a week, each partner names one small touch that filled their tank and one that missed the mark. No blame — just data.

Five-Minute Touch Drill: Set a timer. For five minutes, practice sustained, non-sexual contact (hand-holding, shoulder-to-shoulder, forehead-to-forehead if comfy). Afterwards, say one sentence about how it felt.

Adaptations for Military Couples

For all couples, swap examples that fit your routines ...

If hyper vigilance or PTSD makes close contact hard, scale down: try "contact windows" (30 seconds at first), incorporate grounding phrases ("Feet on the floor— we are safe"), or agree on a safe word if you need space. For same sex and cross branch couples, swap examples that fit your routines — a Navy spouse might choose a dockside walk; an Army vet might prefer a quiet post fielded brief hug.

Closing Thought

Gentle touch isn't flashy, but it's a practical way to reconnect muscle memory and heart memory. Try one small gesture tonight. Afterward, use the Reintegration Reflection prompt to talk about it. Small steps add up — and sometimes a steady hand on a shoulder says more than a speech ever could.

Memory boxes and memorabilia

Deployment photos: pick one good image per deployment, and write a sentence on the back about where you were and how you felt.

- Service medals: place them on a felt backing and note the event connected to each.
- Letters: fold one or two meaningful letters and label the date and context.

Civilian transition mementos:

- Welcome-home signs or airport photos: tuck a small photo into an envelope with the arrival date.
- First civilian-purchase photo: snap a pic of the new car keys or tool set and print it for the box.

Celebrating Individual Growth

Reserve a section for personal wins. This portion honours who each of you became after service.

- New skills/hobbies: include a business card from a class, a photo of a completed woodworking project, or a picture of a certificate.
- Personal achievements: ticket stubs from a graduation, a snapshot of a first day at a new job, or a small token that represents a milestone.

Revisiting and Reflecting

Schedule a quarterly Memory Box Night. Make it short and intentional:

- Reintegration Reflection: Pull one item and each take two minutes to say what it brings up. No fixing—just listening.

- The "Love Tank" Check: After reflecting, each partner names one small, physical thing that would make them feel seen in the next week (a back rub, a handwritten note, a shared walk).

A Tool for Future Goal Setting

Use the box to set shared aims. Add a folded card labelled "Next Five" with three attainable goals you want to accomplish together.

Prompts to write on the card:

- Honour our military roots by attending one veterans' event this year.
- Celebrate resilience by planning a low-key anniversary ritual.
- Look forward: list one skill you'll learn together (gardening, cooking a regional dish, photography).

Keep updating the card as goals shift.

Final thought: a well-made memory box is not a museum; it's a living object. It holds past chapters and also nudges you toward the next ones. Treat it as a project you return to—part storytelling, part planning, and always a shared reminder that both of you matter in the story.

Mutual support during service life

Cultivating Mutual Support: Practical Strategies for Military Couples

Use these strategies alongside conflict de-escalation techniques during high stress times to reinforce connection and prevent escalation.

Understanding and Validating Each Other's Experiences

Use these strategies alongside conflict de-escalation techniques during high stress times to reinforce connection and prevent escalation.

These practices pair well with conflict de-escalation approaches during high stress periods, helping both partners feel heard before tensions rise.

Reintegration Reflection

Start here: both of you carry weight, but not always the same pieces. One partner might come home covered in dirt from field training or carry the mental load of mission planning; the other might be juggling bills, school runs, or last-minute home repairs during long stints away. Naming those different loads out loud reduces friction. Use a calm turn taking approach. Try this quick exercise together:

Use this when tensions are high as a calmer way to surface differences before they escalate.

This reflection is especially helpful when reintegration coincides with heightened conflict; use it as a de-escalation tool to slow things down and rebuild understanding.

- Each partner has two minutes to list three things that felt the hardest while the other was away. No interruptions; just listen.

After each list, restate what you heard in one sentence. If you miss the point, ask one clarifying question.

Use this structured turn-taking during or after heated moments to lower arousal and create space for understanding.

That short practice moves you from assumptions to actual understanding. Validation doesn't mean fixing—sometimes it's a nod, a "That packed weeks of stress into one tiny sentence; I get that," and the other person feels seen. Following the reflection, consider a Love Tank Check to gauge how your emotional reserves have shifted.

When emotions run high, validation can de-escalate more effectively than problem solving; consider pairing it with a brief breathing break or a short time out if needed.

"Validation doesn't mean fixing—sometimes it's a nod, a 'That packed weeks of stress into one tiny sentence: I get that,' and the other person feels seen."

Clear communication strategies are important for preventing and de-escalating conflicts under stress.

Military life perks include discipline and routines—use those for connection. Set predictable contact patterns you can both live with: a 10 minute morning check-in before duty starts, a weekly video date, or a handwritten letter that survives bad WiFi and morale dips. Concrete examples:

These predictable patterns can reduce uncertainty that otherwise fuels conflict during high stress periods.

- If a spouse is at drill weekends, schedule a 20 minute call Sunday nights to recap the week.

Consistency in small rituals helps prevent resentments from building into bigger arguments.

- During deployments, try a shared photo album app where each adds one pic per day; no pressure, just a little window into daily life. After deployment, use a Love Tank Check to assess how well you're sustaining emotional connection.

During stressful transitions, use these low pressure connections to keep conflict from building; check in afterward to de-escalate any residual tension.

The 'Love Tank' Check

Every Sunday, each partner names one thing that filled their "love tank" that week and one thing that drained it. Keep it specific (e.g., "your coffee cup left in the sink" vs. "You were distant"). Small honesty, big repairs.

Celebrating Successes and Building Traditions

Celebrate wins, even small ones—finishing a qualification, a job interview, planting a garden. Rituals anchor you through unpredictability. Pick one simple ritual and protect it:

- A monthly "mission debrief" dinner where each shares one proud moment and one learning.

- A yearly "homecoming roast" where you read silly welcome-home notes aloud.

Providing Tangible Assistance and Emotional Support

Tangible help matters—paying a bill before due date, arranging a vet visit, fixing the leaky Faust—these actions whisper: I've got your back. Pair that with emotional presence: ask open questions ("What worried you most this week?"), Then resist the urge to solve immediately. Often, the first need is to be heard.

Practical Task List for Deployments

- Create a shared calendar for bills and appointments.

- Designate a trusted friend or family point-of-contact for

emergencies.

- Pre-pay or automate utilities if possible.
- Keep a short instruction sheet for home systems (garage, router, alarm).

Championing Individual Growth

Supporting one another's goals builds mutual respect. If one partner wants to finish a degree or start martial-arts training, identify tangible support: childcare swaps, a small monthly budget, or celebrating milestones with a favourite meal. Encourage "solo projects" that maintain identity outside the couple.

Ranking Needs

- Each partner writes top three personal goals and top three household needs. Swap lists. Pick one item from each list to actively support this month.

Wrap-up prompts

- What did I hear my partner say that surprised me?
- What is one small thing I can do this week to back their personal goal?

These practices create a steady, predictable support system—practical, human, and a lot less stressful than guessing. Keep practicing; muscle memory for care works wonders.

Digital boundaries and privacy

Navigating the screen side of life is now part of the packing list for any military household. Just like you wouldn't leave a weapon unsecured, think of your devices and accounts as things that need careful handling. Below are practical ways to set shared expectations about presence and privacy, with specific examples and short exercises to get you talking.

Defining What Stays Private

Start with a short conversation: each partner names three things they're comfortable sharing on social feeds and three things that stay off-limits. Concrete examples:

- Okay to share: base photos without operational details, graduation snapshots, light-hearted memes.
- Keep private: duty schedules, maps of training areas, photos from intimate moments, kids' exact school locations.

Reintegration Reflection: After a deployment, review what you posted while apart. Did anything make you uneasy? If yes, agree on a plan for editing or deleting posts and set a rule for future deployments.

Social Media Rules and Comment Management

Set clear rules for how you interact with other people online. Some prompts:

- Acceptable comments: friendly check-ins, supportive emojis, congratulatory messages.
- Not acceptable: flirtatious back-and-forth, detailed personal rants, or private jokes that exclude the partner.

When negative comments appear, agree on a response protocol: ignore, block, or respond together. Example: if a former unit mate posts a heated comment, the partner on base drafts a calm reply and the home partner approves before posting.

Phone-Free Shared Time

Designate device-free windows—dinners, Sunday mornings, the first hour home after shift. Try a pilot: one week of "no screens during dinner." Compare how conversations change. The point isn't strict policing; it's creating predictable windows where attention is available.

Setting Boundaries for Messages and Notifications

Agree on expected response times for different message types. Sample rules:

- Emergency: call immediately.
- Routine work messages: reply within 12 hours unless on duty.
- Personal texts from partner: reply within a few hours when possible, or send a short "I'll reply tonight" note.

The "Love Tank" Check: Rate your partner's digital responsiveness this week (1–5). Talk about one small tweak each of you can try next week.

Respecting Digital Alone Time

Acknowledge the need to scroll or play games as downtime. Create a "do not disturb" code phrase for when someone wants solitary screen time without being socially checked. Honour that silence without judgment.

Shared Passwords and Account Access

Not every account needs to be shared. Use these options:

- Joint accounts for bills and subscriptions with shared credentials.
- Personal accounts kept private, but with agreed check-ins for important items.

If sharing passwords, set an expiration review every six months and change them after major events like a deployment return.

A Simple Security Plan for Two

Make basic security habits standard practice:

- Use strong, unique passwords and two-factor authentication for email and finance accounts.
- Install antivirus on laptops, back up photos to an external drive, and keep software updated.
- Be cautious about clicking links in messages that claim to be from the service—confirm via a separate call.

Action Item: Set a 30-minute “security date” to update passwords together and enable two-factor on key accounts.

Final prompt for partners: Schedule a 20-minute talk this week. Each person brings one boundary they want and one habit they’ll adopt to protect your shared privacy. Write them down and revisit in a month.

Conflict resolution during high-stress periods

If the answer is yes, avoid piling guilt on top of stress; use this recognition as a cue to shift tactics.

Practical Strategies to Manage Stress and Talk Better

Pause and Breathe Before You Speak

This is not fluffy advice. Try counting to five and taking a breath before answering when a topic feels heated. One partner can say, “Pause?” And the other agrees to take a breath. It’s a signal that you’re choosing response over reaction.

“I” Statements: Concrete Examples

Instead of “You never help with the bills,” try: “I feel overwhelmed when I handle the bills alone and could use a planning session this week.” For veterans who prefer practical phrasing, script short lines and practice them: “I need a ten-minute heads-up before a big talk.”

One Issue at a Time

Set a rule: no laundry-listing. Example: If the argument started over weekend chores, agree to keep the focus on scheduling chores rather than bringing up last year’s deployment-related fights.

Prioritize Understanding Over Agreement

Try a quick check: after your partner speaks, repeat back two things you heard, then ask, “Did I miss anything?”. This builds clarity and lowers defensiveness.

Schedule Tough Talks

When stress is high, pick a calmer slot: "Let's talk Thursday after dinner for 30 minutes about finances." Make this a promise you keep. If emotions spike, agree on a break time and a return time.

Cultivate Empathy with a Simple Exercise

Each person spends five minutes describing their current stressors—no interruptions, no fixes. Then switch. This creates space for empathy and reduces immediate corrective responses.

Reconnect After Conflict

Finish difficult conversations with a small, deliberate act: a shared snack, a short walk, or ten minutes of non verbal closeness. It signals that the argument didn't define the whole partnership.

Reintegration Reflection

- What recent conversation escalated because of stress? Write the trigger and one small behaviour you can change next time.
- Rank the three biggest stressors right now. Which one can you act on together within one week?

The "Love Tank" Check

Once a week, each partner names two things that helped their "tank" feel fuller and one request for the coming week. Keep it short and specific—no long speeches.

Stress changes the way we communicate, but with intentional pauses, clear statements, and agreed routines for tough conversations, couples—especially those moving from military life to civilian—can rebuild clearer, safer patterns of talk. Use the prompts here as short drills to practice calm, controlled communication when stress tries to step in.

Real-world examples of successful strategies

Real-World Examples of Successful Reconnection Strategies

Okay — stories time. Real couples, real tactics, real results. These snapshots show how simple, specific moves tied to the five love languages can bridge the gap after service-related separation or transition. Use them as blueprints: copy, modify, or flat-out steal the approaches that fit your life.

Finding Strength in Words of Affirmation

The partner at home sent a short voice note each morning—e.g., "I heard you on that inspection call and felt proud," or "Thanks for always checking on the kids before lights out." No essay required; consistency was the point. For the veteran returning home, hearing those recorded messages later helped counter the mental noise of stress and reminded them that they were seen.

Reintegration Reflection: for one week, each partner records a 15–30second message praising something specific the other did recently. Play them aloud together on your first evening, with no phones at the table.

Navigating Transition with Acts of Service

An Army veteran and their spouse rebalanced the household by creating a short "mission plan" for chores. Instead of vague promises, they wrote tasks on index cards (laundry, oil change check, kids' school forms) and swapped cards weekly. The veteran found that completing a card with measurable outcome eased the return to civilian anxiety, and the spouse felt genuinely supported rather than carrying all the invisible load.

Actionable tip: The Task Swap: pick three household responsibilities you can fully own and complete for two weeks. At the end of each week, report back—what worked, what didn't, and one change for next week.

Prioritizing Quality Time

An Air Force pilot gave quality time a combat-style plan: weekly mini-dates that lasted 60–90 minutes and had a single rule — no problem-solving allowed. The one week was backyard stargazing with a thermos of coffee; another week featured a retro video game night. These focused, low pressure windows let them laugh and reconnect without the strain of "big conversations."

Before each mini date, both partners answer aloud a single word rating their emotional tank on a scale from 0 to 10. If either tank reads below 5, plan a next day follow up focused on listening; this quick check also works well when pairing civilians and veterans in friendship building activities, signalling when participants are ready for connection and helping community partners know when to pause and prioritize listening.

The Power of Thoughtful Tokens

Small, meaningful gifts can bridge gaps between civilian and veteran experiences by signalling attention to what matters to the other person.

A Marine Corps veteran leaned into small, meaningful gifts—not expensive items but things tied to shared history, such as an old unit patch sewn into a jacket lining or a paperback copy of a novel they used to read together on deployments. Those tokens signalise attention to private details and created touch points of gratitude during stressful seasons.

Try this: Ranking Needs: list five small items or events that would make you feel appreciated. Swap lists, then commit to giving one item from your partner's list within-the-month. This exercise can be run one-on-one or as a paired activity in community groups to help civilians and veterans learn concrete ways to express appreciation.

Finding Solace in Physical Touch

Physical touch can be deeply restorative, but it requires consent and sensitivity. When adapting these practices to civilian–veteran friendship networks, always check comfort levels and offer non-physical alternatives so all participants feel safe.

For a Guard member and their partner, reintroducing touch was gradual and intentional. They established brief touch rituals: a 30second hallway hug when one returns from work, holding hands during morning coffee, and a Sunday "no screen cuddle" in the evening. These tiny, repeated touches lowered defences and rebuilt comfort with closeness. In friendships between civilians and veterans, similar gradual, agreed upon rituals (or non-physical equivalents like a shared walk or a timed check-in) can foster connection while respecting boundaries.

Exercise: Touch Check — agree on three non-sexual touch rituals to practice for two weeks and note changes in mood or connection. If you're working within a civilian–veteran network or group setting, include non touch rituals (a brief verbal check-in, a shared quiet moment, or a gratitude note) so everyone can participate comfortably.

Diverse Applications of Love Languages

These examples can be adapted beyond romantic partnerships to strengthen civilian–veteran friendships and informal support networks; the key is small, consistent actions that reflect the other person's primary need.

These examples show how each love language can be adapted to the constraints of deployment, reintegration, and civilian life. In civilian veteran friendship networks, the common thread is small, consistent actions that reflect the other person's primary need.

Partner Dialogue Starter: Which of these five examples feels most doable? What would the first step look like for you tomorrow? As a variation for civilian–veteran friend pairs, ask: which action would help you feel understood by someone from a different background, and how might you start that conversation this week?

Relationship-Building with Civilian Friends

Having established a stronger connection with your partner, the focus now shifts outward. Reintegrating into civilian life means actively building a network beyond the immediate circle of family and former service members. This is where the art of connecting with neighbours and local acquaintances comes into play. You'll learn how to initiate friendly conversations, share your background in a way that builds understanding, and participate in the rhythm of your new community. We'll cover how to find shared interests and offer support, translating the bonds of service into meaningful civilian friendships that create a sense of belonging.

Building civilian-veteran friendship networks

Embracing the Civilian Perspective: Building Bridges Between Military and Civilian Life

Moving from military to civilian circles can feel like stepping into a town where everyone speaks slightly different slang and orders drinks in sizes you've never seen. The goal here is simple: make civilian friends feel seen and let their world feel less foreign to you. Below are practical ways to do that without losing who you are.

Understanding and Respecting Differences

Start with the assumption that your experiences are not the default. Civilians won't always grasp the specifics of a deployment, rank structure, or life under orders — and that's okay. Respectful curiosity beats impatience every time. Try a conversational opener: "I did X while deployed — what's something at work that's been intense for you?" That flips the script from a monologue into a two-way exchange.

Bridge-Building with Relatable Sharing

Translate military moments into universally human ones. Instead of mission jargon, tell a story about a teammate who taught you how to laugh in hard times, or a small daily routine that kept you sane. Concrete example: rather than saying "we ran convoy security," say "we had to be on high alert for long hours; one night my buddy made instant coffee taste like a five-star brew." Small human details invite connection.

The Power of Active Listening

Active listening is the social equivalent of good maintenance checks: it keeps things working. Put your phone away, ask open questions, and reflect back what you hear. Try: "So it sounds like you've been juggling a lot at home — how are you handling it?" Validation matters. You don't need to have served to be supportive and you don't need others to have served to deserve your attention.

Discovering Shared Passions

Find common ground that isn't uniform patches and formations. Join a local hiking group, a community choir, a cooking class, or a weekend carpentry meet-up — something you actually enjoy. Concrete tactic: pick one club this month and commit to two meetings. Invite a civilian friend along and frame it as a low-pressure hangout: "Want to try this trail with me Sunday? No pressure — bring snacks."

Cultivating Patience in Friendship Development

Friendships take time to deepen. If you feel urgency to rebuild a social circle, slow down. Swap quantity for quality: rather than chasing many acquaintances, invest in two people who return your effort. Reintegration Reflection: who are two civilians you'd like to know better? What shared activity could you invite them to in the next three weeks?

Extending Invitations and Sharing Your World

Open doors gently. Invite civilians to an event that shows how you socialize now — a game night, a unit reunion picnic, or a veteran-run community service day. Make the invitation specific: "We're grilling at 4 on Saturday — want to come for an hour?" Specifics increase the chance they'll say yes.

Expressing Gratitude for Support

When civilians show up for you — whether by listening, helping with a move, or attending an event — say thank you and mean it. A short note, a quick text, or a small gesture of appreciation goes far. The 'Love Tank' Check: who helped you this month? Send one message of thanks by Friday.

Putting these steps into practice means you'll gradually feel less like an outsider and more like someone with a wider circle that includes both former service friends and new civilian friends. It takes patience, plain talk, and a few invites — plus recognizing that ordinary shared moments often build the strongest connections.

Boundaries for civilian relationships

Redefine Civilian Friendships

You have built bridges, and now it's time to look at what those bridges carry: expectations, limits, and new rhythms. Reconnecting with civilian friends after service often means rethinking what friendship looks like for you now. This section gives practical ways to do that without sounding like a lecture—more like a coffee chat with someone who gets the basics and wants to help.

Reflecting on Evolved Friendships

Start with a quick check-in. Your priorities and values probably shifted during service; your friends' lives moved on too. That's normal. Use this prompt:

Reintegration Reflection

- List three things that matter most to you now (example: reliability, quiet time, and community service).
- Next to each, write one way a civilian friend could support that need.

Look for overlap. Maybe you both love fishing, or weekend DIY projects, or a good podcast. Those shared interests are easy wins to rebuild rapport without forcing conversations about deployments. If a friend keeps missing plans, consider whether it's timing, priority mismatch, or something personal on their end—and give yourself permission to step back.

Communicating Your Military Narrative

You control how much of your story you tell. That's not hiding—it's self-care.

Audience Assessment

- Before sharing, ask: "Is this person emotionally steady right now?" If they've just lost a job or are in a rough patch, this might not be the moment.

Set a boundary example: "I can tell you about that deployment, but I prefer not to go into graphic details." Use simple signals: a phrase like "I'm done talking about that topic" or a hand gesture if needed in social settings. For couples, try this together—agree on short phrases that mean "pause the story" during gatherings.

Recognizing Different Life Rhythms

Civilian life often moves at a different beat: weekend soccer practices, or PTA meetings, can feel foreign after a cadence of alerts and orders. Accept that this is okay. Two practical moves:

- Timing Trick: Schedule social time during windows that suit your rhythm (early morning runs, late-night calls) instead of forcing big day events when you're drained.

- Priority Mapping: Write down the top three obligations for you and your friend for the next month. Compare lists—then pick one shared action you both can do without stress.

Setting Boundaries and Prioritizing Self-Care

Saying 'no' matters; practice makes it easier.

Practice Assertive 'No's'.

- Script: "I can't commit to that right now, thanks for asking." Short, firm, no explanation needed.

- Energy Audit: After a week, jot down which social activities boosted you and which depleted you. Adjust invites accordingly.

Fostering Understanding and Patience

Teach a little, expect a little. Invite a friend to a low-pressure event—a charity run, a veterans' meet-and-greet, or a backyard BBQ—and use it as a short teaching moment. Pair explanation with a personal anecdote that's human, not tactical. Then give them time to process.

The final prompt:

The "Friendship Ranking"

- Rank your friendships by two axes: emotional support and mutual activity.
- Decide which two to invest in this quarter and one to let cool off.

Redefining friendships isn't about pruning for loss; it's about tending what energizes you and protecting what keeps you steady. Keep the cues short, the invites simple, and the boundaries clear—and you'll build civilian ties that fit your new life.

Inclusive social activities and events

Bridging Worlds Through Shared Experiences

You've worked through expectations, set boundaries, and learned how to speak about service in ways that feel safe. The next step is practical: create moments where the military side and the civilian side can meet, without pressure or performance. These are simple, repeatable interactions that build familiarity and trust.

Embracing Interests and Comfort Levels

Pick activities where anyone can show up as themselves. Not a parade, not a debrief—just a neutral place to be human.

- Pot luck with a twist: ask guests to bring a dish tied to a memory (a hometown dinner, a field mess favourite, or "first-baseball-game" snack). Short stories encouraged, but optional.
- Low-commitment volunteer shift: park clean-ups or food pantry sorting for two hours. Working side-by-side reduces forced small talk and creates shared purpose.
- Game night with rule-lite options: offer card games, board games, and a quiet corner with conversation starters for those who prefer listening to loud dice.

Cultivating Open Communication

Set expectations ahead of social gatherings. A little upfront clarity reduces awkwardness later.

Prompt to try before an event:

- "What would make tonight comfortable for you?"
- "If you need a quiet break spot, where should we point you?"

These questions signal care and give people permission to honour their needs. At the event, casually remind people that stepping away for a breather is fine—no explanation required.

Respectfully Honoring Service

Honour doesn't need to be loud. Small acknowledgment mean a lot.

- Mark meaningful dates quietly: a morning coffee raise, a simple note on a calendar, or a short toast at a gathering.
- Offer to host a low key recognition—think a framed photo wall where people can pin a service memento, or a short storytelling slot during an evening gathering, with a timer and "pass" option.

Promoting Mutual Learning and Understanding

Create formats that let people share without feeling exposed.

- Story circle: three questions, two minutes each, pass when ready. Questions like "One thing my service taught me" or "A civilian moment that surprised me" keep the focus personal, not political.
- Panel or Q&A with mixed guests: veterans and civilians swap five-minute talk slots on topics like job transitions, parenting after service, or moving into civilian neighbourhoods.

Fostering Casual, Low-Pressure Interactions

Repeatable, small events build momentum. Host a monthly backyard barbecue, rotating hosts, or a Saturday coffee meet-up near the gym. Consistency beats spectacle.

Acknowledging and Respecting Boundaries

Respect looks like options. Offer quiet rooms, opt-out signals (a wristband colour or a "text me" cue), and no-press conversation norms: no interrogation, no unsolicited advice.

Celebrating Shared Milestones

Make wins public and simple: deployment homecomings, certifications, job offers, promotions—celebrate with a dinner, a cake, or a play list and a short speech. Small rituals create communal memory.

Reintegration Reflection

- Who would you invite to a low-key shared event?
- What three options could make a gathering comfortable for you?

The 'Love Tank' Check

With your partner, list two ways civilian friends could show up during a milestone. Rank them by which would actually make you feel supported.

These practices help people cross a social bridge one relaxed step at a time—no formation, no salutes required.

Explaining military life to civilians

Translating Military Jargon into Everyday Language

If you've ever felt like you and your civilian friends are using two different dictionaries, you're not alone. Let's pull some common military terms into civilian-speak and add quick exercises to help partners talk about them without the translation app.

Demystifying Core Military Concepts

- Deployment: Think of it as a long, high-stress work assignment away from home. It's like someone taking a six-month project in another city where they can't pop home on weekends, and the stakes feel higher than a typical job. Prompt: Reintegration Reflection — write three things your partner noticed changed about home life while deployed, and one small routine you both can reintroduce together.

- Rank: Picture the corporate ladder. Rank dictates decision-making power and responsibility, but it also shapes how people are treated in daily interaction. Prompt: Ranking Needs — each partner lists what authority and responsibility look like for them at home (childcare, finances, chores) and compares notes.

- Acronyms: They're shorthand that speeds conversation among those who share context. If your civilian brain short-circuits at "PCS" or "OPSEC," ask for the plain-English version — most service members welcome the question. Quick tip: Keep a short glossary on your phone with three acronyms you run into most and what they mean to your household.

Universal Themes That Translate Well

Teamwork, duty, sacrifice, and camaraderie show up every day in non military life too. Frame examples in household terms: teamwork = splitting morning routines efficiently; sacrifice = one partner taking a late shift so the other can finish school. Prompt: The "Love Tank" Check — list two ways your partner shows duty or sacrifice that you may not have noticed, then thank them for one tonight.

How Military Communication Styles Land at Home

Directness is often practical training carried into civilian life. It can feel blunt in a casual setting. If you prefer softer phrasing, practice adapting without asking someone to change who they are. Concrete exercise: Two-minute role swap — one partner speaks in concise, mission-style requests for two minutes about the week's tasks; the other replies in the same style. Then swap and name one thing that felt useful and one that felt jarring.

Challenges Specific to Military Couples

Frequent moves and long separations teach adaptability but also create gaps in networks and routines. Practical move: create a "home setup checklist" that travels with you — favourite comfort items, a go-to recipe, contact list — to help re-establish a sense of stability fast.

Emotional Impact and Healing

Service can leave invisible marks: sleepless nights, startle responses, or distance during intimate moments. If those show up, small steps help. Concrete actions: schedule a weekly 20-minute "state check" where each person shares mood and one need for the week. If trauma symptoms appear, gently guide toward specialized care and use direct language: "I'm worried about your sleep; can we talk to our provider?"

Personal Anecdote (Practical Angle)

One friend described deployment as "being single again with kids suddenly." She kept a tiny ritual: a published calendar sticker marking the return date and a small welcome-back meal plan. That ritual gave structure and a shared goal—it's the kind of tiny, repeatable plan you can borrow.

Closing Prompt

Talk tonight: pick one military term you hear often, say what it means to you, and ask your partner what it means to them. Compare and agree on a plain-English phrase you'll both use going forward.

Translating military terms and acronyms

Bridging the Civilian–Military Communication Gap

If you've ever finished a sentence with an acronym and watched someone's eyes glaze over, you're not alone. Many veterans find themselves switching mental gears when they leave service: one foot in the world of orders, brevity, and dark humor; the other in late-night PTA meetings and bedtime stories. That split can make everyday chat awkward. The good news: small shifts in how we explain things change how people understand us.

Decoding Military Slang and Jargon

Start with a mini-translation habit. When you use a slang term—SNAFU, chow, or a throwaway like "we got hammered"—pause and give the civilian equivalent. Try: "It was a SNAFU—basically everything that could go wrong did, but we managed." Toss in a quick hint of tone (light joke, serious, frustrated) so it lands as you intend. This saves misreadings and keeps relationships easier.

Common Military Acronyms and Their Meanings

A handful of acronyms crop up in conversation and make civilians feel left out. Below are four you'll probably hear. Use them in context, and add the civilian translation the first few times.

- PT — Physical Training (the early-morning run you either love or hate).
- RTO — Radio telephone Operator (the person who handles radio commas).
- ROE — Rules of Engagement (what's permitted during a mission).
- SIT REP — Situation Report (a quick update on what's happening).

Practice prompt: Next time you say SIT REP, follow with: "SIT REP—basically an update from HQ." Watch how the other person relaxes.

Fostering Empathy through Understanding

Sometimes a phrase like "adapt and overcome" lands like a shrug. To avoid that, add a short line about what you meant. Try: "We had to adapt and overcome—meaning we lost critical gear and had to improvise, which was stressful." That turns a slogan into a story, and stories build empathy.

Building Bridges through Communication

Here are quick, usable moves that work in real conversations:

- Ask questions: If someone says something strange, ask what they mean instead of filling the silence.
- Explain context: When you use jargon, offer one line of background.
- Listen actively: Mirror back what you heard ("So you mean…"), then ask if that's right.
- Be patient: New terms take time to land; repetition helps.

Reintegration Reflection

Take five minutes with your partner or a civilian friend and run this tiny checklist: name one military term you used recently, give its civilian translation, and say how hearing the explanation changed what you thought. Swap roles. That quick exercise cuts confusion and widens the conversational bridge.

Thesc practices aren't about making anyone fluent in military speech. They're about turning shorthand into stories, so the people who care about you can truly get what you meant—and you can be understood without editing your whole self.

Building civilian mental health support networks

Cultivating a Civilian Support Network That Actually Helps

Okay — you've decoded the slang, slowed down the acronyms, and practiced letting civilians ask curious questions without snapping into drill-sergeant mode. Now comes the part that matters day-to-day: building civilian friendships that provide emotional ballast and real-world perspective. This section gives practical steps, quick examples, and short exercises to help you find people who will stand with you while you transition.

Identifying the Right Civilian Friends

Start with three simple criteria: good listeners, non-judgemental, and varied life experience. Think of it as recruiting for a team that won't hand out PT at 0500.

You'll meet people who share a focus on organized activities but talk about everyday topics—careers, family, gear—making it easier to relate.

- Concrete example: If you enjoy bikes, join a weekend group ride. You'll meet people who share a task-focused mindset but talk about normal-life things — careers, family, gear — which can make relating easier.
- Vet check: after a few meetings, ask yourself: Does this person let me talk without immediately offering solutions? Do they ask follow-up questions? If yes, keep showing up.

Benefits of Civilian Friendships

Civilian friends give perspective without military framing. They can point out when you're stuck in a habit that no longer serves you, or cheer on a new civilian goal (starting a small business, finishing a degree, or learning to cook).

- Small win illustration: a civilian friend notices you avoid small talk and suggests a short improve class. Turns out practicing looseness in a low-stakes setting makes talking about heavier topics easier later on.

Practicing Vulnerability — Little By Little

Vulnerability doesn't mean unloading a deployment memoir at the first coffee. Use a slow-burn approach.

- Try this: share a short, concrete anecdote — one moment, one feeling. Example: "Once, during a patrol, I had to make a split decision about a roadblock. It stuck with me; I still replay it sometimes." Pause. See their reaction. If they ask, share one more detail.

- Reinforcement tip: give yourself a small reward for each honest conversation — a favourite meal, a walk, or ten minutes of breath-focused calm.

Encouraging Civilians to Learn About Military Life

Invite people in without expecting them to become experts.

- Practical invitations: share a short article, recommend a 30-minute documentary, or bring a friend to a public military appreciation event. Frame it casually: "This helped me explain one part of service — curious what you think?"

- Boundaries: pick what you're willing to explain. You don't owe a full debrief; give what feels safe.

Adapting Your Communication Style

A little code-switching goes a long way.

- Concrete adaptation: replace acronyms with short phrases when you first explain: "SIT REP — an update on what's happening." Over time, people will catch on.

- Try the "Reframe and Check" method in conversations: after saying something military-flavored, pause and ask, "Does that make sense?" This invites clarification and keeps the exchange mutual.

Reintegration Reflection

- Who are three civilians you could invite to a low-pressure activity this month?
- What small story could you share that gives them insight without overwhelming you?
- Which communication habit will you try to adjust first (acronyms, clipped answers, or immediate problem-solving)?

The 'Love Tank' Check (for couples)

- Share with your partner one civilian friend you trust and why. Ask how they feel about you expanding your outside support.

Building these civilian ties takes time, patience, and testing new ways of talking. But each honest conversation and each shared activity stacks up, making the post-service phase less isolating and more manageable — with company that gets you, even if they don't wear the same uniform.

Mutual aid and community service connections

Building Meaningful Connections through Shared Community Service

If you're wondering how to get out of the house, meet people who aren't in PT gear, and do something that actually matters, volunteering together is a fast track. Shared community service gives you a purpose-driven way to spend time with civilian friends or your partner while making tangible contributions to a place you now call home.

Finding Your Passion

Start with what matters. Pick two or three causes and try them for a couple of hours each. Examples:

- Environmental: Join a weekend river clean-up or a tree-planting crew. Bring water, gloves, and a stubborn sense of duty.
- Food security: Volunteer at a local food bank; organize an efficient packing line—your military logistics skills will shine.
- Animal welfare: Walk dogs at an animal shelter; reward: unconditional tail wags.

Reintegration Reflection: List three causes that trigger a "yes, I'd do this" reaction. Next to each, write one practical way you and a friend or partner could help on a monthly basis.

Bridging Military and Civilian Life

Volunteering is an easy translation device. When you sort canned goods or build a raised bed, you're speaking a language everyone understands: action. Use those settings to share parts of your service in bite-sized bits—what drew you to help, how planning saved time, or how teamwork matters whether you're on a base or in a community centre. This reduces the gap between past structure and current, less-ordered life.

Exploring Opportunities for Mutual Aid

Mutual aid is neighbourhood-level support—think pot lucks that turn into meal swaps, or a tool-lending library that becomes a hangout. Practical steps:

- Check community bulletin boards, Next door, or church/rec centre volunteer lists.
- Offer one skill: lawn mower repair, resume help, or basic first aid classes.
- Start small: commit two hours monthly to a local group and invite one person to join.

The Power of Shared Acts of Service

Doing good together builds trust and communication the same way any shared challenge does. One couple we worked with signed up for a weekly soup-kitchen shift; between shifts they planned menus, split errands, and learned to communicate under low-stakes pressure. Result: better teamwork and a stack of new memories.

Getting Started — Quick Checklist

- Research three nearby organizations that match your values.
- Ask a friend or partner to pick one and schedule a trial shift.
- Make it routine: block time on the calendar—weekly, bi-weekly, or monthly.
- Debrief after each shift for five minutes: what went well, what could change.

The "Love Tank" Check (after service)

After volunteering together, ask your partner: "Did that fill my tank—Connection, Accomplishment, or Fun?" Rank which it hit most and plan the next service time based on that answer.

Parenting collaboration with civilian friends

Building Bridges: Collaborating with Civilian Friends on Parenting

If you've mastered convoy ops and family BBQ logistics, adding civilian friends into your parenting circle is a smart move—if handled with common sense and clear communication. The goal here is practical: create a dependable network of adults who share values, can help when duty calls, and expose your kids to a variety of positive influences.

Aligning Parenting Philosophies: Discussing Shared Values

Before trading weekend babysitting favours, have a frank conversation about core beliefs. Sit down with a friend over coffee (or protein shakes) and run through a short checklist:

- Discipline styles: Are you both fans of positive reinforcement, limited screen-based consequences, or a time-out approach? Share an example: "If Jamie hits, we remove toy privileges for 20 minutes." That level of specificity prevents awkward conflicts later.
- Education goals: Do you favour public school, supplemental tutoring, or hands-on learning? If your friend volunteers to help with science projects, make sure their approach matches your expectations.
- Child-rearing priorities: Talk about values like respect, empathy, and independence. Say, "We're trying to encourage responsibility—can you help with chores when you babysit?"

Establishing Effective Communication for Co-Parenting

Set up simple systems so everyone stays informed.

- Regular check-ins: A 15-minute monthly call or text thread keeps updates flowing: behaviour changes, school notes, sleep regressions.

- Active listening: When a friend raises concerns, paraphrase back: "So you noticed the child's anxiety at bedtime—tell me what you observed." That shows you're paying attention.
- Clear boundaries: Spell out practical rules—bedtime, screen limits, allergy alerts—so volunteers don't improvise in ways you'd rather avoid.

Harnessing Civilian Friendships for Practical Parenting Assistance

Turn goodwill into usable support.

- Babysitting swaps: Offer a calendar block for reciprocal weekend coverage. For example, you trade three Saturday afternoons for one full weekend.

Ask a teacher friend for weekly 30 minute math check-ins; small consistent help beats crisis tutoring.

- Emotional support: Create a small text chain for quick venting or encouragement—"Two-minute lifeline" messages work wonders.

Navigating Different Parenting Styles with Empathy and Respect

You'll encounter different habits. Use curiosity instead of judgment.

- Avoiding judgment: If someone uses a different tactic, ask for the thinking behind it: "What worked for you when your kid did that?"
- Asking questions: Invite specifics—"How do you set limits at your house?"—And compare notes.
- Focusing on shared goals: Agree on the basics—safety and kindness—and let smaller differences slide.

Enriching Children's Lives with a Variety of Adult Role Models

Different adults bring different assets. Encourage that mix.

- New experiences: Let a friend who's a hiker take the kids on a nature walk; it builds confidence and curiosity.

- Mentorship: Ask a musician friend to lead a short weekly class; small commitments create big benefits.
- Emotional support: Allow trusted adults to be extra ears when kids need someone besides Mom or Dad to talk to.

Practical Prompt: Reintegration Reflection

With your partner, list three qualities you want friends to model for your kids and three ways to test-fit a friend into that role over the next month.

The 'Love Tank' Check (for parenting help)

Rank on a scale of 1–5 how supported you feel asking friends for help. Discuss one specific favour you'll request this week.

Done well, civilian friendships become reliable checkpoints and rich resources for your children—and for your own sanity. Treat these relationships like any important mission: clear orders, good Intel, and after-action feedback.

Trust, miscommunication, and repair

Building trust with civilian friends takes intentional moves, not silence or a stoic stare. Start by spotting the gap between military life and civilian routines—call it noticing two different operating systems. Your service shaped habits, deadlines, and loyalties; civilians grew up in a different rhythm. Pointing that out gently, without placing blame, opens space for honest talk.

The Power of Active Listening

Active listening is simple to describe and harder to do when you're tuned to brief, mission-focused updates. Practice by slowing down and using three small habits: repeat back one sentence, ask one open question, and wait two seconds before responding.

- "Repeat back one sentence: "So you felt X when Y happened?"" This shows you heard the human, not just the words.
- "Ask one open question: "What mattered most to you there?"" Keeps the conversation going.
- Wait two seconds before responding. Silence is where meaning surfaces.

Quick example: At a barbecue, your civilian friend mentions stress about a promotion. Rather than pivoting to your deployments, try: "That sounds rough—what's the hardest part?" You create safety; they may return the favour later.

Expressing Gratitude and Apologies

Gratitude is low-cost, high-return. Say thanks when a friend asks about a military detail, or when they include you in a family event. If a remark from you lands poorly—maybe dark humour about risk—own it. A short apology like, "I misspoke; that came out wrong," repairs faster than a lecture. Small acknowledgment show you value the other person's feelings and the connection.

Finding Common Ground

Shared interests shorten the trust-building time line. Try these moves:

- Host a casual skill-share: teach basic first aid, in exchange for a friend leading a backyard grilling session.
- Join a co-ed rec team or a book club about real-world topics (history, politics, sports).

Notice: common ground isn't about agreeing on everything; it's about having places to meet.

Navigating Misunderstandings

When things go sideways, skip defensiveness. Use curiosity: "Help me understand what you heard." That reframe conflict into a problem you solve together. Give a concrete next step—agree on a wording or plan—and check back in a week.

Consistency and Reliability

Trust rebuilds through steady behaviour. If you commit to a monthly dinner, show up. If plans shift because of appointments, text with a new time. Small, dependable actions add up.

Sharing Military Perspectives

Offer context without expecting full understanding. Short stories work better than long lectures: one moment that shows why you reacted a certain way, then pause for their questions. You don't have to carry the whole explanation—invite dialogue.

Quick prompt: Reintegration Reflection

- Who in your civilian circle has asked you a thoughtful question this month?

- Pick one small step (a thank-you note, a skill-share invite, or a follow-up text) to practice this week.

Neighbor relationships and social rituals

Strengthening Civilian Reintegration: Cultivating Connections with Neighbours

You might not think of your next-door neighbours as part of your support network, but they can be surprisingly helpful as you reenter civilian life. Simple ties at the block level reduce isolation, increase safety, and give you little pockets of normalcy—those tiny, repeatable interactions that make a neighborhood feel like a place you belong.

Bridging Worlds Through Local Engagement

Start by noticing what already happens where you live. Is there a weekly farmers' market, a veterans' table at the library, or a PTA meeting that looks tolerable? Pick one local event this month and go—alone or with your partner. Small commitment, high payoff: you show up, learn a few names, and you get a sense of how civilians spend their weekends. Practical example: volunteer for a two-hour shift handing out water at a community run. You get exercise, a reason to talk to people, and you're useful without needing to over share.

Initiating Neighborly Bonds

Begin small. Introduce yourself and your family when you see someone outside. Ask for one piece of local advice—best plumber, nearest dry cleaner, where to get a decent cup of coffee—and you've started a conversation that puts others at ease. Offer help when it's obvious and simple: lending a ladder, taking in a package, or watching a dog for an afternoon. If you want to accelerate connection, host a low-pressure get-together: a block pot luck, a backyard barbecue, or a "pizza and board games" night. Keep the invite casual and the food familiar.

You don't owe anyone a full service history, try this rule: ...

Try this rule: share what helps the moment, not everything at once. A quick line—"I did a lot of work with logistics"—opens a window without dragging a person into heavy details. Watch their cues. If they ask more, give a little more. If they back away, switch topics. Reintegration Reflection: What part of your service feels safe to say in a 30-second intro?

Embracing Local Traditions & Practicing Acts of Service

Attend one local festival or parade this season. Join a community clean-up or sign up to coach a youth sports team for a month. Offer acts of service that match your strengths: if you're handy, mow a neighbour's lawn when they're ill; if you have a reliable vehicle, give someone a ride to an appointment. These practical contributions make you visible as someone who cares.

Joining Community Celebrations & Discovering Shared Interests

Put three things on your calendar: a holiday event, a club meeting, and a casual hobby class. Ask neighbours about their hobbies, swap a skill (guitar lesson for car maintenance tips), and try one neighbour-recommended class together. The shared activities create memories and easy conversation starters.

Prompt for partners: The "Love Tank" Check — Which neighbours activity would refill your tank this month? Rank needs: quiet, social time, practical help, or new friendships. Schedule one small action together and report back at your weekly check-in.

Non-military celebrations and shared experiences

Embracing civilian life means more than showing up at neighborhood events—it's about trying on different parts of civilian culture until some of them fit comfortably. Think of this as testing civilian traditions, not auditioning for a role you don't want. Below are practical ways to pick up new habits, invite others in, and build memories that belong to this chapter of your life.

Discovering New Traditions and Interests

Start small and specific. Sign up for one class, one team, or one meet up this month—pick something with a regular schedule so you get repetition and faces. Concrete examples:

- Try a weekly cooking class where couples rotate hosting a themed dinner. It's low-pressure, social, and gives you a reason to invite neighbours over later.
- Join a coed rec sports league (softball, soccer, pickle ball) that has mixed-skill levels; the post game beers are where friendships form.
- Pick one new Friday-night ritual—visit a different local restaurant each week for a month and keep a shared "menu diary" with your partner.

Reaching Out and Building Connections

Pick one new Friday night ritual: visit a different local restaurant each week for a month and keep a shared 'menu diary' with your partner.

Make invitations specific and easy to accept. Instead of "Wanna hang out?" Try, "Coffee Thursday at 8 a.m. at the diner?" Or "Block pot luck this Saturday—could you bring a salad?" Examples for veterans:

Host an informal open garage night where you fix a neighbour's lawnmower or show a simple DIY skill—practical help plus conversation.

Ask a co-worker to join you for a lunchtime walk twice a week, and two consistent outings build familiarity quickly.

Navigating Social Norms and Dynamics

Civilians often run on a looser timetable and different expectations. Practice patience: if someone is late, treat it like a small etiquette difference, not a slight. Tips:

- Observe first, then ask a clarifying question if something feels odd ("Do people usually split checks here?").
- Use humour to bridge gaps: a light comment about the difference between a drill sergeant time line and a "civilian five minute window" can diffuse awkwardness.

Communicating Expectations and Boundaries

Say what you need without lecturing. Example phrases to try with partners, friends, or family:

- "I'm up for the party, but I need an hour alone afterward to recharge."
- "I'll lead the grill at the cook out if you handle desserts—that gives me both a role and a break."

Set boundaries early and revisit them after events.

Celebrating Milestones and Creating New Memories

Mark civilian milestones intentionally. Plan small rituals that make these moments sticky:

- For a new job: a "first-pay check dinner" tradition with your partner or friends.
- For anniversaries: write two brief notes—one about what you

appreciate from your service life and one about what you're building now—read them aloud together.

Reintegration Reflection

- What civilian tradition do you want to try this month?
- Who will you invite, and what exact words will you use to ask?

The 'Love Tank' Check (quick prompt)

- After a social event, each partner rates their energy: 1 (drained) to 5 (refuelled). Discuss one tweak for next time.

Trying new things, reaching out with clear invites, honouring boundaries, and creating rituals for milestones will help this phase feel less foreign and more yours. Keep testing options—some will stick, some won't—and the ones that do will become the memories you share with others in civilian life.

Storytelling to normalize veteran experiences

Sharing Personal Stories: Building Bridges Between Military and Civilian Worlds

Stories are the short, human-sized bridges we build when the big structural ones are still under construction. For many veterans, the impulse is either to keep military experiences private or to give a rapid-fire, acronym-heavy report that leaves civilians blinking. Neither helps connection. Below are practical ways to share without oversharing, and to invite curiosity instead of confusion.

The power of vulnerability in storytelling

Start small. A short, honest anecdote about a struggle or surprise can open a room more than a long debrief. Example: instead of recounting every operational detail from a deployment, try this: "There was a week of nonstop storms and our shelter kept leaking; it taught me to laugh with people when nothing else worked." That line names a challenge, shows emotion, and points to a lesson—teamwork and resilience—without turning the listener into a trainee.

Reintegration Reflection

Prompt: Think of one moment in service that still shows up in your daily habits. Share that memory with a friend using one sentence describing the event, one feeling it brings up, and one way it shows up now. Pause for their question rather than launching into a monologue.

Explaining Military Culture and Jargon

Translate, then contextualize. When a civilian asks what 'PT' is, define it ("physical training") and add why it mattered ("it set the pace for our day and kept morale steady"). A quick, two-step approach prevents glaze-over: what it means and why it matters. Use analogies civilians know—sports, workplaces, family roles—to make the significance tangible.

Practical tip: create a "Translator Line" for social conversations. Keep one or two plain-English versions of common phrases ready. For example:

- "TO" -> "task order; like a project deadline at work."
- "CQ" -> "guard duty; think overnight campus security."

Connecting Past to Present

Your stories should link to who you are now. After a succinct memory, add a sentence that maps the skill or value forward. Example: "I learned to read weather and terrain quickly; now I use that same habit to plan family trips so we avoid the ruinous rainy-day scramble." That simple bridge helps civilians see continuity rather than a closed chapter.

Ranking Needs

Prompt for couples: each partner lists three things their service taught them that they rely on now (discipline, punctuality, hyper awareness, etc.). Share lists and rank which need the most support at home. This clarifies how military habits show up in daily life—and which ones need adjustment.

The Impact of Shared Experiences

Sharing stories creates empathy and breaks down stereotypes. When a civilian hears about fear, humour, boredom, or pride in plain terms, it humanizes service. Invite reciprocal sharing: ask friends to tell you about a stressful job, an embarrassing moment, or a proud win. Mutual exchange prevents the veteran from being the only one "on display."

The "Love Tank" Check

Prompt for couples: after sharing, ask your partner one question—"Did that feel supportive or intrusive?"—And one action—"Name one thing you want me to stop or start saying." Quick feedback keeps storytelling safe for both parties.

Final note: be selective and intentional. Vulnerability is powerful, but you get to pace it. Use short stories to teach, translate jargon clearly, connect past to present, and give civilians a place to respond. Small, honest exchanges add up to stronger bonds between military and civilian life.

Case studies of civilian-veteran circles

Bridging the Gap: Powerful Case Studies of Civilian–Veteran Friendships

The first months after service can feel like stepping off a ship into fog. Practical routines vanish, the mission changes, and social cues that used to make sense suddenly don't. Real friendships with civilians can cut through that fog. Below are grounded case studies that show how civilian friends helped veterans rebuild a day-to-day life that felt worthwhile again.

Diverse Support Networks: The Key to Successful Reintegration

Case: Jack and Sarah

Jack came home from a deployment with his confidence dented and his calendar emptier than it had been for years. A co-worker named Sarah — not a veteran, just someone who liked order and knew how to get things done — became a mentor and friend. She helped him draft a civilian resume, coached him through interviews, and invited him to casual meet-ups where he met others outside the military. The mix of job help, social invitations, and steady listening gave Jack practical structure and a sense of belonging.

Reintegration Reflection

- Who in your life could offer one practical item this month (help with a resume, a job lead, or a weekly hangout)?
- Rank Needs: list three immediate needs (income, social contact, mental health) and put a civilian friend next to each who might help.

Building Trust and Forging Connections

Case: Alex and Mike

Alex was guarded about his time overseas. Mike, a weekend hiker and patient listener, didn't ask for dramatic stories — he shared trail maps, snacks, and quiet hours. Over time, Alex opened up in small, honest increments. The key: non-pressured shared activity that created safety.

Practice Prompt: The Trail Test

- Plan one low-pressure activity with a civilian friend (hiking, woodworking, cooking).
- Keep it routine: two hours, same day each week for six weeks. Track comfort levels each time from 1–5.

The Power of Shared Experiences

Case: Community Group

A veteran joined a local volunteer chapter that paired civilians and vets to restore a community garden. Working side-by-side on measurable tasks created rapid trust and friendly banter. Shared goals (finish the raised bed, fix the irrigation) turned acquaintances into allies.

Gaining a Deeper Understanding

Case: The Volunteer Who Became an Advocate

A civilian volunteer learned about veterans' common stressors while helping at an outreach event. She used her professional skills to set up workshops and became a community advocate. Small exposure led to concrete action — and that action helped change local attitudes about mental health support.

Mutual Growth and Understanding

Case: Business Partners

A veteran launched a small business with a civilian friend. The civilian brought sales experience; the veteran offered discipline and logistics. Each learned skills from the other: negotiation, public speaking, running payroll. The result: a healthier social network and improved self-efficacy for both.

Supporting Resilience

Case: Group Support Circle

A veteran struggling with adjustment found a group of civilian friends who connected him to resources, accompanied him to appointments, and cheered small wins. That web of ordinary support rebuilt his daily coping tools.

The 'Love Tank' Check

- Who refills your tank? Identify three civilians who provide emotional, practical, or informational support. Send one a thank-you message this week.

A Vital Counterpoint to Isolation

Case: Solace in One Friendship

For one veteran managing post-traumatic symptoms, a single attentive civilian friend provided a non-judgemental space to talk and to be silent. That consistent presence made the difference between retreating alone and staying connected.

Final prompt for partners and friends

- Pick one story above that feels closest to your situation. Write down two small steps you could try this month to create a similar connection (invite someone to a shared activity, ask a friend to help with a practical task, or join a local project).

These cases aren't polished hero narratives; they're practical examples of how ordinary civilians, with curiosity and consistency, became anchors. Use the prompts, try the small actions, and keep the list of civilian allies handy — your daily life will start to look a little less like fog and more like a route you can follow.

Post-Service Realities: Life, Family, and Forward Momentum

Post-Service Challenges for Couples

After the blur of packing and the inevitable questions of "where did that go?", Military life often leaves partners yearning for a settled sense of home. This constant motion, while a part of service, can leave a deep desire for stability, a place to truly root down. It's more than just finding a house; it's about actively building a shared sanctuary that reflects both of your needs and dreams. This next part focuses on transforming that desire into reality. We'll look at how to make unpacking and setting up your new space a collaborative effort, turning a logistical challenge into a team win. We'll also address the crucial financial conversations needed to secure your future, and how the shifts in environment impact individual well-being. Then, we'll turn our attention to the exciting, yet often complex, transition into civilian professional lives, including how to support each other's aspirations and manage the financial adjustments that come with it. Finally, we'll acknowledge the mental health shifts that can surface and how to redefine your partnership and social connections as you move forward.

Relocation and housing transitions

There's something about moving that feels like being tossed on a roller coaster you didn't volunteer for. One week you're unpacked and confident; the next you're staring at boxes with labels that lie, "Kitchen," but somehow the coffee maker is missing and the kids' drawings are in a tub marked "Fragile." For military families, this ups and downs is routine: orders, packing, new base, repeat. That rhythm brings pride and purpose, but it also brings wear.

The Stress of Frequent Moves

Frequent moves place pressure on every member of a household. Think of it as emotional carry-on you can't check. Research shows military families face unique stressors — increased anxiety, depression, and even post-traumatic stress symptoms — and repeated uprooting can intensify those reactions. Kids may switch schools midyear, losing classmates and teachers who understood their quirks. Spouses may watch a career stall again because a license didn't transfer or because the next post expects a different set of hours. Service members juggle deployments and training while trying to keep the family steady. None of this is a failing; it's reality.

Quick prompt — Reintegration Reflection

- Name one thing you miss consistently after a move (friend, routine, workspace).
- How long did it take last time to feel "settled" emotionally?

The Desire for Stability

After years, people begin to crave a steady landing spot—one that keeps emotional spikes flat. Stability means fewer unknowns: a familiar school district, neighbours who know your name, a weekend coffee shop that sees you as more than "the new family." Many military families want less frantic packing and more time cultivating a place that soothes, not stress.

Ranking Needs exercise

- List your top three needs for a home (examples: quiet backyard, short commute, supportive neighbours).
- Share with your partner and compare lists; mark overlaps.

Building a Shared Sanctuary

Creating a home that feels safe across moves starts with honest talk. Sit down — not in the car between stops, but at a kitchen table or on the couch — and lay out preferences. Discuss specifics: do you want a walkable neighbourhood or a yard big enough for a dog? Is being near a veteran support group a priority? Call out deal-breakers such as noisy streets, long commutes, or homes that lack a bedroom on the main floor—especially if you have mobility concerns.

Concrete action: make a "Home Non-Negotiables" sheet. Include three must-haves and three no-go items. Use it when scouting rentals or buying.

Teamwork Makes the Dream Work

Turning a new space into a sanctuary is a team sport. Divide tasks by skill: one partner handles utilities and paperwork, the other focuses on creating a daily rhythm for kids and unpacking what matters most first (beds, kitchen staples, comfort items). Set weekly check-ins: a 20-minute chat to swap progress, frustrations, and what feels missing. Small shared wins — hanging a photo, finding a paediatrician — builds the sense of belonging.

The 'Love Tank' Check (short exercise)

- Each partner lists one practical thing that fills their sense of home (e.g., "fresh coffee every morning," "quiet hour to read").
- Commit to providing that thing twice a week for the next month.

Moving forward, the next sections will dig into teamwork techniques, practical financial moves for stability, and how new environments affect mental health. Consider this your starter kit: honest talk, clear priorities, and shared tasks can turn a transient address into a place you both want to protect.

Career transitions for both partners

Redefining professional identities

When service ends, the uniform comes off but the habits, skills, and pride don't. That can be inspiring—and confusing. Many veterans describe the post-service period as a strange mirror: you recognize yourself, but the label that used to explain everything is gone. Give yourselves permission to ask, 'Who am I outside that role?' Without rushing to an answer.

Practical prompt — Reintegration Reflection:

- Each partner writes three things they loved about their military role and three things they'd like to leave behind. Share and discuss one overlap and one surprise.

Aligning Career Aspirations

Talk like a team planning a mission. Lay out individual goals, short-term needs (income, benefits, licensor), and long-term hopes (purposeful work, stability, flexibility). Use this to craft a shared roadmap that respects both partners' ambitions.

Actionable steps:

- Inventory transferable skills together (leadership, logistics, training, clear communication). Put them next to civilian job titles you both find interesting.
- Pick two realistic target roles together and research typical pay, certification requirements, and commute/time demands.
- Set a six-month checkpoint to compare progress and adjust.

Identifying Transferable Skills (concrete examples)

- Leadership: describe leading a small unit; civilian translation — project manager or operations lead.

- Training and Instruction: teaching weapons handling or first aid; civilian translation — corporate trainer or safety instructor.
- Logistics and Planning: mission planning and supply tracking; civilian translation — supply chain coordinator or event planner.

Navigating Civilian Career Paths

This is where practical hustle meets strategy. Networking is not just schmoozing at mixers—it's reconnecting with former military mates who moved into civilian roles, Linked In messages to alumni and reaching out to veterans already doing what you want.

Job-search checklist:

- Create a civilian-friendly resume that converts military tasks into business outcomes (e.g., reduced downtime by X%, supervised Y personnel).
- Role-play interviews at home. Practice answering 'Tell me about a time you led under pressure,' using a clear problem action result structure.
- Use veteran-focused hiring fairs and local workforce centres for targeted leads.

Supporting Each Other Through Transition

Be each other's editor, coach, and alarm clock. The partner who's not in job mode can offer honest feedback on resumes, mock-interview questions, and a realistic time line.

Support moves that work:

- Schedule two weekly "job support" blocks—one for application work, one for feedback.
- Celebrate small wins (phone screens, interviews) with a simple ritual: favourite meal, a walk, or a high-five and a minute of praise.

Addressing Financial Realities

Money talks can be awkward; make them routine. Lay out best- and worst-case salary estimates for target roles and build a buffer plan. Create a temporary spending plan that trims non-essentials while training and interviewing.

Quick budgeting tool:

- Rank needs: mortgage, utilities, insurance, groceries, childcare. Then rank wants. Reduce one want for three months and track the difference.

Balancing Career Demands and Relationship Needs

New jobs can be all-consuming. Protect the partnership pro-actively.

The "Love Tank" Check: Protect the partnership pro-actively by setting clear boundaries and scheduling regular check-ins to discuss work related stress.

- Weekly 10-minute check: each partner names one work stress and one thing the other could do that week to help keep connection strong.

Exploring Shared Professional Growth

Think team projects you can do together: taking a certification class in the same field, co-hosting a veteran support group, or piloting a small business that uses both your skills.

Ideas to try:

- Sign up for one course together (project management, small-business basics) and commit to a shared project.
- Find a mentor who's been through the civilian switch and meet quarterly.

Final prompt — Ranking Needs:

- Individually list top three professional goals and top three household priorities. Swap lists, discuss overlaps, and create one combined action plan for the next 90 days.

These steps make the post-service phase less like a Free-handed and more like controlled descent—one decision and one shared check-in at a time.

Debt management and budgeting

Navigating Financial Stress: A Crucial Part of Post-Service Reintegration

Financial stress shows up in many homes after service—unexpected bills, gaps between paychecks, student loans, even different habits around spending. It's normal and fixable. The point here isn't to shame anyone for past choices; it's to give you practical tools so you and your partner can handle money like a coordinated team rather than two solo players.

The Importance of Open Communication

Start with a money conversation that's low-pressure and regular. Pick a weekday evening, grab take out, set a 30-minute timer, and agree that this is a no-blame zone. Share concrete numbers: current balances, monthly obligations, and any looming payments. If one partner is embarrassed about a credit-card balance or missed payments, agree to focus on solutions instead of assigning fault.

Reintegration Reflection: What money topic gives you the most anxiety? Share one small fact about it with your partner during your 30-minute check-in.

Creating a Shared Financial Vision

Turn goals into a household plan. Use SMART thinking—not because it's fancy, but because it works. Examples:

- Short-term: "Pay off $4,000 in credit-card debt in 12 months by adding $340 a month to debt payments."
- Long-term: "Build a retirement account that we both contribute to monthly, starting with 5% of each pay check and increasing by 1 % per year."

Ranking Needs: Each partner lists top three financial goals. Compare lists aloud, then merge them into one joint list with timeliness.

Budgeting and Mindful Spending

Try the simple split: 50 % essentials, 30 % wants, 20 % savings, adjusted to your life.

Concrete example: If rent and utilities are $2,000/month (50 % of a $4,000 net income) and you earmark $800 (20 %) for savings and debt, the remaining $1,200 (30 %) can cover flexible spending.

The "Love Tank" Check: Once a month, ask: Is money stress draining our connection? What can we cut this month so we can schedule a low-cost date that fills both tanks?

Seeking Support and Resources

You don't have to do this alone. The VA offers financial counselling tailored to veterans, and groups like the National Foundation for Credit Counselling can help draft repayment plans. FINRA's resources explain investing basics in plain language. Schedule a session with a credit counsellor if debt feels overwhelming—many offer sliding-scale or free first meetings.

Supporting Each Other Through Challenges

Celebrate small wins: paid-off bill, one month of sticking to the budget, the emergency fund hitting $500. When setbacks happen—unexpected medical bills, a job gap—use a simple script: "I'm stressed about X. Can we look at options together?" That keeps the tone team-oriented, not accusatory.

Understanding Debt and Financial Healing

Inventory everything: list creditor, balance, interest rate, and payment due date. Find the root cause—was it a deployment gap, schooling, or impulse spending? Then choose a plan: snowball (smallest debt first for momentum) or avalanche (highest interest first to save money). If you're unsure, bring the list to a credit counsellor or a trusted financial advisor who works with veterans.

Debt Repayment Plan Prompt: Write down one small action you can take this week—call a creditor, set up auto pay, or schedule a counselling appointment—and commit to it together.

Working on money together strengthens more than just the bank account; it builds trust, reduces sleepless nights, and gives you both a clearer path forward. Keep the conversations regular, the goals specific, and the attitude practical. You've handled difficult missions before; this one just needs planning, patience, and two people willing to tackle it side by side.

Parenting and child development changes

Understanding Military Parenting: What Makes It Different

If you served, you already know that military life comes with its own rhythm—orders, moves, deployments, training cycles. For parents, that rhythm turns parenting into a pattern that often pauses and restarts. Picture a roller coaster that stops mid-loop: kids learn to cope with ups and downs, but they can also pick up anxiety when the stops are long or unpredictable. That's the core of what makes military parenthood different from civilian family life.

Recognizing the Impact on Children

Kids react in ways that make sense once you put it in context: missed birthdays, teachers who change every few years, a parent gone for six months and then back but different. You might see anxiety (night waking, clinginess), sadness (withdrawn play, loss of interest), or anger (outbursts, testing limits). These are signals, not defects. A simple first step: map behaviour to events. When did the changes start—before, during, or after deployment? That timing helps you know whether the child needs routine, talk time with the deployed parent, or extra emotional support at home.

Adapting to Changing Developmental Needs

As kids grow, their needs shift. A toddler needs consistent routines and comforting rituals; a teen needs autonomy plus clear boundaries. During transitions, tighten the routines that matter most. Example: For a 7-year-old, keep bedtime, dinner, and story time steady. For a teen, keep the weekly family check-in and household expectations steady while giving latitude on music choices or curfews.

Concrete support steps:

During transitions, tighten the routines that matter most. For example, for a 7 year old, keep bedtime, dinner, and story time steady.

- If a preschooler regresses (bed wetting, clinging), add a short calming ritual—five minutes of shared breathing or a "goodnight hand squeeze" to rebuild security.
- For school-age kids struggling with new schools, ask their teacher for a quick "what I'm seeing" email each week for a month.
- For teens showing withdrawal, set a neutral check-in: 20 minutes with no lecturing, just asking "What's one thing that felt hard this week?"

Shifting Roles When a Parent Returns

When the deployed parent arrives, the household power shift can feel like a surprise inspection. The returning parent might expect to slide back in; the at-home parent has learned to be commander of the logistics. Give yourselves a phased reintegration:

- Phase 1 (first two weeks): low-pressure reconnection. Small tasks, shared meals, no heavy decisions.
- Phase 2 (weeks 3–8): renegotiate responsibilities. Use a short "who does what" checklist on paper.
- Phase 3: resume joint planning for kids' activities, finances, and personal time.

Reintegrating as a Couple: Quick Exercises

The "Love Tank" Check: Each partner says their top two needs this week (emotional, practical). Swap and repeat back what you heard. No problem solving—just reflection.

Aligning Parenting Philosophies

Sitting down together and agreeing on consistent rules matters more than who set them. Pick three non-negotiables (bedtime, screen limits, respect language) and present them as a united front to the kids. If you disagree, use a "time-out" rule: pause the debate, tag it with a time to revisit, and commit to a provisional choice until then.

Supporting Children Through Behavioral Changes

When a child acts out, try this three-step response: acknowledge emotion ("You look really mad"), set the boundary ("You can't hit"), and offer a safe alternative ("Let's stomp our feet together until it cools down"). Follow up later with a short conversation about what happened and one thing you both can try next time.

Integrating Self-Love Practices for Parents

Self-care isn't luxury—it's a baseline. Practical examples:

- For a male veteran who prefers movement: 20-minute runs three times a week, plus a 5-minute progressive muscle relaxation before bed.
- For a female veteran who prefers quiet: a 10-minute guided breathing app session each morning and one weekly craft or reading hour.
- Shared: a 15-minute "disconnect" nightly where both phones are off and you sit together, even in silence.

Strengthening the Partnership

Create shared parenting goals (e.g., "We will handle bedtime together Monday–Thursday") and schedule small rituals—Friday pizza night, Saturday park walk—to rebuild connection. Use short reflection prompts as a couple:

- Reintegration Reflection: What felt hardest about the return? What felt surprisingly good?

- Ranking Needs: Each partner lists three needs, ranks them, and the couple picks one to address this month.

These practical moves help stabilize the kids and give you both a clearer, less frantic way to adjust to the repeated starts and stops of military family life. Keep the prompts visible—on the fridge, or in a shared notes app—and check in regularly. Your consistent actions matter more than perfect answers.

Mental health transitions and stress

Navigating Mental Health Transitions in Post-Service Reintegration

Coming home from service can bring a weird mix of relief, gratitude, and—surprise—old stress that didn't go on leave with you. Mental health transitions after leaving the military are common and normal; they deserve attention without stigma or theatrics. Nearly one in five veterans will face conditions like PTSD, depression, or anxiety after service, so this is not a personal failing; it's a predictable response to a high-demand past. The good news: there are practical ways couples can work together to manage this phase.

Understanding the Impact of Cumulative Stress

Think of stress from military life like an invisible rucksack you carried for years. Each deployment, long separation, late-night watch, or traumatic event added another item. When you step out of uniform, that pack isn't magically light. The strain can surface as irritability, trouble sleeping, numbness, or sudden emotional reactions to small things.

Concrete example: a veteran who used hyper vigilance to stay safe in a war zone may startle at loud noises during a fireworks show, then feel guilty for overreacting. Recognizing the origin of the response helps remove self-blame and opens the door to better coping.

Reintegration Reflection:

- List three stressors you carried during service.
- Which of these still shows up in daily life? How often?

The Importance of Open Communication

Talking about mental health is easier said than done, especially when training taught you to "suck it up." But shutting down tends to widen the gap between partners. Start small: a daily check-in that's low-pressure and time-limited (five minutes, phone off) can loosen tight lids.

Actionable technique: The "Ground-and-Share" check-in

- One partner names one emotional state (tired, on edge, blank).
- The other mirrors without fixing: "You sound tired—what helps?"
- No problem-solving unless asked.

The goal is to create a safe habit of expression. This prevents resentment and reduces isolation.

The "Love Tank" Check (for couples)

- Each week, pick one method to refill each other's tanks (physical touch, acts of service, words of affirmation, quality time, gifts).
- Keep it simple: a 10-minute walk, making a favourite coffee, or a genuine "I see you."

Developing Shared Strategies for Managing Stress

Shared coping beats going it alone. Build a short list of household anchors that both partners can use during rough patches.

Concrete shared strategies:

- Daily micro-routines: 15 minutes of shared movement (push-ups, a short run, or yoga) to lower cortisol.
- Breathing cue: when one partner says "Reset," both do a 4-4-4 breathing set together.
- Social plan: schedule one civilian-friend meet-up monthly to practice civilian social muscles (bring an easy topic list to avoid military-centric only talk).

Specific self-love techniques (for him and her):

- For male veterans: guided progressive muscle relaxation app for

10 minutes before bed to ease tension and reduce night replay.

- For female veterans: a short evening journal prompt—three wins today—to counteract negative spiral.
- For any partner: a hobby "date" where you each spend 30 minutes on a solo hobby and then share what you did.

Ranking Needs:

- Each partner lists top three needs (sleep, help with kids, time to decompress).
- Trade and negotiate priorities for the week.

Seeking Professional Support

There is strength in getting help. PTSD, depression, and anxiety respond well to properly trained clinicians and couples therapy. Couples-based therapy can reduce symptoms and improve connection—it's not about blame; it's about tools.

Action steps:

- If symptoms interfere with daily work or parenting for two weeks or more, call a licensed clinician.
- Ask your VA or local clinic about trauma-informed couples therapy options.
- Consider a trial of six sessions before deciding on long-term care.

Reintegration Reflection (wrap-up):

- Which two strategies will you try this week?
- How will you check back in next Sunday to report progress?

If you treat mental health transitions like maintenance—regular, small, practical actions—you and your partner can move from surviving to building a life that feels more like yours.

Identity negotiation as a couple

Redefining Roles and Responsibilities as a Couple

Coming home means more than moving boxes and dusting off civilian clothes — it also means redefining who does what, why, and how. The military often handed you a blueprint: wake-up times, duties, contingency plans. Now you and your partner get to draw the blueprint yourselves. That can feel freeing and messy at the same time. The trick is to do it together, with clear communication and small experiments.

Letting Go of Service-Dictated Structures

If you were used to orders and schedules, the sudden lack of external structure can be disorienting. Instead of letting frustration build, try intentionally removing one old rule and replacing it with a shared choice. For example, pick one weekday when chores are split differently: maybe one person cooks, the other handles dishes and mail. Test it for two weeks, then adjust. The goal is not perfection — it's learning how to decide together.

Reintegration Reflection

- Which military routines do you miss the most? Which felt restrictive?
- Which civilian routines would help you feel steadier right now?

Write one routine to try for 14 days and check in weekly.

Navigating Individual Identities

Both of you carry new experiences and different versions of themselves after service. A good starting point is a short, structured conversation: each partner lists three things they want to keep from their military identity (discipline, team focus, technical skills) and three new things they want to develop (a creative hobby, a school plan, a side business). Share these lists without judgment and ask each other two follow up questions: "How can I support that?" And "What would feel like too much pressure?"

Communicating Evolving Needs and Expectations

Expectations shift — sometimes slowly, sometimes overnight. Set a recurring check-in (15 minutes, no problem-solving, just updates) where you cover:

- How civilian adjustments are going
- Where you're stuck and where you feel good
- One specific way your partner can help this week

Short check-ins keep small issues from turning into resentments.

Establishing New Couple Rituals

Rituals don't need to be grand. Commit to at least one shared ritual that fits your life:

- Weekly dinner date with phones in another room
- Sunday thirty-minute planning session for the week
- A monthly "try something new" night (cooking class, a museum, or backyard stargazing)

Treat these like assignments at first—habits build connection.

The "Love Tank" Check

Each partner names one thing that "fills their tank" (quality time, acts of service, gifts, physical touch, and words of affirmation). Rank them in order of importance and share concrete examples: e.g., "My tank is mostly filled by helping with the lawn," or "I feel held when we sit and talk for 20 minutes." Use this list to guide small, regular gestures.

Balancing Individual Growth and Mutual Support

Support each other's goals while reserving time for couple goals. If one person signs up for school, agree on how household tasks will shift for that term. If the other starts a fitness plan, schedule shared or solo workout windows. Compromise matters, but so does protecting personal growth time — both keep the partnership lively.

Finding Common Ground and Shared Interests

Try a three-month "new-things" plan: each partner picks one activity the couple will do together (cooking class, volunteering at a veteran centre, joining a weekend hiking group). Rotate choices so both people lead. These shared experiences build memories and help civilian life feel more like a team effort.

Honoring and Validating Each Other's Experiences

Your re-entries into civilian life may differ—acknowledge that out loud. Create a weekly "what stood out" moment: one sentence about a tough day, one about a small win. Listen without fixing; validation is often the most useful support.

Ranking Needs

- Each write three needs in order of importance.
- Swap lists and discuss where priorities match and where they don't.
- Identify one practical step toward meeting a mismatched need this month.

If you do this work—talking, testing small routines, honouring changes—you're less likely to fall into the trap of passive resentment. You're building a way of living together that fits both of you now, not the one someone else designed for you years ago.

Social integration and new friends

Transitioning from the close-knit world of service to civilian social circles can feel like arriving at a party where everyone else already knows the punchline. The easy camaraderie you had with fellow service members—shared shorthand, trust under pressure, and built-in activities—doesn't always show up in the civilian neighborhood or at the office. That doesn't mean meaningful connections are off the table; it means they take deliberate effort, patience, and a willingness to be open in new ways.

Building New Civilian Connections

Start small and practical. Attend a local meet up for a hobby you actually enjoy rather than what looks impressive. Try:

- A weekly adult rec league (softball, basketball, or ultimate frisbee) where attendance and banter build bonds over time.
- A community class—woodworking, photography, or a fixer-upper workshop—where projects create natural conversation starters.
- A volunteer shift at an animal shelter or food bank; consistent presence matters more than instant chemistry.

Action Prompt: Reintegration Reflection

Write down three civilian activities you could try this month. Rank them by ease and interest, then commit to attending at least two sessions before deciding whether to continue.

Discovering Shared Interests and Hobbies

Shared activities create shared stories—plain and simple, low stakes experiences that become the glue for friendships. Bring a partner along sometimes; it helps you both test new settings together and shows civilians another side of you beyond the uniform.

Concrete Example: If you loved tactical drills, try a team sport where strategy matters. If you liked technical gear, join a maker space and work on a beginner project you can finish in a weekend—people will ask about it, and you'll have something to talk about.

The Role of Military Couples in Social Exploration

Couples can multiply opportunities for friendly integration. Make a habit of introducing new acquaintances to each other, and rotate hosting small gatherings—cookouts, game nights, or movie marathons—that emphasis low-pressure interaction. When both partners are active in developing networks, social life becomes shared and protective rather than competitive.

Boundary Basics: Protecting Intimacy While Expanding Circles

Having more friends is great, but so is preserving your private life. Set limits on social commitments you say yes to. Try a "two event rule": attend no more than two large social events per week, and reserve at least one evening for partner time. Communicate these boundaries out loud: let friends know when you're unplugging and why—it's honest and sets expectations.

Understanding Military vs. Civilian Friendships

Recognize the different soil these friendships grow in. Military bonds often form under stress and time pressure; civilian friendships usually require more small-thing trust-building—coffee chats, shared errands, light favours. You might miss the intensity, and that's normal. Allow civilian connections to develop at their own pace rather than measuring them against service bonds.

Reflection Prompt: The "Love Tank" Check

With your partner, list three social goals (e.g., "make two civilian friends," "host a monthly game night," "join a volunteer group"). Discuss what support you need from each other to reach them and when to pull back and prioritize couple time.

Be patient with this social rebuild. With steady presence, clear boundaries, and joint effort, your social life can include both the deep, rapid bonds you miss and the slower, steady connections that sustain civilian living.

Maintaining intimacy under stress

Transition hits more than boxes and schedules; it also moves the ground beneath how couples connect.

Transition hits more than boxes and schedules; it also moves the ground under how couples connect. When one or both partners leave military life, closeness—both emotional and physical—can feel awkward or diminished. This next section focuses on practical ways to recognize what's changing, respond without blame, and rebuild closeness with intention and a dose of patience.

Recognizing the Impact of Stress on Intimacy

Stress after service shows up in odd places: sudden irritability, avoidance of tight spaces, or being present but feeling emotionally distant. These are not signs of failure; they are normal reactions to massive change. Partners should watch for shifts in desire, touch comfort, or patience for conversation, and call them out gently.

Concrete check:

- Reintegration Reflection: Each partner writes three stress signs they notice in themselves and three they see in their partner. Share them out loud in a calm setting (5 minutes each). No arguing—only clarifying questions.

Prioritizing Intentional Time for Connection

Life fills up fast: job interviews, classes, VA appointments, kid logistics. If you don't carve time, connection slips away. Schedule is not romantic, but it works. Plan concrete slots for connection—date night, a morning coffee ritual, or 20 minutes of "no screens, real talk" before bed.

Examples:

- For couples with opposite schedules: try a rotating 15-minute check-in at different times each week so both partners get a turn when they're most alert.

- For couples with small kids: use a babysitter swap with another couple for one evening a month to buy uninterrupted time.

Communicating Openly and Honestly

Honest talk can feel risky—especially when habits from service trained you to bottle up. Start small: name one fear about intimacy and one desire. Use "I" statements: "I feel distant when we don't plan touch" instead of "You don't try." Aim for curiosity rather than fixing.

Practice prompt:

- The 'Love Tank' Check: Each partner lists one thing that fills their affection tank and one thing that drains it. Swap lists and ask, "How can I help fill your tank this week?" Keep it practical—actions, not promises.

Cultivating Patience and Compassion

Adjustment takes time. Give yourself permission to be inconsistent. That's both partners' work: offering grace when someone's flat, frustrated, or needs more space. Try a compassionate phrase you agree on in advance—something like, "I'll give you space, and I'll check back at X time."

Self-care examples for both men and women:

- Short solo routines: 10-minute breathing or grounding before bed to reduce hyper arousal.

- Physical safety checks: one partner practices non-sexual touch (handhold, shoulder rub) to rebuild comfort without pressure.

Embracing the Changing Nature of Intimacy

Intimacy will shift as careers, health, and identities shift. That's normal and workable. Treat intimacy like a toolbox: sometimes you need long talks, sometimes shared chores, sometimes quiet presence. Keep trying new tools and tracking what sticks.

Reflection Prompt

- Ranking Needs: On a scale of 1–5, each partner ranks emotional closeness, physical touch, shared activities, and solo time. Compare scores and plan two small experiments (one week long) to move closer together.

Closing note: This is not about returning to a single "before" state. It's about building a new rhythm where both partners feel seen, safe, and desired. Little, steady changes—time set aside, honest words, agreed-on compassionate responses—add up to real recovery of closeness.

Sleep routines in post-service life

Sleep Disturbances: A Challenge for Veterans and Their Partners

If you've ever felt like your bed is more of a staging area than a sleep zone—lights on, phone buzzing, one of you awake staring at the ceiling while the other is snoring like a wounded bear—you're not alone. Sleep problems after service are common and they affect both partners. When sleep is fractured by nightmares, hyper vigilance, or chronic insomnia, irritability, distance, and misread signals can pile up fast. The good news: there are practical steps you can try together.

The Impact of Military Experiences on Sleep

Military training and deployments teach constant alertness. That instinct helped keep folks safe overseas, but at home it can keep the nervous system keyed up at night. Nightmares and sudden waking are common. For partners, sharing a bed with someone who startles awake or needs the TV on to feel safe can be draining. Acknowledging that these sleep patterns are reactions—reasonable reactions—to past conditions reduces blame and opens the door to teamwork.

Cultivating Consistent Bedtime Routines

Small, repeated actions send a clear signal to your body that sleep time is coming. Try this—set a 'lights out' window that both of you agree on, even if one of you stays awake for a bit. Build a five-step routine: dim lights, switch to a low stimulation activity (read or listen to a calming podcast), do five minutes of paired breathing or progressive muscle relaxation, jot down tomorrow's top three tasks to clear the mind, and settle under the covers. If reading together sounds cheesy, make it tactical—rotate short passages or news free essays. Shared rituals create safety and connection.

Communication is Key

Talk about sleep like you'd brief a mission: specific, clear, and without blame. Use concrete sentences—"I sleep best with the white noise at 45 dB" or "When you wake me up by turning on the light, I feel anxious"—and avoid "always/never" language. Try this prompt after a rough night: "What helped you sleep? What made it worse?" Make it a short daily check-in, not a debrief marathon.

The Importance of Patience

Resetting sleep rhythms can take weeks. If one partner's hyper vigilance eases before the other's, don't treat that as failure—treat it as progress. Celebrate small wins: a night without nightmares, a stretch of deep sleep, a morning without tension.

Managing Common Sleep Disturbances

Nightmares: try imagery rehearsal—write the nightmare, then rewrite it with a less threatening ending, and practice that new script during the day. Hyper vigilance: incorporate grounding exercises before bed (five senses check) and limit stimulants in the evening. Insomnia: keep the bed for sleep and intimacy only—no work or stressful talks.

Creating a Sleep Sanctuary

Make the bedroom a simple, calm zone. Blackout curtains, a fan or white-noise machine, cool temperature, and a comfortable mattress go a long way. If one partner needs a light on, consider eye masks or directional reading lights. Small adjustments can protect both people's sleep without asking either to give up their needs.

Seeking Professional Support

When sleep problems persist, bring in a clinician. Cognitive-behavioural therapy for insomnia (CBT-I), trauma-focused therapies for nightmares, or a sleep medicine consult can be transformative. Couples therapy that includes sleep-focused strategies can help partners support each other without getting stuck in blame.

Quick Checklist

- Establish a consistent sleep schedule.
- Create a calming bedtime routine you share.
- Use specific communication prompts about sleep needs.
- Try relaxation or imagery techniques for nightmares.
- Build a sleep-friendly bedroom.
- Seek professional help when needed.

Reintegration Reflection: Tonight, each partner list one bedtime habit you'd add and one bedroom change you'd make. Share and pick one to start this week. The "Love Tank" Check: after a week, note who slept better and what helped—small data, big impact.

Health and wellness routines

Establishing Consistent Couple-Centric Wellness Practices and Health Routines

You did the hard work getting through deployment and transition; now it's time to tie a new set of habits to the life you want to build together. Think of this as team training—less "push-ups at dawn" and more "how do we both stay healthy and connected without making it a chore?" The next pages give simple ways to make wellness something you do together, not just something you each try to squeeze in between shifts, appointments, and whatever civilian life throws at you.

Navigating individual versus shared

One partner may swear by early-morning runs, while the other prefers slow-flow yoga at dusk. That's fine. The aim is to create a plan that honours both pursuits and still lets you spend time together. Try this:

Schedule alternating shared sessions: Monday/Wednesday/Friday is partner A's run, (partner B joins with a brisk walk or a mobility routine), Tuesday/Thursday is partner B's yoga (partner A does strength or stretching nearby). Weekend time is for a joint activity you both enjoy.

- Create a "fitness trade" list: If you skip your partner's session twice in a month, you owe them a massage or cooking their favourite meal.

Schedule alternating shared sessions: Monday/Wednesday/Friday is partner A's run, partner B joins with a brisk walk or a mobility routine; Tuesday/Thursday is partner B's yoga, partner A does strength or stretching nearby.

Reintegration Reflection: Which of your individual goals can you do side-by-side with your partner this week? Write one compromise and one shared win.

Integrating Physical and Mental Health Support

Wellness routines that mix body and mind are powerful. Small rituals can make a big difference:

- Weekly mental-health check-ins: Set 15 minutes on Sunday to say, in one sentence each, how you're doing emotionally and one thing you need that week.
- Joint relaxation practice: Try a five-minute guided breathing exercise before bed, or a two-minute progressive muscle relaxation after dinner.
- Meal teamwork: Pick one night a week for joint meal prep—one cooks, one preps, then swap. It's practical, nourishes both of you, and reduces decision fatigue.
- Sleep priority: Keep the bedtime routine you already read about consistent, and add a short "decompression chat"—a calm ritual to shift from daily stresses to rest.

The "Love Tank" Check: On a scale of 1–10, how full is each of your emotional tanks? Share what would move the needle by two points.

The Influence of Service Branch Experiences on Health Habits

How you trained and deployed affects how you approach health now. Couples who spent time in different branches may need to translate those habits into civilian life. Examples:

- If one partner comes from a branch that emphasized constant readiness, introduce deliberate "off" times—scheduled rest blocks where no performance is required.
- If high-intensity training was the norm, build gradual transitions to lower-impact choices: interval sessions interspersed with mobility work, or swapping a weekly ruck for a family-friendly hike.

Ranking Needs: List three habits from your service time that help you feel secure, and discuss one way to keep the benefit without the extremes.

Re-Establishing Routines That Build Connection and Mutual Well-Being

Routines are comfort. Pick small, repeatable acts that bring joy and closeness:

- Date-night loop: Rotate who plans the date. Keep it low-cost—board games, a sunset walk, or cooking a new recipe.
- Shared hobby block: Book an hour on Thursdays to try something new together—photography, birding, or a language app.
- Nightly check-ins: Two quick questions—what was the best part of your day? What do you need tomorrow?—Can prevent small resentments from growing.

Supporting Each Other's Evolving Health and Wellness Aspirations

People change. Encourage growth without pressure:

- Monthly "goal pulse": 10 minutes to update each other on new goals and where you want help.
- Try-it-together days: Commit to one new activity each quarter—climbing, dance class, or a 5K—and treat it as data, not a test.
- Celebrate small shifts: Did your partner swap soda for sparkling water? A quick "good job" goes a long way.

Reflection Prompt: What new wellness goal do you each want to try this month? How can your partner help in a specific, small way?

Action Steps to Get Started This Week

- Pick one shared wellness habit to try for 14 days (even 10 minutes a day counts).
- Schedule a 15-minute mental-health check-in.

- Choose one service-based habit to adapt into a civilian-friendly version.

Close with a low-pressure attitude: the goal isn't perfection; it's making wellness a regular part of your life together so both of you feel stronger, calmer, and more connected.

Community involvement and volunteering

Transition & Resilience: From Uniformed Structure to Community Action

After the routines and orders of service, stepping into civilian community life can feel like being handed a map with no legend. That map becomes less intimidating when you treat community involvement like a new mission—with roles, objectives, and a team to build. Start small and intentional, and let your service skills guide you.

Rebuilding and Expanding Social Circles

Begin with these simple ops:

- Pick one local group that matches an interest—dog-walking meet ups, a gardening crew, or a veterans' woodworking class—and attend two events before deciding. The first is reconnaissance; the second is where people start recognizing your face.

- Volunteer at a cause you both care about for a single weekend. Shared low-commitment tasks reduce pressure and create natural conversation starters.

Reintegration Reflection: List three civilian activities each of you might enjoy. Circle one you'd try together this month.

Discovering and Establishing New Community Connections

Look for repeated, low-barrier interactions—weekly farmers' markets, library programs, or neighbourhood clean-ups. These create reliable touch points where acquaintances can become friends. Try hosting a small pot luck or board-game night within a month of meeting a few neighbours; inviting others over accelerates familiarity.

Understanding the Value of Service Experience

Your military training gave you concrete assets: planning under pressure, leading small teams, training newcomers, and logistics. Those are useful in civilian roles that need structure. Think of your experience as practical currency—use it where it helps others get organized or improve systems.

Averaging Acquired Skills for Community Engagement

Action steps:

- Make a two-column skills list: "What I did" (e.g., coordinated shipments, taught weapon safety) and "How that helps civilians" (e.g., supply-chain help for a food bank, safety training for youth programs).
- Match the top three civilian organizations in your area with those skills. Reach out with a targeted offer: "I can help set up inventory tracking for your pantry."

Exploring Shared Volunteer Opportunities

Volunteering together checks a lot of boxes: time spent, mutual purpose, and shared stories. Try these pair-friendly options: crisis-response teams, youth mentorship, habitat builds, or park restoration. Rotate roles—one handles logistics, the other manages volunteers—to play to strengths while learning new ones.

The "Love Tank" Check: After two volunteer sessions, check in on how the work affected your connection. Did doing good together pull you closer, or did one of you feel sidelined? Talk candidly and adjust.

Navigating New Roles and Responsibilities

Civilian communities won't assign ranks, but informal leadership often emerges. Discuss which roles you want: visible organizer, behind-the-scenes planner, or occasional contributor. Keep communication direct—pick a time each month to reassign tasks so neither partner feels overburdened.

Creating a Shared Sense of Purpose

Finally, craft a short joint mission statement: one sentence that captures why you volunteer together (e.g., "We build safe spaces for kids to learn skills"). Use it to guide which opportunities you accept. This shared purpose helps replace the common mission you had in service with a new, civilian one that fits both of you.

Ranking Needs: Each month, rate on a 1–5 scale how much purpose, social connection, and time together you're getting from community work. Compare scores and adjust plans accordingly.

Financial planning for future goals

Navigating Financial Histories and Futures Together

Money talks are rarely romantic, but they can be clarifying—and in military-to-civilian life shifts, they're essential. Start this chapter at the kitchen table, not in a financial planner's office: put out two mugs, set a timer for 30 minutes, and treat this as relationship maintenance. Keep the tone curious rather than accusatory.

Understanding Your Financial Past

Begin by trading short stories about money. Each partner takes five minutes to answer: What was your first money memory? What financial mistakes taught you the most? What gives you anxiety around money now? Speak plainly: list debts, past bankruptcies, times you bounced a check, or periods of tight savings. Also name the wins—first paid-off loan, a year you built an emergency stash—because those show what you can do together.

Reintegration Reflection

- What financial fear from service years still shows up in your daily choices?
- Which habit would you like to stop repeating this year?

Bridging Aspirations with Practical Considerations

Once past histories are addressed, align on short- and long-term aims. Write down three shared goals (e.g., purchase a modest house in two years, fund professional schooling, or take a sabbatical to travel). Next to each, note realistic constraints: current monthly take home pay, upcoming relocation, or a partner's plan to return to school.

Ranking Needs

Use a simple grid: column A = big dreams; column B = current reality; column C = one step this month toward each dream. This keeps plans actionable rather than aspirational wish lists.

Establishing Shared Post-Service Priorities

Decide what matters most now. Is stability, with an emergency fund and steady savings, the top priority, or is paying down high interest debt the immediate priority? Agreeing on three core priorities creates clarity for daily choices.

Creating a Joint Budget

Turn the priorities into a working budget. Cover these headings together:

- Income: list all steady pay and likely changes in the next 12 months.
- Fixed Expenses: rent/mortgage, utilities, insurance.
- Variable Expenses: groceries, gas, and hobbies—set realistic caps.
- Debt: list balances, interest rates, monthly minimums.
- Savings: emergency and goal accounts.

The Love Tank Check

Each month, each partner answers: Did the budget help fill my "love tank"—emotional safety, autonomy, and shared fun? If not, adjust a line item so that small pleasures are not cut. Budgets that feel punitive won't last.

Managing Debt and Building Savings

Pick a pay-down method together:

- Debt Snowball: celebrate paying off the smallest balance first to build momentum.

- Debt Avalanche: attack the highest-interest debt to save money over time.
- Consolidation: if qualifying, move multiple balances into a lower-rate loan.

Aim to save 10–20% of income when possible; if that's unrealistic now, start with 3–5% and increase quarterly.

Planning for Unexpected Financial Challenges

Create a 3–6 month emergency fund target and a checklist of contingency steps (cut discretionary spending, pause non essential subscriptions, and tap vocational benefits). Decide in advance who handles which phone calls or paperwork if a crisis hits—clarity removes friction when stress is high.

Seeking Professional Guidance

When the math gets complex—tax implications of VA benefits, investment choices, or starting a business—book a session with a certified financial planner or a military-friendly counsellor. Ask for a written plan, clear fees, and at least one follow-up review. Professionals don't replace your conversations; they sharpen them.

Closing Prompt

Schedule a monthly money date: 20 minutes to review the budget, one item to celebrate, one adjustment to make. Use a low-pressure tone: you're teammates setting the compass for financial calm and future options—together.

Case studies and practical solutions

Navigating Post-Service Relationship Challenges: Case Studies and Strategies for Military Couples

Case Study: John and Sarah — When Combat Memory Shows Up at the Grocery Store

John came home after multiple deployments carrying more than a duffel bag. Loud noises, crowded aisles, or even bright fluorescent lights could snap him back into a state where his body remembered danger before his mind did. Sarah loved him and wanted to help, but when his anxiety turned into anger, she started pulling away to protect herself. They were stuck in a loop: John shut down or snapped, Sarah retreated or lectured, and both left evenings feeling alone.

Concrete moves that helped them:

- Small exposure steps: Instead of diving into the busiest mall, they practiced short grocery trips during off-peak hours, with a pre-agreed signal John could use if he needed space. That signal meant Sarah stayed calm and offered a distraction or suggested stepping outside for five minutes.

- Therapy options: John connected with a clinician familiar with combat trauma and with couples therapy experience. They did some sessions together to teach Sarah tools for grounding John (breathing patterns, naming five things in the room) and to give John space to explain what triggers felt like.

- Rewriting the script: They created a one-page plan for "when a trigger happens" — who calls whom, who leaves the room, and how they reconnect afterward (a text, a hug, or a short check-in).

Reintegration Reflection

- What three situations make you feel most on-edge? Rank them from 1–3 and describe a low-stakes way to practice handling number 3 this week.

- What's your calm down signal with your partner? If you don't have one, pick a word or gesture tonight and test it during a low pressure moment.

Strategies for Civilian Adjustment — Practical Tools

Communication is the foundation, but that doesn't mean "talk more" as vague advice. Try this:

- The 10 minute Check: Set a timer. Each person gets five uninterrupted minutes to speak about feelings—no fixing allowed from the listener. After both sides speak, share one small support action you'll take before the next check.

- The Debrief Walk: Leave screens behind. Walk 10–20 minutes and talk about one specific thing that went well that week. It trains the brain to notice positives.

Seeking Support — Specific Paths

- Couples therapy: Look for therapists listed on veteran-focused directories or through VA partnerships. Ask if they use trauma-informed approaches.

- Peer groups: Find civilian-military couples meet ups, or veteran spouse groups at local community centres. If in-person feels hard, start with online groups that meet by video.

Building Civilian Friendships as a Couple — Actionable Steps

civilian military couples meetups

Civilian Military Couples Meetups

Shared-interest onboarding: Pick one hobby both are curious about (gardening, a recreational sports league, cooking classes). Commit to attending three sessions before deciding whether it fits.

- Shared-interest onboarding: Pick one hobby both are curious about (gardening, a recreational sports league, cooking classes). Commit to attending three sessions before deciding whether it fits. Double-intro method: When meeting new people, introduce each other with a tiny story—'This is Alex; he can build anything out of duct tape.' That humanizes military experience without centering it.

- Volunteer date: Choose a two-hour volunteer shift together. It gives a purpose-driven setting to meet folks outside your service circle.

Self-Love Techniques for Post-Service Life — Practical Examples

- Mindfulness in motion: For someone who prefers activity, try a five-minute "box-breathing" routine before workout sets; for someone who prefers sitting, use a guided 7-minute body-scan app before bed.
- Self-compassion script: When you catch negative self-talk, say aloud: "I did what I could with what I had." Repeat three times. (Works for anyone—male or female veterans.)
- Micro-rewards: Build a small list of three things that bring calm—hot shower, favourite song play list, or a 15-minute woodworking or knitting block—and schedule one each day.

The 'Love Tank' Check (Quick Partner Exercise)

- Each partner lists one thing that fills their emotional tank and one behaviour that drains it. Swap lists. For seven days, try to add at least one "filler" item to each other's week.

Post-service adjustment takes time and some trial and error. Use small, specific experiments—short trips, timed check-ins, role-played conversations—so you can test what works together and discard what doesn't, without making each attempt feel like a final exam. If triggers or symptoms elevate, reach out to qualified providers and urgent support lines; getting help early saves months of friction. You don't have to get this perfect; try stuff, keep what helps, and keep checking in.

Shared Goals and Identity Beyond the Uniform

The transition from military life to civilian existence marks a significant personal shift, a period where the structured world you knew gives way to new possibilities. While your service has undeniably shaped your experiences and capabilities, it doesn't represent the entirety of who you are. This section is dedicated to the process of rediscovering and integrating your individual self within this new chapter. We will look at identifying and nurturing personal interests that may have taken a backseat, and articulating the core values that now guide your decisions. It's about consciously weaving the discipline and skills acquired during your service into a civilian identity that feels authentic and fulfilling, and importantly, doing so with your loved ones. This is your opportunity to define yourself anew, unburdened by previous expectations, and to co-create a shared vision for your family's civilian life, one that honors both individual aspirations and collective well-being.

Rediscovering individual identities

Reintegration and Rediscovery: Navigating Life After Military Service

You left one world and stepped into another that asks different questions. That doesn't mean who you were in uniform is gone — it just means some parts of you get dusted off, others are set aside, and a few surprising interests show up like old friends. This section gives practical steps to help you claim a civilian identity that fits, without discarding the strengths you built in service.

From Soldier to Civilian: A New Chapter Unfolds

Start small: pick one hobby you stopped during service and try it again for a month. If you used to play guitar, set a weekly 30-minute practice slot. If you liked running, sign up for a local 5K with a friend. These tiny commitments remind your brain that you're allowed to enjoy things that aren't mission-critical.

Reintegration Reflection

- Which personal interest did you put on hold during service? Rate your desire to restart it from 1–5.
- What is one concrete step you can take this week to give that interest airtime?

Identifying Core Values

Military life often cements values like duty, loyalty, and teamwork. In civilian life, those same values can translate into different choices—volunteering on a community board, mentoring a younger colleague, or carving out protected family time. Make a short list of the three values that matter most now, and write one decision you'll make this month that reflects each value.

Ranking Needs (quick exercise)

- Duty/Loyalty: ______
- Autonomy/Choice: ______
- Community/Belonging: ______

Rank these and discuss with your partner where your rankings match or differ.

Integrating Military Skills into Civilian Life

Concrete examples work best here. If you ran logistics for a 100person company, your planning, scheduling, and resource tracking skills map directly to project management roles in the private sector. Translate bullet points into civilian language on your resume and in conversations. Practice a 90second pitch that says: "I led operations for X people, managed Y budget, and cut process time by Z%." Rehearse it at the kitchen table or with a friend until it sounds natural.

For everyday life, use military routines as tools, not rules, keep a weekly family planning meeting (10 minutes), use after action review skills to talk about arguments without blame, and set clear SOPs for chores that drive realistic expectations rather than rigid control.

Communicating with Loved Ones

Make the talk more specific. Instead of "I want to be seen differently," say, "I want you to know I still value responsibility, but I also want to try painting on weekends." Invite your partner into the process: schedule a "Who am I now?" Conversation, each taking turns to describe how you want the other to see you and what support you need.

The 'Love Tank' Check (couples prompt)

- This week, what filled your tank? (Of service, quiet time, words)
- What drained it?

Share answers and pick one small behaviour change to try for seven days.

Embracing Freedom and Authenticity

Freedom here means permission to choose. Try a month of experimental identities: volunteer for a new role, take a night class, or switch your weekend routine. At the end of the month, note what felt true and what felt forced. Authentic choices often feel slightly vulnerable, but energizing.

Supporting Each Other's Growth

Pair up growth goals. One partner might want to finish a certificate; the other offers childcare or household coverage midweek. Set check-ins: a 15 minute weekly meeting to report progress, troubleshoot hurdles, and celebrate small wins. Mutual encouragement makes reinvention less lonely and more doable.

Closing prompt

Set a 30-day plan with one personal restart, one value-driven decision, and one shared conversation with your partner. Small, concrete steps move identity changes from abstract hopes to actual living choices — and that's how a new civilian life gets built, one honest habit at a time.

Aligning family goals and values

Re-discovering Your Family's Shared Purpose in This New Chapter

You've already been working on who you are now — here's the next step: bring the family into the process. Service changes routines, roles, and expectations. When one person shifts from military life to civilian life, the household chart changes, too. That can be a good thing, if you intentionally create a shared purpose that fits where everyone actually is today.

Articulating What's Truly Important

Start with a kitchen table conversation that feels less like a briefing and more like a team huddle. Use these prompts to keep it practical:

- Reintegration Reflection: Ask each person to name three values they want the family to stand for right now. (Give examples: respect, empathy, resilience, gratitude, authenticity.)
- The "Why This Matters" Check: For every value listed, have the family member explain one concrete behaviour that shows it — e.g., "Respect means we listen without interrupting during family meetings," or "Gratitude means we share one thing we're thankful for at dinner."

Make it simple and specific. Veterans tend to respond well to concrete rules over vague slogans.

Defining Collective Aspirations and Dreams

Once values are on the table, map them to goals. Use a whiteboard or a shared note in a phone app. Try these prompts:

- What are two things we want to achieve this year as a family? (Examples: one parent finishes a school program, family takes a road trip, start volunteering once a month.)

- What does a successful week look like for our household? (Work-life balance specifics: number of shared dinners, weekend chores schedule, screen-free hour.)

Turn big dreams into small, trackable steps. If the goal is "get more involved in the community," the first step might be attending one local event together next month.

Identifying and Prioritizing Values

Have each person rank their top five values. Then read them aloud and look for overlap. Try this exercise:

- Ranking Needs: Each member lists five values, ranks them 1–5, then you total the scores to see which values rise to the top as shared priorities.

Co-Creating a Family Mission Statement

With top values and a few goals, draft a one- or two-sentence mission statement. Keep it honest and short. Example:

"Our family commits to supporting each other's growth, maintaining respect and empathy in how we speak, and contributing to our neighbourhood through small, regular actions."

Write it down and put it somewhere visible. Revisit it quarterly.

Integrating Personal and Professional Growth Goals

Mix individual ambitions with shared plans so no one sacrifices their aims. Try this mode:

- Individual: Set one education or job goal per adult and one personal-growth goal (e.g., running a 5K, learning to paint).

- Shared: Pick one family project (garden, home improvement, monthly service day) and one discretionary-spend goal (vacation fund).

- Check-ins: Establish a monthly 20-minute meeting for progress and course-corrections.

Building a Shared Vision for Civilian Life

Create a checklist of lifestyle priorities: work-life balance, community involvement, relationships, health. Assign one small action per week that reflects each priority. For instance, "health" could be a Sunday family walk; "community" could be attending a local council meeting.

Fostering Open Dialogue and Adaptability

Treat this plan as a living document. Use these habits:

- Schedule regular family meetings.
- Encourage honest feedback with a "Start / Stop / Continue" format.
- Be willing to adjust goals as careers, schooling, or health needs shift.

The 'Love Tank' Check: At each meeting, ask everyone to rate their emotional tank (0–10) and name one thing that would move the needle up by one point. Small changes accumulate.

When the family creates a shared purpose, reintegration stops being a solo project and becomes a cooperative mission. That doesn't remove bumps, but it gives everyone clearer instructions and a shared map to follow.

Crafting a joint after-service plan

Articulating Your Shared Vision and Beyond

You've sketched your mission and checked values off the list. Now it's time to get specific: what does life after service actually look like for both of you, and where do those pictures overlap? This is more than wishful thinking — it's the planning that stops small disagreements from turning into big ones.

Starting with Open Dialogue

Set aside a neutral hour (no devices, no chores) and run a two-part check-in. First, each person speaks for five uninterrupted minutes about personal goals, dreams, and fears. Second, swap and summarize what you heard to confirm accuracy. Use prompts like:

- Reintegration Reflection: What would a good week look like for you in civilian life?
- Ranking Needs: List your top three priorities — work, family time, health, side projects, friendships — and compare.

Research shows couples who share a clear future picture report higher satisfaction. It's also okay if the pictures aren't identical; the point is to notice overlap and differences early.

Embracing Evolving Identities

Military roles shaped habits and identities. Outside that structure, new versions of you will show up: student, small-business owner, hobbyist, caretaker. Talk openly about what feels lost and what's exciting. Try this prompt together:

- Identity Check: Name one thing you miss from service and one thing you want to try that you couldn't before.

Example: Alex wanted to start a landscaping business he'd daydreamed about on deployments; Mia discovered she really likes pottery. Supporting small experiments like a weekend market booth or a community art class helps new identities take shape without pressure.

Co-Creating Your Practical Roadmap

Now move from talk to action. Build a three-column plan: short-term (0–6 months), medium (6–18 months), and long-term (18+ months). Include:

- Career alignment: List certifications, networking steps, or job applications that each of you will tackle. Example: enrol in a VA-funded certification, attend one industry meet up per month.
- Living situation: Do you want a city apartment, a suburban yard, or family nearby? Pin down must-haves and negotiable.
- Finances: Create shared priorities — emergency fund target, debt repayment order, saving for a house. Schedule a monthly money check.

Fostering Mutual Personal Growth

Agree on ways to support individual growth. That might mean trading childcare for study time, celebrating course completions with dinner, or agreeing to a "no guilt" solo hobby night. Try The "Love Tank" Check: once a month, each rates how full their tank feels (0–10) and lists one concrete thing their partner could do to add fuel.

Weaving in Civilian Connections

Build civilian networks intentionally. Action steps: join a local club tied to a shared interest, volunteer two hours monthly, or host a small dinner for new neighbours. Practical tip: each partner picks one new person to invite into your social circle every quarter.

Scheduling Intentional Connection

Block time for dates and low-key connection. Put a recurring "we" appointment in your calendars — a cheap dinner, a hike, or a tech-free hour to talk about non-logistics topics.

Building a Flexible Framework

Finally, treat this plan as a living document. Check it quarterly, adjust goals when life shifts, and celebrate progress—no matter how small. Flexibility keeps plans useful and keeps you both moving forward together.

Building a Flexible Framework: Keep it dynamic by reviewing it quarterly.

Quick prompts to finish:

- What's one short-term goal we can achieve in 30 days?
- Which identity do I want to try on for six months?
- Who will we each invite to dinner this season?

Answer those together, and you've taken another solid step toward a satisfying life after service.

Education and career planning together

Charting a Shared Civilian Future: Talking About Your Own Wants and Making a Shared Plan

You've sketched a shared vision and set up some habits. Now it's time to get specific about what each of you wants, and how those wants can be woven into a life you both can actually live. This section gives a practical how-to: talk about your individual hopes, place them on the common board, and pick next steps together.

Understanding Individual Aspirations

Start with a short exercise: each partner takes 15 minutes to write down five concrete goals—no clichés, next vague ambitions. Think: "Finish my HVAC certification within 12 months," "run a half-marathon," "retrain as a school counsellor," or "open a food truck." The goal list should include the why: what personal value or need it answers.

Reintegration Reflection

- What goal would you pursue if money and time weren't an issue?
- Which goal did you pause for military life?
- Which new interest has shown up since you left active service?

Communicating openly means more than stating goals; it means naming fears. One partner might worry about losing steady pay while starting a business. The other might fear being left out if their partner returns to long hours of study or training. Say these things out loud. When fears are visible they become manageable tasks instead of silent resentments.

Envisioning a Shared Future

Once both lists are on the table, look for overlaps. Maybe both of you list "stable home base" or "more time with kids." Those are signals to prioritize shared goals first. If priorities conflict—say one wants to move to a small town while the other wants city life—try a time-limited compromise: "Two years in the city, then reassess."

Identifying Common Goals

- Pick three shared goals and assign timeliness.
- For each goal, list two concrete actions and who takes the lead.

Exploring New Opportunities together is also practical: enrol in a weekend community-college class, volunteer at a VA event on Saturdays, or test a hobby with a month-long commitment (try woodworking, dog training, or a cooking class). Small shared trials reduce risk and build joint confidence.

Navigating the Transition Together

Couples don't have to do this alone. A counsellor who understands military-to-civilian shifts can help mediate planning conversations and teach conflict tools for scheduling, finances, and shifting roles. Look for providers who have experience with service members and partners.

The "Ranking Needs" Prompt

What goal would you pursue if money and time weren't an issue? (If money and time weren't an issue)

- Each partner ranks five needs (income stability, social time, personal study, family time, alone time).
- Merge duplicate entries: compare lists and negotiate the top three shared commitments for the next six months.

Celebrate wins—big or tiny. Did one of you finish a certification? Mark it on your calendar with a small dinner out or a favourite snack.

These moments build momentum.

Final Action Steps

- Do the 15-minute goal list this week.
- Pick three shared goals and set a 6-month check-in.
- Book a session with a counsellor or peer-support group if talks stall.

This work isn't a one-off—keep checking and adjusting. When each person's goals are visible and given a place in the shared plan, the two of you move from surviving post-service change to intentionally building a life you actually want to live together.

Community service and civic life as a couple

Discovering Shared Purpose through Community Service

If you've been talking about shared goals, here's a practical next step: get out and do something together that matters to your neighbors. Community service gives couples a shared identity that isn't built on rank, MOS, or last deployment—it's built on action and shared stories. Think of it as teamwork with civilians as teammates.

Exploring Volunteer Opportunities

Start small and pick something you both can commit to for a few months. Concrete options:

- Weekend shifts at a food pantry: one of you sorts donations while the other runs intake. Low stress, immediate impact.
- Monthly park or beach clean-ups: set a monthly "mission day" and bring coffee and gloves.
- Animal shelter support: if one of you is better with paperwork and the other with handling animals, split tasks to play to strengths.
- Tutoring or mentoring veterans' kids: use military structure to offer routine and reliability.

Reintegration Reflection: Which of these options fits your schedule, skills, and values? List two that sound doable and one you're willing to try for three months.

The Benefits of Civic Involvement

Doing good together does more than check a box. Specific gains couples report:

- You notice how your partner solves problems under stress—useful Intel for daily life.

- Working side-by-side builds trust faster than talking about trust.
- Shared tasks create rituals (the volunteer coffee run, the "end-of-shift debrief") that keep connection strong.
- Serving publicly solidifies a shared identity—people will call you "that volunteer couple," which feels good on hard days.

The 'Love Tank' Check: After a volunteer shift, ask each other: What filled my tank today? What drained it? One-minute answers—no debate.

Averaging Your Unique Strengths

Make a short list of skills each of you brings: logistics, medical training, leadership, social outreach, carpentry, grant writing. Then match those to roles at the organization you choose. Example: if one of you has first-aid training and the other is good at organizing, run a community safety workshop together.

Ranking Needs: Which partner prefers visible roles (public speaking, leading teams) and which prefers behind-the-scenes support? Rank 1–3 to avoid clashes.

Supporting Local Causes

Pick a local cause and commit to it for at least a season. Showing up consistently matters more than grand gestures. Consider sponsoring a community event, helping a small non-profit with a skills-based project, or creating a mini volunteering tradition—like always volunteering at the same holiday drive.

Making It Part of Your Life

Turn service into a recurring date: calendar it, set reminders, and celebrate milestones. If regular volunteering is too much, plan quarterly community projects and one annual signature event you co-lead. Keeping it predictable helps both partners make plans around civilian jobs, family, and self-care.

Partner Prompt: Schedule your first volunteer date this month. After the activity, use the 'Love Tank' Check and jot down one thing you learned about each other.

Putting time into your community together creates shared memories, teaches new ways to cooperate, and gives your partnership a public, positive role. It's practical work with emotional pay-offs—plus, you get to meet people who'll likely become part of your civilian support circle.

Housing and relocation decisions

Finding Home After Service: Collaborative Decision-Making and Emotional Resilience

When the last orders come through and the dust settles, the idea of "where to land" moves from a logistics problem to an emotional one. For military families, home quickly becomes more than a mailbox or a mortgage—it's where people feel steady, known, and safe. The sections that follow give you hands-on ways to decide together, protect the kids' stability, and handle the grief that comes with repeated moves.

Defining "Home" as a Shared Vision

Start with a quick couples' exercise: each partner lists five things they need for a place to feel like home—these can be concrete (good schools, access to VA services) or softer (walkable neighbourhood, a front porch for coffee). Share lists without debate for five minutes, then circle the overlapping items. Those overlaps form the core of your shared vision. Reflection prompt: what are the top three non-negotiables we both can live with?

Collaborative Decision-Making for Housing and Relocation

Make relocation a team project. Create a decision grid with columns for factors like commute time, school ratings, nearby family, housing cost, and access to medical care. Rate each potential location 1–5 on each factor, then add up scores together. Keep communication clear: set a weekly check-in to update research and air frustrations. Practical tip: assign one partner researcher and the other community-scout—one handles online facts, the other calls neighbours, schools, or local groups to get the human side.

Balancing Individual Career Wants with Geography

Talk openly about career goals early. One model that works: set a three-year plan. If Partner A needs a specific market for their job, agree on a trial period—six to twelve months—to test whether the move supports both careers. If work can't bend, look for hybrid solutions: remote roles, commuting pods, or job-share timeliness. Reintegration Reflection: what career compromises are we willing to try for short-term stability?

Prioritizing Kids and Family Stability

For parents, school placement, pediatric care, and social support are top priorities. Map the nearest hospitals, pediatricians, after-school programs, and playgrounds for each candidate town. Talk to school administrators about transfer policies and special programs before signing a lease. The "Love Tank" Check: how are the kids adapting? Track sleep, appetite, and social play for six weeks and flag any downward trends.

Processing the Emotional Impact of Repeated Moves

Acknowledge loss plainly: missing friends, routines, neighbourhoods. Book professional support if feelings pile up—many clinicians offer Healthcare for veterans. Peer groups help too: find local veteran meet ups or online forums to swap tips and vent. Self-care examples: short daily walks with a partner, journalling one "small win" each night, or a monthly ritual that marks endings and beginnings.

Creating Belonging and Setting Realistic Expectations

Plant small roots fast: join a volunteer group, sign up for a class, or host a simple neighbourhood barbecue. Establish routines—Saturday breakfasts, Sunday calls with family—that act as anchors. Give yourselves a grace period: it often takes months to feel settled. Compromise is part of the deal; list three trade-offs you're willing to make now and revisit them after a year. Quick couple prompt: rank these needs—schools, work, health access, proximity to family in order of priority and compare answers. Use this ranking when choosing your next base for building a real sense of home.

Memory making and legacy projects

Actively Create Shared Memories to Honor Your Time Together

You've moved enough times to know where the toaster goes by feel alone. Now, intentionally building shared memories turns those small domestic victories into something deeper: a record of who you were on active duty and who you are now. Pick one simple medium and start: a joint notebook, a shoe box of tickets and letters, or a phone album labeled "Our Post-Service Stuff." The point isn't perfection—it's putting the story somewhere you can return to.

Documenting Your Story: Practical Options

- Couple's journal prompt: once a month, each write one page titled "That month we…" and swap. Keep both entries together.
- Scrapbook sprint: set a two-hour evening, lay out photos, ticket stubs, patches, glue, and play lists. Make it low-pressure—snacks encouraged.
- Phone archive: create a shared cloud album with folders for deployments, PCS moves, and "Firsts after service." Add a one-line caption to each photo: who, where, one emotion.

Reintegration Reflection: Who Are We Now?

Ask each other: What moment from service shaped how we handle stress today? What post-service moment made you feel most like "us"? Write answers separately, then read them aloud over coffee.

Defining Your Legacy, One Conversation at a Time

Legacy isn't a monument; it can be small and practical. Talk through values you want to pass on—honesty, service, curiosity—and pick one tangible expression for each. If "service" is on the list, maybe your legacy project is a monthly volunteering date. If "curiosity," pledge to try one new local class every season.

Creating Meaningful Legacy Projects (Concrete Ideas)

- Volunteer together at a veteran centre twice a month. Rotate responsibilities so each partner leads one month.
- Start an annual scholarship fund for a local cadet or student, even if it's small—set a dollar goal and a deadline.
- Build a family cookbook with favourite meals from each duty station, and make one recipe together every holiday.

Building New Traditions That Stick

New rituals anchor ordinary days. Try a weekly "Recount & Rank" where each person names the week's high, low, and silly win. Or institute an annual "Where We Were" night: pull out photos, tell three stories, and vote on which memory becomes next year's tradition.

Preserving Family History: Hands-On Projects

Give each other one praise and one wish each month, turning the Love Tank Check into a quick celebration habit.

Create a simple family tree poster together, add photos and captions. Have kids (or friends) interview you both and record the conversation—then archive it. These artifacts are instructional and bonding.

The "Love Tank" Check (Quick Celebration Habit)

Once a month, list three things each of you accomplished—big or tiny—and give each other one praise and one wish. Celebrate wins: a printed photo, a small dinner, or a framed page from your scrapbook.

Final Prompt: Pick one memory-preserving task for this week. Who's responsible? Set a 30-minute window on the calendar and do it. Small, steady acts like this turn accumulation of moves into a shared record that clarifies purpose and keeps you moving forward together.

Financial and legal planning for the future

Establishing a Joint Financial Vision

Money talk often feels like a no-fly zone—awkward, tense, and full of landmines. But for couples coming out of military service, creating a shared plan for money can be one of the most stabilizing things you do together. Think of it as a mission brief: clear objectives, roles, contingencies, and regular check-ins. Below are concrete steps to help you craft that vision together.

Aligning Individual Aspirations with Collective Goals

Start by listing what each of you wants to accomplish with money. One partner may want a quiet retirement on a small farm, the other may want to finish a degree or launch a business. Put everything on the table—short-term wins (a family road trip, new appliances), medium goals (pay off student loans), and long-term targets (retirement, a mortgage). Then mark which items overlap. Those become the backbone of your joint financial vision.

Sergeant First Class Anna wants to finish her certification in welding within two years; her spouse Mark wants a reliable vehicle for a side contracting gig. Shared goal: free up $400 per month by trimming subscriptions and reallocating combat pay bonuses to a skills and tools bucket.

Discussing Shared Financial Responsibilities

Be explicit about who pays what and why. Do you split everything 50/50, or contribute proportional to income? Who handles bills, who tracks reimbursements like VA benefits, and who is responsible for debt payments? Put this in writing—even a simple bullet list in a shared note app helps.

Prompt: The "Money Map" — write down monthly income streams (VA, civilian pay, retired pay, side gigs) and monthly outflows (mortgage, groceries, loan payments). Highlight gaps and overlaps. Discuss for 20 minutes with a timer on.

Benefits of a Joint Financial Vision

When you create and use this vision, you'll see three clear benefits: better communication about resources, less financial stress because you have a plan, and a stronger sense of partnership when tackling money problems. It's teamwork in a practical form—no parade required.

Creating a Collaborative Budget

Turn the vision into a living budget. Start with tracking for 30 days—save receipts, use a phone app, or keep a small ledger, like an old school logbook, to enforce discipline. Categorize: housing, transport, groceries, medical, child care, recreation. Set target amounts and a "flex" line for unexpected costs.

Concrete tip: Use separate envelopes or sub-accounts for 'essentials', 'savings', and 'fun.' Each pay day, automate transfers so savings happen without a decision every time.

Implementing Shared Savings Strategies

Automate savings into named accounts: emergency fund, home fund, training fund. Aim for a 3–6month emergency reserve—if deployments or rehiring delays happen, this covers basics. Consider retirement accounts and simple index funds for longer-term growth.

Action steps:

- Set an automatic transfer of a set dollar amount the day after pay arrives.
- Create a "3-month emergency" target and track progress weekly.
- If you have debt with high interest, make extra payments from any windfalls (tax refunds, bonuses).

Reflection prompts

What financial stressors have followed you from service to civilian life? List three, then name one small money action you can take this week to reduce one of them.

Ranking Needs: Each partner lists top three financial priorities. Compare lists—what is shared, what differs, and what trade offs are acceptable?

The "Money Check": Schedule a weekly 15-minute money huddle. Quick review, one decision, and one encouragement.

A joint financial vision is not a rigid plan; it's a shared tool kit that grows with you. Keep it practical, written down, and revisited—like mission briefings, but with less caffeine and more mutual respect.

Work-life balance in post-service life

Harnessing Service Strengths

You already know the drills, the routines, the way a plan turns chaos into order. Those habits didn't evaporate when you took off the uniform — they're tools. The challenge now is to reshape them for civilian use so they support goals, partnership, and personal well-being instead of creating friction.

Integrating Service Strengths into Daily Life

Start small. Pick one military habit that served you well — waking early, using check lists, briefing teammates — and adapt it. Example: if briefings helped you stay focused, try a five-minute nightly "mission review" with your partner. What went well today? What needs attention tomorrow? That short, structured check-in keeps communication clear without turning evenings into grind sessions.

Concrete routines:

Morning cadence: 20 minutes of focused planning (calendar, priorities, one fitness goal) before email or social media.

- Morning cadence: 20 minutes of focused planning (calendar, priorities, one fitness goal) before email or social media.
- Task tiring: Use three tiers — Must, Should, Can — to prioritize household tasks and career moves.
- Accountability buddy: Pair up with your partner for weekly goal checks; keep them to 15 minutes and stick to facts, not feelings.

Reintegration Reflection

- Which service habit do you miss most? How could a civilian version of it help your life now?
- Pick one habit to test for 30 days. What will be your success metric?

Discovering a New Rhythm

Civilians measure success differently; that's okay. Replace mission success metrics with milestones that matter to you: steady savings, fewer arguments, running a 5K together. Find outlets that echo military camaraderie—join a community league, volunteer on a team, or sign up for a group class. Those settings give structure and peers while letting you explore new roles.

Redefining Success

Give yourself permission to set goals that aren't rank-related. Example goals:

- Financial: automated savings of $200 per month for six months.
- Personal: one hobby night weekly that's just for you.
- Couple: one screen-free Sunday afternoon per month.

The "Love Tank" Check

Weekly, take 10 minutes together:

- Rate your love tank from 1 to 10.
- Name one action to raise it by 1 point.
- Commit to that one action before the next check-in.

Celebrating Progress

Create small rituals for wins. Finished a course? Buy a modest treat. Completed the first month of a new routine? High-five and log it. These rituals build momentum and counter the civilian tendency to overlook small steps.

Establishing Boundaries for Balance

Use clear language with employers and family: "I'm off duty after 7 p.m., unless there's an emergency." Practice saying it once — then enforce it. If you need structure, block non-negotiable downtime on your calendar and treat it like leave.

Prioritizing Shared Recharge & Nurturing the Couple Connection

Schedule recharge together: a monthly date that's already on the calendar. Try alternating who plans it so both partners bring fresh ideas. Plan a "quiet reckon" — 30 minutes of shared silence (reading, sitting on the porch) to recover together without pressure.

Fostering New Routines and Passions

Support each other's experiments. If your partner wants woodworking or coding, give them three months and one uninterrupted hour a week to try it. Offer concrete help: babysit for a class, share tools, or celebrate milestones.

Closing prompt

Pick one service habit, one couple routine, and one personal recharge plan to start this week. Set a 30-day check and note one sign that tells you it's working.

Rebuilding trust and communication

Rebuilding trust and communication after service takes intentional effort and empathy from both partners. Think of it like re-learning a two-person SOP—clear steps, practice runs, and occasional after-action reviews. For many couples, the difficult part isn't a single event but the slow accumulation of small misunderstandings and unmet needs that grow into distance. The good news: small, consistent actions rebuild connection.

Understanding the impact of service

Military time changes people in ways partners don't always see at a glance. Stress responses can shift, priorities can tighten, and what used to be casual banter might now trigger a defensive reflex. Partners need plain-language checks: "When you snap at me, what are you feeling?" Or "I notice you go quiet after dinner—what's happening for you?" These prompts invite concrete answers instead of leaving both people guessing.

Active, empathetic listening—how to actually do it

Try this: sit down, put phones away for five minutes, and use the "three points" rule. One partner shares for three minutes while the other listens without interrupting. Then the listener summarizes three things they heard, focusing on feelings as well as facts. Swap roles. This reduces misinterpretation and shows you tried to understand, which is a trust-building action in itself.

Expressing expectations and unmet needs

Unspoken expectations are like land mines. Make them explicit with a quick "Expectation Check": each partner writes three things they expect of the other this week (e.g., handle dishes after dinner, check in when running late, join therapy session). Exchange lists, ask clarifying questions, and negotiate what's realistic. Concrete examples cut through assumptions and stop resentment from stacking up.

Sharing vulnerabilities

Vulnerability feels risky—especially if your training taught you to keep emotions tight. Start small: share one thing that's been hard this week and one thing you appreciated from your partner. Celebrate the honesty. When both partners practice small disclosures regularly, deeper sharing becomes less scary and more habitual.

Consistent routines and dedicated time

Set a weekly "sync" that's sacred: 30 minutes with no problem-solving—just connection. Use it for short check-ins, planning the week, or the "Love Tank" Check: each partner rates their emotional tank (0–10) and names one refill action that would raise it by two points. Keep it casual but consistent—predictability creates safety.

Celebrate progress

Mark progress with small rituals: a fist bump after a tough conversation, a note on the fridge for a handled conflict, or a shared play list for "we did the work" nights. These micro-celebrations reinforce that improvement is happening and that both of you are on the same team.

Seeking understanding and outside support

Sometimes the couple's tool kit isn't enough. Consider couples counselling with someone experienced in post-service issues, or a veteran peer group where partners can hear other couples' tactics. Support can look like therapy, an online forum, or a weekend workshop for veterans and partners.

Reintegration Reflection

- What one expectation have I not said out loud this month?
- When was the last time I listened without planning my response?
- Name one small habit we can start this week to feel more connected.

These steps are practical, low-friction ways to rebuild trust and communication. Keep the focus on steady, measurable actions—because trust grows from consistent moves, not grand promises.

Managing expectations and change

Embracing the Shift: Navigating Life After Military Service

The moment you swap your uniform for whatever civilian clothes you now prefer, life doesn't magically line up. That emptiness where structure and mission used to be is real, and both partners often feel it—sometimes in different ways. Let's talk about what that change looks like, and how to handle it together without turning every evening into a debrief.

The Reality Check: Expectations vs. Reality

When duty gave you a daily plan, leaving can feel like being handed a blank map. You might expect a smooth transition: job clicks into place, friends keep showing up, routine snaps back. Instead, you may find gaps—less obvious purpose, less automatic belonging. Say it out loud: this is normal. Options for action:

- Reintegration Reflection: Each partner lists three things they miss from service life and three things they want to keep. Compare lists and identify one concrete overlap to try in the next month.

- Practical step: Set a 30-minute weekly planning session where you pick one shared activity (community group, class, weekend hike) and one solo goal (certification, creative hobby).

From Service to Civilian Life: A New Chapter

Community in uniform came with expectation: you showed up and were part of the unit. In civilian life, friendships and shared purpose usually need to be built intentionally. Try small, specific moves:

- Relationship-building with civilian friends: Invite one new acquaintance to a low-pressure event—cook out, volunteer shift, or a sports game.

- Afterward, follow up within three days to keep momentum.

- Shared responsibilities: Create a short, rotating checklist for household tasks and social plans so both partners know who's doing what that week.

Rediscovering Identity

Losing the uniform can feel like losing an anchor. Use this time to try on parts of yourself you might've shelved:

- Self-love techniques: For men—schedule a weekly "skill hour" to work on a hobby (woodworking, bikes, coding). For women—book a recurring solo appointment that replenishes you (yoga, running group, creative workshop). Both: keep a one-page list of strengths tied to service and read it aloud once a week.
- The "Love Tank" Check: Each partner rates their emotional tank (0–10) and names one thing that would add two points this week.

Communication, Patience, and Progress

Talk early, talk often, and lower the pressure. Small wins count: a successful interview, a new friend, a calm night without old triggers. Celebrate those in ways that connect you—text a short thank-you, leave a sticky note, or cook a small favourite meal.

- Ranking Needs: Together, list five needs (structure, purpose, social, quiet, physical activity). Rank them and pick one area to focus on improving for the next 30 days.
- Progress prompt: Set one measurable goal for the month (apply to three jobs, attend two social meet ups, try one new hobby together). Check in weekly and cheer each other when steps happen.

This phase requires patience and plain talk. With steady, small actions and the right prompts, you'll find routines and meaning that fit civilian life—on your terms and as a team.

Celebrating milestones and gratitude

Celebrating Milestones and Embracing Progress

Once the uniform is off and the days stretch out differently, it's easy to forget that small wins add up. Start treating tiny successes like brief but important debriefs: they tell you what worked, who showed up, and where to tweak plans. This isn't about trophy cases; it's about shifting attention from flawless execution to steady forward motion.

The Power of Gratitude

Make gratitude specific and regular. Instead of a vague "thanks," name the act and its impact: "Thanks for driving me to that doctor's appointment—I felt less anxious because you were there." Try a nightly three-item gratitude check where each person shares one practical thing the other did and one feeling it created. For example, a veteran might say, "I appreciated you stepping in with the dishes — it helped me unwind," and a civilian partner might answer, "I appreciated how you listened after my rough day — I felt seen."

Prompt: The Gratitude Call-Out

- Each week, pick one moment where your partner made life easier and say it out loud, with detail. Notice how it changes your tone and your mood.

Creating Meaningful Rituals

Rituals build connective muscle. They don't have to be elaborate. A few examples:

- Weekly mission brief: Over pizza on Sunday, each person shares one win from the week, one struggle, and one plan for the coming week.

- Milestones jar: Write small wins on slips — first interview, completed class, fixed the leaky Faust — and read them aloud at the end of the month.

- Micro-celebrations: When one of you reaches a goal, celebrate with a favourite meal, a hike, or an evening without screens.

Reflecting on Progress

Make reflection regular and low-pressure. Try a monthly review: each partner lists three things they've grown in and two areas they'd like support with. Journal prompts can help: "What surprised me this month about life off active duty?" Or "Which small moment made me feel most at home?" These reflections show how much ground you've covered and highlight realistic next steps.

Embracing Imperfection

Mistakes and setbacks are part of learning. Call them what they are—lessons— and talk about the takeaways, not just the blame. When something falls short, do a quick after-action: what went well, what didn't, and one fix for next time. This reduces repeat friction and keeps the focus on improvement.

Putting It Into Practice

Try these starters this week:

- Schedule a 20-minute check-in to share a gratitude and a tiny win.
- Start a milestones jar and add at least two slips.
- Pick one small ritual (weekly brief, date night, or micro-celebration) and commit to it for a month.

Reintegration Reflection

- Which small victories from this month make you proud?
- What ritual would help you both notice more of those moments?

The goal: live in a place that notices progress, thanks each other for the heavy and the small lifts, and treats imperfection as ordinary work in progress. That habit does more for a couple than chasing some impossible perfect standard ever could.

Stories of growth and resilience

Evolving Partnerships and Redefined Identities

After the celebratory rituals and gratitude practices, a tougher, quieter task often waits: sorting out who you are when the uniform comes off. For many of you, the transition from service means shifting roles at home, at work, and inside your head. That shift affects both partners—whether you both served, or only one of you did—and how you handle it can change the tone of your life together.

Shared Post-Service Experiences and Mutual Support

If you and your partner both spent time in uniform, you already share a language—late-night debriefs that sound like mission reports, an instinct for practicality, and a pile of inside jokes nobody else gets. Use that. Try a weekly "Check-In and Coffee" where each of you spends ten minutes describing one win and one struggle from civilian life. Specific prompt: "One small thing that surprised me this week was…" That short habit keeps empathy active without turning every conversation into therapy.

When only one of you served, the civilian partner can feel like they're reading a manual in another language. Concrete action: the veteran can set aside 20 minutes to explain a specific service memory—what happened, why it mattered, what feelings it still brings up—while the non-veteran listens without problem-solving. Follow with a swap: the non-veteran shares an experience the veteran might not instinctively grasp, and the veteran practices reflective listening. These micro-exchanges build a shared reference bank.

Redefined Individual Identities

Leaving service can be freeing and disorienting in equal measure. Practical step: create a "Self Inventory" worksheet together. Column A: skills and traits you know came from service (discipline, logistics, leadership). Column B: new interests you want to try (gardening, coding, coaching youth sports). Then pick one item from column B to try in the next 30 days and name the partner as your accountability buddy. That pairing turns identity work into low-stakes experiments instead of pressure-filled reinventions.

Navigating Reintegration through Shared Journeys

Tell each other the short version and the long version of how reintegration is going. Short version: one-sentence check-ins like "Today, my brain felt scattered." Long version: a 10-minute sit-down where you unpack triggers, wins, and plans. Try this prompt: "What helped me today, and what would have helped more?" Track responses for a month—patterns emerge faster than you think.

The Strength of Vulnerability and Shared Healing

Being willing to show cracks is not weakness; it's an invitation. Start with small vulnerability drills: admit one thing you're nervous about, then ask for something concrete—extra patience, help with a task, or silence. Healing often moves in tiny steps: join a community group together (veteran café night, a couples' workshop) or set nightly "no-device" wind-downs where you share one feeling from the day.

Reintegration Reflection

- What part of my service still feels central to who I am?
- What new activity or role do I want to test this month?
- How can my partner support that experiment in one specific way?

The 'Love Tank' Check

Weekly, each partner names one practical thing that filled their tank and one that emptied it. Small data, big clarity.

These practices turn the hard work of changing identities into a series of small, shared steps. You don't have to reinvent yourselves at once—try an experiment, report back, adjust. Over time those small moves build a new, honest sense of self and a partnership that can handle the surprises civilian life brings.

Communication, Rituals, and Homecoming: The Language of Connection

Communication Adaptations for Military Couples

When life calls for service, distance and unique challenges can reshape how you and your partner connect. The rhythm of your communication, so familiar in peacetime, might shift when one of you is deployed or when service leaves its mark. This part of our discussion is dedicated to understanding and strengthening that connection, especially when the military life creates its own set of communication hurdles. We'll look at how to keep your lines open, how to bridge the gap between military language and everyday life, and how to build a shared understanding that honours both your individual experiences and your life together. We'll also discuss how to process difficult moments, create emotional safety, and recognize the silent language that often speaks volumes. Finally, we'll touch on how to manage stress, make decisions as a team, and express your affection in ways that truly matter.

Intentional check-ins and schedules

Establishing Intentional Check-Ins: The Key to Maintaining Connection

You know that feeling when the deployment clock starts to tick and suddenly your texts turn into code words, emojis, and long pauses? That's not just distance—it's a new way your daily contact is disrupted. This section is about taking back some control: setting up intentional check-ins so the two of you stay connected even when miles and stress make everything harder.

The Impact of Deployments on Communication

Deployments change how people talk and how safe they feel saying things. Some veterans pull inward and clip emotions short; others get clingy, asking for constant reassurance. Both reactions are normal responses to stress, yet they may surprise the partner at home. Notice the shift—"they're quieter" or "they're texting me three times an hour"—as the first step to prevent small ripples from turning into big arguments.

Proactively Addressing Communication Differences

When service members come home, the person who left isn't always the exact person who returns. The experiences during deployment can be hard to explain, which leaves partners guessing. The solution isn't magic; it's scheduled honesty. Set a time to talk about what changed, what each of you needs, and what's non-negotiable. Reintegration Reflection: List three things your partner did during deployment that surprised you and then ask them to list three things they felt but didn't say. Use that list as the opening for a calm, no-blame talk.

Making Dedicated Time for Undivided Attention

"Think of conversations like physical workouts: they need a time slot and focused energy. Block out a video call or phone check-in the same way you would a medical appointment—no notifications, no multitasking." The "Love Tank" Check: once per week, each partner names one thing that filled their tank and one thing that drained it. Five minutes. No fixing allowed—just listening.

Averaging Communication Tools and Strategies

Technology can help—schedule video calls, share a joint calendar for phone times, or create a private message thread just for small joys. But rules help tech work: agree on no work calls during your check-in, decide what counts as an emergency, and pick one app for quick updates so nothing gets lost. Practice: pick three app you already use and assign each a role: urgent, fun, and logistics.

Planning for Shared Routines and Rituals

After returning home, reintroduce small, repeatable rituals to rebuild closeness. Dinners together twice a week, a walk on Sundays, or a ten-minute "what's one good thing" at bedtime—all create a predictable rhythm that heals awkwardness. Try a 30-day "reset": choose one shared ritual, do it daily, and jot how it affects mood and connection.

Putting it All Together

Intentional check-ins are a deliberate habit: schedule them, acknowledge how deployment shaped your communication, make space for focused attention, use tools with boundaries, and create routines to bring you back in sync. Implemented consistently, these steps help you build a stronger, more resilient connection, cut down on conflict, and restore trust and intimacy. Quick prompt: Ranking Needs—each partner lists their top three emotional needs this week and trades lists; talk for ten minutes about what surprised you.

Translating military shorthand for civilian partners

Deciphering Military Acronyms and Jargon

If you've ever sat at a backyard barbecue while your partner's buddy dropped a string of letters and you smiled and nodded like a trained seal, this section is for you. Military talk can sound like a different dialect—fast, efficient, and full of shorthand. Learning a little of this language does more than help you follow conversations; it builds connection and shows you care enough to understand an important part of your partner's daily life.

Understanding the Military Language

Start with the basics: many military terms exist to speed up communication in high-pressure situations. PT is Physical Training; a TO is a Tactical Officer or Team Officer, depending on the branch; and yes, FUBAR is a salty way to say things went very wrong. The trick is noticing context. If someone mentions PT at 0600, they probably mean a workout routine. If they say "on mission," the meaning will shift depending on whether they're talking about training, deployment, or a household project with military-style planning.

Why it Matters

Knowing these terms helps you make sense of stories and stressors. When your partner talks about being on a "detail" or "standby," you can ask useful follow-up questions instead of guessing. That turns small talk into meaningful conversation and reduces the accidental isolation many civilian partners feel at unit events.

Quick Tips for Learning

- Ask without guilt. A short, 'Can you unpack that one for me?' Is better than nodding along. Most service members appreciate the curiosity.

- Build a running glossary. Keep a note on your phone labelled "Base Lingo" or "Unit Terms." Add entries when you encounter new acronyms and review them before social events.

- Match context to meaning. If someone mentions "situation report" or SIT REP, it's likely updates, not drama. If "OPORD" comes up, it's an operation order — think plan, not paperwork.

- Use reputable resources. Military-focused websites, veterans' forums, and branch-specific handbooks can clarify terms and acronyms quickly.

Translating Military Language into Everyday Terms

Try re framing. A "mission" can be a shared objective like renovating the kitchen; a "briefing" becomes a family check-in. That doesn't dilute the original meaning—it bridges worlds so conversations land for both partners.

Empower Your Civilian Partner — Practical Moves

- Reintegration Reflection: After a drill or event, set five minutes to ask, "What was the highlight and one thing I should know?" This keeps explanations bite-sized and digestible.

- The 'Love Tank' Check: If your partner uses military shorthand for stress, translate it aloud: "So when you say 'tight time line,' you mean you're feeling rushed and need help with priorities?" Saying it back builds trust.

- Ranking Needs: Keep a simple list of terms you both agree to explain immediately during group chats—this avoids repeated confusion at unit gatherings.

This work isn't about becoming an expert overnight. It's about small, respectful steps that make social settings easier, reduce miscommunication, and deepen connection. Keep the glossary handy, ask the occasional clarifying question, and use simple translations at home to turn military shorthand into shared meaning.

Debrief routines after incidents

Establishing a Debrief Routine for Resilience and Reconnection

You've learned the language; now let's set up the habit that helps you process the hard stuff. A debrief routine is a predictable, intentional way to talk about difficult events so they don't pile up like unread emails. Think of it as a short, regular check-in that combines objective sharing, emotional validation, and small planning for next time.

Creating a Safe Space for Open Discussion

Pick a place and a time that signals "you're switching out of mission mode." That could be a corner of the couch with the lights dimmed, a walk after dinner, or a ten minute sit down before bed. The point is consistency. Use a simple rule set:

- No interruptions for at least ten minutes.
- No judgments or "should have" statements.
- One person speaks; the other listens and paraphrases back what they heard.

Debrief Prompt: "Tell me what happened in facts first — what you saw, when it started, what changed." Then pause for a minute. The factual piece helps slow the replay-loop so emotions don't instantly hijack the conversation.

Focusing on Objective Observations and Emotional Validation

Start with sequence: what, when, who, where. Keep it factual for a minute or two. After facts, shift to feelings. This two-step makes it easier to see what actually happened and how each of you experienced it.

Concrete steps for this part:

- Speaker: Give a 60–90 second factual recap.
- Listener: Repeat back the facts in one sentence. ("So you were on-site at 0700, the commas failed, and you waited two hours for a solution.")
- Speaker: Share emotions tied to the event. ("I felt frustrated and guilty that I couldn't fix it.")

Speaker: Share emotions tied to the event—"I felt frustrated and guilty because I couldn't fix it."

Quick script to avoid blame: "I noticed that X happened, and I felt Y." Swap roles after a short breath.

Lessons Learned and Future Preparedness

Turn a debrief into a micro-action plan. Identify one thing to try next time—nothing huge. Small, specific changes build confidence.

Examples:

- If a mission call became chaotic, agree on one pre-check to reduce uncertainty next time (e.g., confirm commas before movement).
- If an argument followed stressful duty, agree that either person can call a 20-minute pause with a code word.

Exercise — "One Thing Forward": Each partner names one tweak they'll try next time and one resource they want (a contact, a checklist, five minutes of silence).

Reinforcing Mutual Support and Understanding

Finish the debrief with appreciation. That sounds a bit cheesy, but it works. Acknowledge stamina and whatever coping worked, even if small: "Thanks for telling me. I know that wasn't easy." Positive closure helps both people feel safer and more connected.

Transitioning Back to Home Life

Set a short, intentional decompression routine after the debrief: make tea, take a 10-minute walk, put on a play list you both like, or do a quick breathing exercise together. These closing actions mark the return to day-to-day home time.

The "Reintegration Reflection" Prompt

After a debrief, answer these aloud or in a note:

- What helped me the most about that talk?
- What felt unsafe or missing?
- What small action will I take to be better prepared next time?

Why keep the routine? Because the payoff is concrete: better communication, less emotional carry-over, and a clearer sense of teamwork. It takes practice, but regular debriefs reduce reactivity and help you both show up steadier for each other—on duty and off.

Emotional safety and active listening

Cultivating Emotional Safety: The Foundation of a Strong Connection

If the debrief routine is the tool you use after a rough mission or a long shift, emotional safety is the ground you stand on while using it. For couples with military backgrounds, that ground can feel uneven at times — orders, deployments, post-service stressors — so let's make it solid. Below are concrete ways to build a secure emotional space at home, with examples that work for both partners.

Creating a Secure Space

Start with active listening. That sounds simple, but practice makes it reliable. Turn off the TV, put the phone face down, and use small verbal cues that show you're present: "Tell me more about that" or "What happened after that?" Mirror what you hear back in one sentence: "So you felt shut out when the team changed plans?" That little rewrite shows you heard the content and the emotion without arguing about either.

Quick drill: schedule a 10-minute "clear air" session each evening. One partner speaks for five minutes uninterrupted about anything weighing on them; the other listens and then paraphrases for one minute. Swap roles. No fixes allowed during the speaker's time—just listening and paraphrasing.

The Power of Validation

Validation isn't agreement; it's saying "I see your experience." For example, if a partner says, "I'm on edge after that training," a validating response is, "I can see why you'd feel on edge; that was intense." Short, concrete statements work best. Try: "That sounds exhausting," or "I can tell that stuck with you."

Validation can also be physical: a hand squeeze, a quiet "I'm with you," or staying in the room rather than leaving. These small actions communicate safety more quickly than a long speech during a tense moment.

Identifying and Addressing Triggers

Triggers come from service, but they also come from things as ordinary as certain smells, phrases, or sudden movements. Make a trigger map together: list known triggers, rank how intense they are, and note what helps when they flare up. Example entries: "Fireworks — intensity 7 — helpful response: turn on lights, deep-breathing together, offer space if requested." Another: "Unexpected loud conversation — intensity 5 — helpful response: brief exit and regroup in the kitchen."

Practical tactic: use a pre-arranged "pause" phrase—something neutral like "Time-out check"—that either partner can say when they feel overwhelmed. That phrase signals temporary de-escalation and a plan: 20 minutes to breathe, then come back and debrief using the objective-observation method covered earlier.

Reassuring Each Other

Reassurance isn't just grand gestures; it's regular, small bets on your commitment. Leave a sticky note in a gear bag: "You got this. Back here later." Bring home coffee on a rough morning. Schedule a weekly check-in where you each say one specific thing you appreciate about the other that week. These acts reduce uncertainty and increase trust.

The "Love Tank" Check (short prompt)

- Partner A: Name one thing I did this week that filled your tank.
- Partner B: Name one thing I could do next week to top up your tank.

Keep answers specific: "You texted me a goofy selfie — that made me smile during the meeting" beats "You're nice."

Reintegration Reflection

- Where do I feel safest in my day-to-day? At home, at the gym, with a friend?
- What one action from my partner helped me feel safer this week?

Write one sentence each, share, and discuss for five minutes.

Building emotional safety takes practice, like running drills together. The payoff: fewer misread signals, faster reconnection after stress, and a clearer sense that you're on the same team. Try the drills this week, and report back to each other at your next debrief.

Non-verbal communication cues

The Silent Language of Love: Non-Verbal Communication in Military Partnerships

If words sometimes fail when stakes are high, non-verbal signals often pick up the slack. In military partnerships, where deployments, briefings, and high-alert days limit chances for long talks, what you say without saying it can carry the load. Below are practical ways to notice, interpret, and use those silent signals to stay connected.

Tuning In to Non-Verbal Cues

Start by broadening your awareness. Spend a week intentionally noting small signals from your partner: posture, facial expressions, tone, and how close they choose to sit. Jot one observation per day in a notebook. Over time you'll see patterns — the tell that means "I had a rough day" versus the one that means "leave me be until I decompress."

The Power of Body Language

Spend a week intentionally noting small signals from your partner: posture, facial expressions, tone, and the way they choose to sit.

Concrete examples: when your spouse comes home from shift work with shoulders tight and jaw clenched, try a low pressure approach: set down their gear, make a cup of coffee, and offer a silent touch on the shoulder. If their posture opens after a few minutes, that touch was a bridge. If they shrink away, they may need space — which you can honour with a gentle, "Want company or time?" Action prompt: The "One Minute Pause" — before asking questions after a long separation, take sixty seconds to read body language and decide whether to lead with a hug, an offer to listen, or quiet company.

Eye Contact: A Window to the Soul

Eye contact varies by training and personality. Some veterans were taught to look away in intense moments; others maintain steady contact as a sign of trust. If your partner looks down when stressed, try softening your gaze and matching their pace before gradually lifting it to meet theirs. Exercise: The "Look-Up Test" — sit quietly across from each other for thirty seconds and aim to hold eye contact for ten. Debrief: how did it feel? Too intense? Comforting? Use results to calibrate.

The Comfort of Physical Touch

Touch is portable therapy. For dual-military couples, a pre-shift squeeze or a post-debrief hug sends a clear message: you're backed up. For partners separated by deployment, pack small, scented items or a worn T-shirt to exchange; these provide tactile memory cues. Try a daily micro-touch habit: a squeeze when passing in the doorway. Track how often it prompts a smile versus an awkward glance — adjust timing accordingly.

Interpreting Shared Silences

Silence can mean 'we're tuned in' or 'we're shutting down.' Context matters: long quiet after a ceremony might be processing; long quiet after an argument could be avoidance. Reflection prompt: Reintegration Reflection — after a tense silence, write what each of you thinks it meant, then compare. Often the mismatch is where the work — and relief — lives.

Developing the Skill of "Reading" Your Partner

Reading someone takes practice and humility. Start by naming observed cues rather than assuming motives: "I noticed you avoided eye contact when I mentioned the move; are you worried?" This reduces misreadings and opens dialogue. Practice weekly with small, safe check-ins and celebrate when a non-verbal nudge leads to an early de-escalation of stress.

Quick Tools to Use Tonight

- Ranking Needs: list five comforting gestures (touch, space, coffee, a listener, a note) and rank them together. Use rankings for the next week.

Non-verbal skill-building isn't mysterious. With attention, simple experiments, and short debriefs, you'll become fluent in each other's silent language — which, in military life, can be the most reliable line of communication you've got.

Conflict de-escalation during high-stress times

Effective Communication Strategies for Couples in Conflict

Conflicts happen — even between two people who've trained to follow orders and operate under pressure. The good news: you can start handling disagreements with the same discipline and teamwork you'd use on a hard mission. Below are specific steps and short drills you can try with your partner to keep arguments from spiraling and to get to solutions that stick.

Acknowledge the Stress First

When tempers flare, the body is often doing half the talking. Before you tackle the topic, call out the stress out loud. Try a short script: "This is heated right now; my heart rate is up. Can we pause for two minutes?" Saying that absorbs some of the emotional fuel and signals you want a better outcome than trading barbs.

Quick Drill — Stress Check

- Pause. Name one physical sign you notice (clenched jaw, shallow breath, pacing).
- Each partner says a single sentence: "I'm feeling…" then one word (e.g., "overwhelmed," "exhausted," "frustrated").

This resets the tone and gives both of you a chance to be seen before words start swinging.

Agree on a Mutual "Time-Out" Signal

Create a neutral pause button that either of you can use without guilt or escalation. Pick something simple: a phrase like "Need a minute," a hand gesture, or even a two-finger salute. The rule: when the signal happens, both partners step away for a set time (20–30 minutes), no plot-twisting texts, no passive-aggressive comments — just cool-down.

Planning Note

Set the cooldown length together, and if one of you needs more time, ask for a check-in time: "Let's meet again in 40 minutes." That avoids endless cliffhangers.

Focus on One Issue at a Time

Fighting about five things at once guarantees no one wins and resentment grows. Use this tactic: label the topic. Start with "Today's issue:" and finish the sentence. Keep a physical list — write it down and cross off the item when you resolve it. If old complaints pop up, place them on a "parking lot" list for later.

Example

Today's issue: night shift schedule. Parking lot: last year's tax argument.

Use "I" Statements to Express Feelings

"I" statements reduce blame and increase clarity. Replace "You never listen" with "I feel unheard when conversations end abruptly." Short, specific, and tied to action works best.

Practice Script

- Old: "You always put work first."
- New: "I feel unimportant when plans change without a heads-up."

Prioritize Active Listening for Understanding

Active listening means you aim to understand, not to answer. Try the 3-step loop:

- Listen without interrupting.
- Summarize what you heard: "So you felt X when Y happened."

- Ask one clarifying question, then switch roles.

Mini-Exercise — The 90-Second Rule

Take turns speaking for up to 90 seconds while the other person practices the loop. No interruptions. Then swap. This builds the muscle of being heard.

Schedule a Reconnection for Deeper Discussion

If the conversation needs more time or cooler heads, schedule a follow-up when both are ready. Put it on the calendar like an appointment. Name the purpose and expected outcome: "Saturday 10 a.m. — talk about finances, goal: agree on a budget next steps." Treating the talk as a meeting reduces ambushes and sets expectations.

Reintegration Reflection

- What stress signs do I notice most in myself during conflict?
- What time-out signal feels fair to both of us?
- Which one issue should we solve this week?

The tactics above are practical, repeatable, and low-tech — which is exactly what works when feelings get loud. Try one method this week and report back to your partner on how it landed. Small drills add up; soon you'll both handle disagreements with more calm and less collateral damage.

Shared decision-making tools

Fostering Mutual Respect through Shared Decision-Making

Shifting from a military command structure to making choices as equals can feel like trading march orders for a group chat—confusing at first, but eventually less likely to end with someone yelling "Move!" This next part gives concrete ways to turn old habits into new patterns that build respect and trust.

Identifying Common Military Decision-Making Styles

First, get curious about how you made decisions in uniform. Were you the quick-call leader who decided under pressure? The planner who ran options up the chain? The person who waited for instructions? Sit down with your partner and list three decision behaviours from your service years and three civilian situations where those behaviours show up now (home repairs, parenting, bills, job changes). That gap between "how you were trained" and "what this partnership needs" is where small, useful adjustments happen.

Prompt — Reintegration Reflection

Each partner writes: "When I was in the service I decided like this…" and "At home, that shows up when…" Share responses out loud for five minutes each. No interruptions.

Establishing a "Veto" or "Consult" System

A practical fix that reduces power struggles: agree ahead of time on which topics require a consult and which allow a veto. Example: if one partner manages investments, they might have veto power on large financial moves over a set threshold; the other partner gets consultation before weekend plans that impact family time. Put numbers or categories on it—"veto on purchases over $1,000" or "consult for childcare changes." Treat the system like equipment: test it for 30 days, then tweak.

Prompt — Ranking Needs

Make two columns: "Veto" and "Consult." List five items each. Swap lists and discuss where you overlap and where you disagree. Adjust until both feel safe.

Utilizing Shared Calendars and Tools

Shared calendars stop accidental double-booking and reduce the "Why didn't you tell me?" Fights. Use a shared app or a paper wall calendar—whichever you'll actually use. Block deployments, doctor visits, work shifts, and "me time." Add a colour for priorities: red for non-negotiable, yellow for flexible, green for tentative.

Example: Create a weekly check-in event labelled "Sunday Sync" for 15 minutes. Use it to move tasks, confirm plans, and give a quick heads-up if something major pops up.

Creating a Family Budget Together

Make budgeting a team sport. Start by listing monthly income and fixed costs side-by-side, then set one joint goal (emergency fund, car repair, travel). Split responsibilities: one person tracks bills, the other handles day-to-day spending, with both reviewing the app once a week. Make the first budget meeting feel like mission planning—clear roles, timeliness, and contingency plans for surprise expenses.

Practicing Active Listening

Tap into your listening skills like you would survey a new area: observe, summarize, confirm. When your partner explains a concern, repeat back the gist before responding: "So what I hear is…" That small step reduces misreads and signals respect.

The "Love Tank" Check

Weekly, ask each other: rate communication, chores, and money on a 1–5 scale. For any area scoring below 4, spend five minutes discussing improvements. This keeps small issues from turning into all-night arguments.

Wrap-up

These tools—knowing your decision style, a clear veto/consult system, shared calendars, joint budgeting, and actual listening—turn military habits into a civilian teamwork plan. Try one change at a time, measure how it feels, and adjust. You'll build respect not through rules alone, but through consistent small actions that show: we decide together.

Love languages applied to daily routines

Weaving Love Languages into Military Life

Transitioning from the decision-making tools we just covered, let's turn to another practical way couples keep the emotional connection alive: the five love languages. For anyone serving or partnered with someone who does, these simple categories—words of affirmation, acts of service, quality time, receiving gifts, and physical touch—can be adapted to the rhythms and limits of military life so they actually work, not just sit on a shelf collecting good intentions.

Understanding the love languages in military life

Start by picking one language to test for two weeks. Don't overcomplicate it: notice how your partner responds when you try a different approach. If the service member lights up after a casserole and the partner doesn't, that's a data point. If a soldier gets choked up over a text that says "I'm proud of you," that's another.

Words of Affirmation: acknowledging sacrifices

Concrete idea: create a "mission praise" file—short voice notes or texts that highlight specific actions (e.g., "Thank you for staying up late organizing the PCS paperwork" or "I noticed how calm you stayed during that field exercise. Proud of you."). During deployments, record one-minute messages that can be played when homesickness hits. Reflection prompt: Reintegration Reflection — list three specific sacrifices you've noticed in the last month and share one with your partner tonight.

Acts of Service: sharing the burden

Military schedules are a logistics problem disguised as daily life. Split tasks with clarity: one partner handles vehicle maintenance and medical appointments, the other does meal prep and school pick-ups. Example: during pre-deployment chaos, agree that the non-deploying partner will pack the household's important documents while the service member handles personal gear. Quick practice: The "Two-Thing Swap" — each week, trade two chores so the load truly feels shared.

Quality Time: making the most of brief moments

Quality here is about focus, not duration. Try a five-minute "mission check-in" before duty: no planning, just curiosity—"What's one thing that went well today?" Put phones in airplane mode for the first ten minutes of breakfast. If distance separates you, schedule a consistent 10-minute video call at a time that's realistic for the service member's watch schedule. Prompt: The "Love Tank" Check — rate your connection 1–5 each night; if either score is a 2 or below, schedule a focused 20-minute conversation the next day.

Receiving Gifts: tangible symbols of care

Gifts don't have to be expensive. Mail a small packet with an inside joke, a printed photo, or a favourite snack. For long deployments, create a "countdown box" with weekly envelopes—each contains a note or tiny item for the coming week. Concrete example: send a T-shirt with a handwritten note tucked in the collar — simple, practical, and comforting.

Physical Touch: comfort and reassurance

Touch can be scaled to what's possible and appropriate: a steady hand on the knee over morning coffee, a quick hug before a shift, or a massage after a long training day. For couples separated by deployment, create a ritual for reunion—first five minutes are all about presence: no phones, no chores, just meeting each other's eyes and three solid hugs.

Closing prompt and short practice

Ranking Needs — each partner privately ranks the five languages from 1–5, then compare. Discuss one small change you'll try this week to speak your partner's top language. Make it concrete, measurable, and bite-sized.

Adapting these approaches to the unpredictable demands of service will help you keep the emotional bank account healthy. Small, consistent actions—tailored to schedules, duties, and stress levels—often matter more than grand gestures. Try one idea this week and report back to each other at the end of seven days.

Social media boundaries and privacy

Social media has a way of sneaking into the quiet corners of a partnership — the good, the awkward, and the combustible. For couples tied to service life, setting clear expectations for what you share and how you interact online protects more than privacy; it protects trust. Below are straightforward steps and small exercises that help you both set boundaries without turning every post into a negotiation.

Setting Boundaries for a Healthy Online Presence

Start with a front line conversation. Sit down—coffee, beer, or MRE-style snack—and ask: what feels safe to post? Make a list together. Examples:

- Photos: OK to post unit group shots but not home kids' faces.
- Updates: Announce major life events, but skip daily emotional blow-by-blow.
- Location tags: Turn off geo-tagging for home and sensitive locations.

Prompt: The "Post or Pause" Exercise

Each partner names three things they'd post right now and three they'd never post. Compare lists. Anything surprising? Tweak rules.

Defining Acceptable Online Interactions

Break down how you'll communicate with others. Simple rules reduce drama:

- Direct messages from exes: disclose, and discuss, or block.
- Flirty comments: zero tolerance for public back-and-forth that could cause discomfort.

Comment on sensitive posts—such as politics or mission details—only after discussing them first. Avoid posting outright.

The "Red Card" Protocol

Agree on a one word signal (e.g., "red card") that either of you can use in text when an interaction crosses a line. It stops escalation and prompts an in person chat.

The Impact of Presence on Well-being

Online life can amplify stress through comparison, harassment, and pressure to look perfect. If one partner is scrolling late and losing sleep, take a time out. Consider app limits, a bedtime blackout, or muting certain feeds. Mental health is mission-critical; treat online triggers like any other stress or.

Respecting Privacy and Personal Space

Respect looks like granting each other private accounts when needed, not weaponizing passwords, and not pressuring someone to share more than they're ready to. If one of you uses social platforms for decompression (gaming, forums), set clear hours and respect that space like a brief leave.

Creating a Shared Understanding of Behaviours

Draft a short, written agreement — three to five bullet points — that outlines your shared rules. Review it every few months or after major transitions (deployment, PCS, separation).

Putting Guidelines into Practice — Quick Checklist

- Set social windows: no posting after 10 p.m.; no phones at dinner.
- Use private messages for sensitive talk.
- Skip intimate details in public feeds.
- Check in monthly: what's working? What's not?

Reintegration Reflection

After a deployment or move, sit down and ask: how did social media affect us while apart? What should change now? Use this time to update your agreement and keep your partnership strong in both real life and the feeds.

Caring gestures during separations

Nurturing Meaningful Connection Amidst Deployment: Strategies for Maintaining Emotional Closeness Despite Physical Distance

Deployments present a different kind of challenge—time zones, limited bandwidth, and the weird gap between "I'm fine" and "I actually had a rough night." The good news is that a few targeted practices can keep your emotional bond active even when hugs aren't an option.

Establishing a Vital Lifeline: The Importance of Scheduled Communication

Set up a predictable communication rhythm so both partners know when to expect contact. Try these concrete plans:

a 15 minute morning call (or text update) and a 45 minute video call on a day when schedules allow.

- The "priority window": pick a fixed 30-minute slot that's honoured unless mission-critical things come up.
- The message chain: commit to at least one photo, voice note, or handwritten line each day—no pressure for long conversations.

Reintegration Reflection: What communication rhythm would make you feel most stable? Rank options from 1 (most helpful) to 3 (least helpful) and share your picks before deployment.

Tangible Reminders of Affection: Sending Thoughtful Notes and Small Gifts

Small items carry big meaning. Pack a care kit with:

- A handwritten letter to be opened on tough days (include a joke or a memory).

- A scarf, pair of socks, or play list titled "First Dance on the Porch."
- A snack that tastes like home.

Pro tip: label one package "Open when you miss me" and another "Open when you nailed a tough day." The ritual of receiving something physical breaks up monotony and gives the deployed partner a portable piece of home.

Averaging Technology for Shared Experiences

Use app and clever set-ups to build shared routines:

- Virtual movie nights: queue the film, press play together, use a chat or voice call to comment in real time.
- Online cooking class: pick a simple recipe, order the same ingredients if possible, then cook while on video.
- Game night: choose low-pressure games—trivia, Words With Friends, or cooperative puzzle games—that let you team up.

The "Love Tank" Check: After a virtual date, each person names one small thing that filled their "tank" and one thing that felt empty. Use that to tweak future plans.

Acknowledging and Validating Sacrifices

A quick, specific acknowledgement beats a vague "thanks." Try: "I know you missed our anniversary training shift—that was tough. I'm proud of how you handled it." Offer short, routine appreciation messages and ask, "What can I do this week to make things easier?" Small validation reduces isolation.

Cultivating a Shared Future Vision

Keep a forward-facing plan that's tangible:

- Plan a reunion weekend: pick dates, a place, and three activities.

- Start a savings goal for something concrete—a camper, a down payment—with weekly progress notes.
- Create a shared scrapbook (digital or physical) where each adds one future wish per week.

The "Future Vision" prompt: Write one specific thing you'll do together within 90 days of reunion and three reasons it matters.

Brightening Their Days with Surprise Messages

Surprises are morale boosters: random GIFs, voice clips of a silly story, or a brief scavenger hunt of clues leading to a video message. Keep surprises low-effort for you but high-impact for them.

Planning Reunion Rituals

Decide on reunion rituals before separation: a welcome-home play list, a favourite meal, or a two-day "no schedules" rule. Make it concrete—who cooks, where you'll sleep that first night, one thing you'll both do to decompress. Rituals reduce post-reunion awkwardness and create something to look forward to.

Quick Partner Exercise: Pick one communication plan, one surprise to send this week, and one reunion ritual to plan. Share these three items with your partner tonight and set a date to check in on how they landed.

Small, steady actions keep the emotional thread taut. With intention and a little creativity, you can keep close while apart—and come back with a connection that feels stronger for the effort.

Non-sexual touch routines

The little things you touch—the ones that aren't sexual—can do a lot of lifting when you're rebuilding closeness after deployment or stressful tours. Think of non-sexual touch as a short, reliable signal that says: "I see you. I'm here." It's low drama, high impact.

Why Non-Sexual Touch Matters

When words are clipped by fatigue or conflict, a brief physical contact communicates support without requiring a perfect script. A quick hug can reduce tension; a palm on a shoulder can steady someone mid-story. For veterans who are used to non verbal cues in the field, these small touches can feel familiar and grounding.

Daily Moments That Add Up

Make a handful of tiny rituals part of normal life. Practical examples:

- Morning reset: two-second hug before stepping out the door—no speech required.
- Check-in squeeze: while talking about the day, reach for their hand and give a gentle squeeze to signal attention.
- Wind-down rub: five minutes of a light back rub after dinner to ease shoulders and shut off adrenaline.

Try the 'Touch Break' experiment

Label it, schedule it, and see how your home life shifts. A "touch break" is a deliberate pause to reconnect physically for a few seconds. Set gentle reminders for yourself the first week—an alarm at midday or a sticky note on the coffee machine—and do one of these:

- A forehead kiss while passing in the kitchen.
- Five seconds holding hands on the couch.
- A pat on the back and a quick "good job" after a small victory.

Rebuilding closeness with consistent gestures

Restoring intimacy often takes patience. Small, repeated physical cues rebuild trust faster than a dramatic, one-off grand gesture. Use these moves to:

- Re-anchor each other after a rough day.
- Show solidarity when one of you faces hard memories or stress.
- Open doors for deeper talk later, because physical safety often precedes emotional safety.

Practical integration tactics

Make non-sexual touch normal, not staged.

- Sit closer during TV time. If you're both scrolling, nudge in and let knees touch.
- Offer comfort when needed: a hand on the back during a tough phone call, an arm around the shoulders while listening.
- Be spontaneous sometimes: a surprise hug from behind or a forehead kiss—small surprises matter.

Prompts for reflection and dialogue

Reintegration Reflection: Which three non-sexual touches feel most natural to you? Rank them.

The "Love Tank" Check: Once a week, ask each other if your "touch tank" is full, low, or empty. What small touch would refill it?

Ranking Needs: Which situations make you want touch most—stress, celebration, boredom? Share examples.

Small, intentional touches become a language you both learn to use. For veterans and their partners, these simple signals can create a steady thread of comfort and connection during and after deployment. Try them, jot down what changes, and use the prompts above to build a routine that fits your life.

Communication during relocations

Chapter: Moving Day Protocols — Keeping Each Other in the Loop

Military moves throw a lot at a couple: timelines that change overnight, a garage full of labeled boxes, and the odd feeling that the world is shifting under your boots. Treat the move as a shared mission. That doesn't mean you both have to do everything the same day, but it does mean planning and communication are non-negotiable.

Fostering Open Conversations

Set a weekly "move briefing"—15 minutes where you sit down, look at the calendar, and say what's stressing you out. Use simple prompts:

- What's the biggest unknown right now?
- What help do I need this week?
- One win from last week.

Be specific. If one partner is worried about school enrolment for the kids and the other is worried about shipping the motorcycle, write those down and assign the next step. Tone matters: use a soft opener ("I feel...") and avoid blame. If things escalate, take a five-minute break, then come back.

Prioritizing Couple Connection Time

When you're surrounded by boxes, romance doesn't have to be a production. Try micro-dates:

- Date-before-the-pickup: a take out dinner on a folding table, candles (battery-powered), and no packing talk for 45 minutes.
- Five-minute check-ins: set an alarm twice daily to hold hands,

breathe, and name one thing you're grateful for.

These rituals remind you both that you're more than logistical partners.

Establishing New Routines Quickly

In a new place, small routines anchor you. Pick one ritual to start in week one: a Saturday morning walk, a nightly 10-minute kitchen clean-up together, or Monday coffee at the nearest shop. Make it simple and repeatable. If you both like morning runs, scout a route within the first three days and run it together once—routine beats loneliness faster than waiting for "someday."

Rebuilding Social Networks

Go on offense together. Sign up for a volunteer gig at the base, join a local veteran group, or attend a community meet-and-greet. Bring a teammate mindset: approach these events with the goal of making one new connection, not conquering the whole town. Role-play quick intros beforehand—who says your branch, interests, and one question you'll ask. That removes awkward pauses and makes conversations easier.

Maintaining Existing Friendships

Keep remote friendships alive with structure: schedule a monthly video game night, a rotating "mail call" where one friend shares life updates, or an annual visit plan. Use shared calendars to block time for calls so they don't get pushed aside. If a friend helped during a past move, send a short update and a photo of the new place—those small reciprocations go a long way.

Celebrating Resilience

Mark wins. Unpack one room and celebrate with pizza. Take a photo of your first morning coffee at the new kitchen table. Call out effort: "You handled that landlord conversation like a pro." These moments build a positive record you can flip through when stress returns.

Reintegration Reflection

- Rank three needs (emotional, practical, social) for this move.
- Which one can we tackle this week, together?

The move is messy, but with a system and little rituals, you and your partner can come out steadier and more connected than when you started.

Real-life scenarios and scripts

Understanding the Unique Communication Landscape of Military Couples

If you've lived military life, you already know it's not your typical nine-to-five relationship test. Long absences, shifting schedules, and the mental load of service create a communication environment that needs intentional care. This next section gives straight-up tools—scripts, activities, and quick checks—to help you and your partner talk through separation, reintegration, and the everyday stuff that gets messy when one of you is gone for months.

Common Challenges in Military Communication

Real talk: being apart makes small problems grow. Deployment, training, and temporary duty often mean you miss the little things—inside jokes, bedtime routines, who takes the trash out that keeps smooth days smooth. Add stress from operational experiences, and a service member may seem emotionally distant or shut down. Partners at home may become full-time problem-solvers and caretakers, then feel invisible when the service member returns.

Quick prompt: The "Missing Moments" List — each partner lists three small daily things they miss or notice changed. Share for five minutes, no fixing, just listening.

Triumphs in Military Communication

There are wins here. Many couples get creative: handwritten notes in a sock drawer, scheduled video dates, or voice messages that play while making dinner. These approaches turn limited time into high-quality contact.

Action idea: Set up a "signal"—one-minute voice clips labelled "need a laugh," "tough day," or "big news." Commit to replying within 24 hours when you can. Keep emotions from piling up.

Bridging the Gap: Reintegration and Sensitive Topics

Coming home is joyful and awkward at once. Practical scripts help when both of you are rusty with new roles.

Script starter:

Service member: "I want to hear what it was like here while I was away. Can we talk about the good and the hard so I don't make assumptions?"

Partner: "Thanks. I handled a lot solo, and it felt heavy sometimes. I want to support you, and I need time to hand things back."

Reintegration Reflection: Schedule a 20-minute check-in the first week home. Use open questions, keep tone low-pressure, and take notes—literal or mental—about what needs negotiation.

Adapting Love Languages

The five love languages still work; they just need practical tweaks when distance is in the mix.

- Words of Affirmation in Action: Send short voice notes that say two specific things you appreciate—easier to record than write, and more human than text.
- Acts of Service for Homecoming: Partner at home might prep a "welcome back" drawer with pay stubs filed, favourite snacks, and a list of household changes. Service member can offer to take over a recurring chore for a month.
- Quality Time: Block five consecutive evenings (no screens, no catching up on chores) to rebuild rhythm.
- Receiving Gifts: Think symbolic—photos, a patch-up of a favourite worn item, or a small token with a note about the memory it ties to.
- Physical Touch: Start small; a 30-second hug before bed can reset

closeness after a long separation.

The "Love Tank" Check: Each week, rate your tank from 1–5 for each language and share results—no judgment, just data.

Navigating Civilian Friendships and Family Dynamics

Post-deployment social life can be tricky. Civilians may mean well but not get certain experiences. Practice short role-play phrases to introduce your partner to new circles:

"When I was deployed, we did X. It's different than what you might imagine, and I'm still processing it. If I seem quiet, that's part of it."

Activity: Plan one low-pressure social outing where your partner leads a two-minute story about something ordinary that happened at home. It humanizes both sides.

Closing prompt: "Ranking Needs" — each partner lists top three needs for connection this month. Share and pick one concrete action to meet each need. Small steps add up fast.

Symbols, Rituals, and Homecoming

The moments following a service member's return are charged with emotion and the need for deliberate connection. The transition from separation back to shared life requires intentionality, moving beyond the simple relief of presence to actively rebuilding the partnership. This next part of our discussion focuses on creating meaningful structures and practices that acknowledge the unique experiences of deployment and honor the reunion. We will look at establishing welcoming spaces, designing personal ceremonies, and the importance of open dialogue about the deployment itself. Furthermore, we'll address the gentle process of readapting to civilian routines and the value of celebrating every step, both individual and shared, as you move forward together. Finally, we will introduce a tangible way to preserve your story through a shared memory box, a collection of mementos that speaks to your resilience and enduring bond.

Homecoming rituals and celebrations

Intentional Homecoming Rituals

The first hours and days after a service member returns are full of relief, awkwardness, joy, and a little chaos. That mix is normal. What helps is planning a few intentional rituals that make reconnection easier and clearer for both partners. These don't have to be elaborate; they should simply mark the transition from separation mode into partnership mode.

Creating a Welcoming Haven

Think of the homecoming as a short, concentrated reset. Small, tangible things tell your returning partner, "You belong here." Some practical ideas:

- Cook their favourite comfort meal (bonus points for the exact recipe they grew up with).
- Set up a quiet corner with soft lighting, a throw blanket, and headphones — a place to sit without questions for a while.
- Assemble a photo album or a simple slide show of the kids, friends, pets, and silly moments. Put it where you can watch it together later.
- Deliver a stack of handwritten notes or a video montage you made during the separation. Read one out loud together.

Reintegration Reflection (prompt): Before the first dinner, ask, "What do you need most tonight: space to decompress, a low-key check-in, or a big celebration?" Write the answer down and agree on a time to revisit it.

Developing a Shared "Welcome Home" Ceremony

A repeatable ceremony creates predictability and emotional safety. Ideas you can adopt or adapt:

- A "first meal" routine: always eat the same starter or dessert during reunions.
- An exchange: a small token from the time apart — a patch, a stone, a note — and a sentence about why it mattered.
- Lighting a candle or ringing a bell together before the first conversation.
- A family circle: everyone shares one positive moment from the deployment period.

The "Love Tank" Check (prompt): Each partner names one thing that filled their "love tank" while apart and one thing they want now. Short answers only.

Honoring the Deployment Experience

Give the deployment its own space. That means listening without fixing and asking questions that invite, not pressure. Useful moves:

- Ask open-ended prompts like, "Tell me one thing that surprised you," or "What was the hardest day?" Pause. Let silence do some of the work.
- Validate feelings: 'That sounds like it wore you down' is often better than offering solutions.
- If stories are too heavy, agree on timing: a short debrief now, a longer talk later, or a therapist-facilitated session if needed.

Graceful Reintegration into Daily Life

Practical patience beats good intentions. Set short-term agreements: who handles which chores for the first two weeks, how to manage sleep schedules, and when to check in about work or schooling. Keep expectations low and flexible.

Ranking Needs (prompt): Each partner lists three non-negotiables for the first month at home. Compare lists and trade or negotiate one item.

Celebrating Milestones

Mark endings and new starts. Celebrate the final day of deployment with a modest ritual, acknowledge individual wins that happened while apart, and plan at least one shared treat — a weekend away, a picnic at a favourite spot, or even a quiet movie night with no phones.

Wrap-up prompt: Schedule one shared activity within the first 30 days that is just for fun and undemanding. Put it on the calendar now.

These rituals, small and repeatable, help turn a chaotic reunion into a steady, human reconnection. Try a few, tweak them, and keep what actually helps you both settle back into life together.

Memory boxes and memorabilia

Create a Shared Memory Box

If you're into keepsakes and sentimental clutter (guilty as charged), a shared memory box gives you one curated spot for the stuff you actually want to keep. Think of it as a physical scrapbook with fewer glue sticks and more emotional pay-offs. Here's how to put one together so it actually helps you reconnect instead of collecting dust.

Gather Individual and Shared Symbols

Start by collecting items that mean something to each of you and that represent the life you share now. Concrete examples:

- Photographs: a candid from the first reunion, a goofy selfie from a backyard cook out, a formal unit photo.
- Military pieces: unit patches, dog tags, a challenge coin, a bootlace from dress shoes.
- Personal mementos: a small piece of jewellery, a ticket stub from a show you saw together, a handwritten letter saved from deployment.

Reintegration Reflection: Sit down with your partner and spread your items out. Each picks one item and explains why it matters. Ask: "What feeling does this bring up for you?" And "Did this moment change how you see us?"

Acknowledge Unseen Sacrifices

Some of the heaviest things aren't obvious. Add tokens for the invisible work: a coffee cup to represent long late-night shifts, a folded napkin representing missed dinners, a blank index card to stand for the nights you held it together when you were exhausted. Naming the small, unseen costs helps both partners face them aloud.

Share and Understand Meanings

Make time to tell the short story behind each item. That freed-up detail—who gave it, where it was, what you were feeling—bridges a lot of silent distance. If your partner pauses or gets quiet, give space; sometimes listening is the best part of the ritual.

Use Memorabilia as Conversation Starters

Pick one object each week to prompt a 10–15 minute talk. Example prompts: "Tell me about the day you got this," or "What scared you most that week?" Keep it low pressure—no interrogation, just curiosity.

Document Civilian Reintegration

Include artifacts that mark your new civilian milestones: diplomas, job offer letters, photos from the first civilian pay check celebration, the first tool or sports gear tied to a hobby you picked up. These remind both of you that a new life chapter is being written, not erased.

Establish Memory Box Rituals

Create rituals around the box: a quarterly review night, adding one new item on anniversaries, or a quiet solo hour where each person writes a short note and places it inside. The box becomes both archive and living practice.

Honor Individual Contributions

Make sure both partners get equal space and say in what goes in. Label items with dates and one-sentence notes so future you won't guess the story. Ownership matters—this is a shared spot, not a museum run by one person.

The 'Love Tank' Check: Once a month, pull an item and use it to talk about what filled or emptied your "love tank" that month. Fast questions. Honest answers. That small habit keeps the box active and useful—just like you planned.

Symbolic gifts and tokens

The Power of Symbolic Gifts and Tokens

Small objects can carry big meaning. After deployments or long stretches apart, a token can do what words sometimes cannot: make absence feel smaller and connection feel real again. Think of symbolic gifts as tiny anchors—one glance, one touch, and a memory, an emotion, or a promise surfaces.

Celebrating Shared Memories and Future Aspirations

- Concrete idea: Build a "firsts" photo frame. Fill it with photos of your first R&R, first home-cooked meal after service, and a snapshot from a meaningful civilian milestone. Label each photo with a date and a one-sentence memory to prompt stories later.

- Future-focused token: Get a map and mark a place you both want to visit. Stick a small pin in it and place the map in your shared space. It's a visual nudge toward planning together and provides a hopeful object to discuss when plans get stalled.

Reintegration Reflection: Which three shared memories would you choose for a frame? What travel pin would you place on a map, and why?

Honoring Individual Achievements and Personal Growth

- Recognition plaque alternative: Create a small, framed certificate that names an achievement—promotions, certifications, even personal growth like 'Completed 12week counselling.' Hang it where it can be seen.

- Growth-support gift: Buy a book or enrol your partner in a class that aligns with an interest they picked up in service. Attach a note: "Keep growing—I've got your back."

Prompt: What achievement of your partner should be publicly acknowledged at home? How would that acknowledgement lift them?

The Significance of "Found" Gifts

- Found gifts work because they show attention. A smooth pebble from a deployment beach, a pressed wild flower from a layover, or a small shell tucked into a care package says, "I was thinking of you in that place."
- Action: Start a "found" jar. Drop in one small found object each month with a sticky note describing where it came from and why you saved it.

The "Love Tank" Check: Which found object would you most want to receive, and what would it tell you?

The Intention Behind the Gift

A gift's real power is the thought that went into it. A simple token with a handwritten line—'For tough days' or 'For our next chapter'—can mean more than anything expensive. Before choosing a token, ask: What memory or promise should this item carry? How will it help when words aren't enough?

Partner Prompt: Write one sentence explaining the intention behind a gift you'd give your partner. Share it aloud and listen to their response.

Small, meaningful tokens help stitch daily life back together after separation. They're practical, affordable, and human—tools for keeping each other close when schedules, miles, and post-service rhythms pull you in different directions.

Deployment- and memory-based rituals

Acknowledging the Impact of Deployments on Your Partnership

Deployments change things. Not overnight, but in ways that pile up—missed birthdays, different rhythms of sleep, movies watched alone, stories that don't get told until months later. Those gaps and events shape how you show up with one another afterward. Naming that reality matters; it gives you something to work on instead of pretending nothing shifted.

Understanding the Emotional Fallout

Expect a cocktail of emotions: anxiety, relief, quiet joy, residual anger, and sometimes numbness. One partner may seem fine and then snap back into stress when a memory appears. Combat or high pressure missions can leave particular wounds—startling reminders, trouble sleeping, or avoidance of certain topics. Talk about specifics: what moments were hardest? Which days felt like the longest? Concrete acknowledgment helps move feelings out of the shadow.

Creating a Safe Space for Shared Experiences

Set aside time—non-negotiable—to talk about the deployment. Call it a Debrief Date: 30 minutes with phones off, one person speaking for five minutes while the other listens, then swap. Use prompts:

- Reintegration Reflection: "What surprised you most about coming home?" And "What did you need that you didn't get?"
- The 'Love Tank' Check: each partner rates connection on a 1–10 scale and names one thing that would add two points this week.

When someone shares something raw, respond with simple validation: "That sounds awful," or "I hear you." No fixing unless asked.

Deployment- and Memory-Based Rituals

Turn hard memories into shared markers. Try these:

- Make a memory book with keepsakes (letters, ticket stubs, photos) and write one line under each item about why it mattered.
- Start a small homecoming ceremony: first meal is the returning person's favourite dish, and the other reads a short letter aloud.
- Keep a shared journal during absences. After return, read it together and highlight entries that show growth.

Symbolic Gestures and Homecoming Routines

Pick a symbol that means something only to you two—a coin, a patch, a phrase—and use it when stress hits or when celebrating reunions. Establish a reliable routine for the first week home: a morning walk, a slow dinner, a no-phones movie night. These small rituals signal safety and consistency.

Navigating Challenges and Celebrating Successes

When memories include trauma, consider professional help together—couples therapy or a peer-support group of fellow veterans. Build a "wins" list: small victories like sleeping through a night, talking about a tough memory, or completing the memory book. Mark these wins publicly at home—put a note on the fridge or announce them over that first homecoming dinner. Those acknowledgment stack up into real healing.

Quick prompts to try tonight:

- Ranking Needs: each partner lists top three needs (emotional, physical, practical) and trades lists.
- Reintegration Reflection (written): one paragraph on "What I missed most" and one on "What I'm nervous about now." Share them aloud.

Working through deployment impact isn't instant. But with time, intention, and a few rituals, you can convert rupture into shared strength—and laugh about the little oddities of reintegration along the way.

Gift etiquette and recognition

The Power of Gifts in Military Life

Gifts are often treated as small currency of care—especially when one partner is on the road, at sea, or on a rotation that makes ordinary time together scarce. In military contexts, a present doesn't just mark an occasion; it can stitch a gap, say "I saw you" after a promotion or tough stretch, and serve as a portable piece of home.

Acknowledging Accomplishments

Milestones in service deserve clear recognition. Think beyond the generic card: a stamped challenge coin turned into a key chain to mark a deployment; a shadow box with patches and a deployment ribbon for a promotion display; or a personalized notebook engraved with call-sign or unit number for a class graduate. These items work because they connect to shared values and inside jokes—two things military couples often keep close.

The Art of Appreciation

The best gifts carry thought, not price tags. A laminated "mission time line" of the couple's major dates (first meet, first deployment, first homecoming) might be low cost but huge on meaning. When you receive something meaningful, say what it meant—"That coin reminded me of the story you told about guard duty; I keep it by my bedside"—and you make the giver feel seen.

Effective Expression of Gratitude

Try short, specific rituals: a voice message describing how you use the gift, or a handwritten note tucked into a uniform pocket. For long separations, send a photo of the item in everyday use—text plus image equals proof that the gift isn't gathering dust. These small communications reinforce effort and deepen connection.

Gift Preferences and Open Communication

Have a brief "gift chat" with your partner. Ask: What makes you feel appreciated—practical, sentimental, humorous? Rank three favourites and three dislikes. Keep a joint list on your phone so when milestones arrive you're not guessing. This prevents misfires and helps both partners hit the mark.

Symbolic Gifts and Recurring Rituals

Create repeatable rituals by giving a custom bracelet after each deployment, or exchanging a postcard from wherever the deployed partner is. Place the postcards in a shared jar for reading on the next homecoming. These recurring tokens build a visible ledger of shared survival and joy.

Prompt — The Gift Inventory

Partner exercise: each list three gifts that made you feel most seen. Discuss why—practical use, memory, or joke—and decide together on one ritual gift to use for the next milestone.

Gifts won't fix every tension, but used well they remind both partners that attention and thought travel with them, even when they cannot.

Shared rituals and religious/ secular practices

The Power of Rituals in Military and Post-Service Life

Rituals give two people a shared rhythm when orders, deployments, and paperwork try to steal the beat. They act like a checkpoint: small, repeatable, comforting. Think of them as habit-based anchors that keep partners connected when schedules, locations, and civilian life all change.

Adapting Existing Traditions

Start by looking at family customs you already have. Pull the parts that matter and remix them. If one partner's family always had a Sunday gravy and the other's had breakfast burritos on holidays, pick a year to do both: gravy burritos, anyone? Concrete option: for your first post-service Thanksgiving, ask each set of parents to bring one dish and add a new item the two of you create together — a signed recipe card tucked into a box becomes the new heirloom.

Creating New Rituals

Sometimes the best rituals are the ones you invent together. Make a short list of possibilities and trial them for three months. Examples:

- Weekly or monthly family game night: rotate who picks the game; loser makes dessert.
- Annual trip or long weekend: pick a theme (history, hiking, food); fund it with a small "adventure jar" where you toss spare change.
- A ceremony for milestones: a simple handshake + a printed certificate for promotions, or a candle ritual after a deployment ends.

Try this prompt with your partner: Reintegration Reflection — each write three small rituals you miss from service and three new ones you want. Share and rank them.

Integrating Religious Practices

If faith is part of your life, put it into the calendar. Attend a service together, schedule a monthly spiritual retreat day, or develop a short morning prayer or intention-setting practice you both say before sleep. These actions build a shared moral compass and quiet spaces for honest conversation.

Embracing Secular Practices

Not religious? No problem. Volunteer together once a month, join a community class, or pick a personal-development book to read and discuss over coffee. These activities create shared values and memories outside of duty or work.

Celebrating Milestones and Achievements

Make celebrations predictable so they offer comfort. Use simple markers: a dinner out for a job change, a framed photo for finishing school, a ritual unpacking party after a move. The "Love Tank" Check — monthly, each partner lists one thing they want celebrated and one small way the other can help make it special. Keep it short, keep it consistent, and the rituals will become the glue that holds your life together when everything else shifts.

Journaling and reflection practices

Cultivating Reconnection Through Journaling

If the idea of "writing things down" makes you think of dusty diaries or performance reports, stick with me. Journaling for reconnection is less about neat prose and more about giving your inner thoughts a place to land—especially during the slow, messy work of shifting from military habit to civilian partnership.

Symbolic Reflection

Start by picking an object that represents your service or a shared moment: a challenge coin, a faded photo, a uniform patch, a ticket stub from a first date. Spend one page writing what the object brings up—words, smells, flashes of memory. Then write a second page as if your partner is reading it aloud. What does that change? Try this prompt together and then swap journals.

Prompt: Reintegration Reflection

- Object: ____________________
- What it makes me feel (3 words): __________________
- One story tied to it: ___________________________________
- If my partner reads this, what would they hear? ____________________

Crafting a Homecoming Ritual Journal

Make a small, dedicated notebook for "homecoming" entries. Record rituals you already do and ones you want to keep alive: Saturday morning pancakes, a monthly grill-and-talk, or a quiet ten-minute check-in after work. Note who initiates each ritual and how it helps you feel seen.

Action step: For 30 days, write the date, the ritual you did, and one line about how it landed (calm, annoyed, connected, tired). After two weeks, sit down together and compare notes.

Discovering Identity Outside the Uniform

Use prompts that separate roles from self. Write: "What I did in uniform was _____. What I want people to know about me now is ____." Follow with three small things that make you feel like yourself outside service—gardening, running a business, listening to a certain podcast. For male and female veterans, include self-care entries: 5-minute morning stretches, a grooming habit that feels good, or a small personal reward for hitting a non-military goal.

Unveiling Unspoken Needs and Feelings

Journals are private practice fields. Try a weekly "needs list": write what you needed this week and whether you asked for it. Rank needs by urgency and then bring just one item to your partner in a short, scripted way: "This week I needed X. Can we try Y?" Use the "Ranking Needs" prompt to clarify.

Documenting Acts of Service and Appreciation

Keep a running ledger of acts—big and small. Did your partner handle the car maintenance? Did you fix a leaky Faust? Note date, action, and impact: "Took the kids to practice — felt like a team." At the end of each month, read three entries aloud and thank each other for those specifics.

Aligning Future Visions

Write a joint entry: "In five years we want…" Each partner adds three concrete items (housing, jobs, travel, family rhythms). Then circle items you both put down and pick one short-term goal to script into monthly steps.

Capturing Moments of Symbolic Reconnection

Finally, whenever you have a moment where something clicks—an easy laugh, a quiet apology, a moment of recognition—write it down immediately. These little records become proof that connection is happening, even when the bigger picture feels uncertain.

Prompt: The "Love Tank" Check

- Today I felt close when: ____________________
- One small thing my partner did that filled my tank: ___________
- One small thing I will do tomorrow: _______________________

Using these practices consistently gives you concrete evidence of growth, helps reveal unspoken needs, and creates shared material you can return to when life gets hectic. Treat the notebook like a tool: not perfect, not polished, but honest—and useful.

Love languages in symbolism

Understanding Love Languages through Symbolic Actions

We've spent time writing about symbols, rituals, and journaling. Now let's get practical: how do you turn those symbols into the kind of everyday gestures that actually refill each other's emotional tanks? Gary Chapman's five love languages—Words of Affirmation, Acts of Service, Receiving Gifts, Quality Time, and Physical Touch—translate well into symbolic actions that are especially useful when military schedules, deployments, or reassignments make regular closeness tricky.

Symbolic Tokens of Appreciation

Think small, deliberate, and portable. For someone whose primary language is Receiving Gifts, a customized token can be a daily anchor. Examples: a dog-tag-style pendant engraved with a shared date, a tiny fleece patch sewn inside a jacket that says "home," or a wristband with coordinates of where you first met. For Acts of Service, a laminated "coupon" that promises one chore handled without being asked — laundry, car maintenance, a grocery run — can mean more than a grand gesture. Place these tokens where they'll be seen: taped inside a locker, tucked into a notebook, or slipped into a deployed service member's rucksack.

"Found" Gifts

Found gifts are scavenger-hunt-level sweet. They show attention to detail and time spent listening. If your partner loves books, bring back a battered paperback from a base town bookshop with a note on the flyleaf: "I thought of you." If they collect patches or coins, find one from a place you visited and add a short journal entry about why it reminded you of them. These items are small but signal active presence even when you're apart.

Shared Acts of Service

Acts of service are about picking up invisible weights. Practical examples: create a shared digital checklist where each person logs errands done — oil change, bill paid, school sign up — and add a one-line "why" (e.g., "Did this so you could sleep in after shift"). Rotate responsibilities after transitions so no one feels single-handedly responsible. During reintegration, schedule two 30-minute "house reset" sessions where you tackle clutter together; the shared activation becomes both chore and connection.

Intentional Physical Touch

Physical touch doesn't have to be dramatic. Post-shift, practice a 20-second hug without talking. Keep a "touch token" like a soft key chain that signals permission to initiate closeness: if it's on the night stand, gentle touch is welcome. When distance is a factor, plan a "welcome touch" ritual for return days — a specific handshake, a forehead touch, or a slow, deliberate hug that signals "I'm here."

Words of Affirmation

Short written affirmations carry weight. Leave sticky notes in boots, send three-sentence voice messages describing one thing you admire, or write a two-line letter before a deployment and date it to open on a future anniversary. Try the "Daily One" prompt: each evening, each partner writes one sentence about something the other did that day that mattered.

Rituals and Symbolic Memories

Rituals stitch these acts into something repeatable. Create a weekly habit — a 10-minute check-in call with a ritual opening line, a Saturday breakfast that uses the same mug, or a shared play list named after your transition year. Use your journals to log each ritual and rate how it felt on a scale of 1–5; this gives you a running scorecard to discuss during reintegration talks.

Reintegration Reflection

Prompt: Which of the five languages feels easiest to receive right now? Which feels most neglected? Schedule a 15-minute conversation where each partner reads one journal entry and says what symbolic action from this section they'd like tried this week.

These symbolic actions make love languages visible and doable. Small, repeatable, intentional moves often matter more than perfection—especially when schedules and distance push hard against closeness.

Non-verbal affirmations and gestures

The quiet stuff matters — the face you make when you walk into a room, the way you reach for a mug and hand it over without saying a word. Those are non-verbal affirmations, and for many veterans and their partners, they become the daily code that says: I see you, I've got you, you're not doing this alone.

Listening with Your Eyes and Heart

Start treating your eyes like a second set of ears. Not in a creepy-stalker way, but as a tuned-in observer. Watch for micro-shifts: a jaw that tightens when radio noise starts on the TV, a tucked chin after a phone call, or the small brightening of the face when a certain song plays. Try this quick drill with your partner tonight: sit back-to-back for two minutes and then turn to share what you noticed—an eyebrow twitch, a sigh, any tiny change. Labeling those observations aloud (calmly) — "You looked tired after that call" — lets your partner know you're paying attention without demanding explanation.

Shared Routines: The Little Rituals That Anchor

Routines don't have to be boring. They're the everyday ceremonies that say "we made it through another day." Pick one low-friction ritual and stick with it: a three-minute debrief after supper where each of you says one good and one hard thing about the day; a Saturday coffee ritual where the veteran makes coffee and the civilian partner brings the newspaper (or a play list) — swap roles weekly. These shared patterns act like check-ins: predictable, safe, and calming.

Simple, Consistent Gestures of Care

Make a list of three micro-gestures you can actually do this week. Keep them specific: heat up the mug before handing it over, replace the batteries in the flashlight without being asked, leave a sticky note on the truck dashboard that reads "fuel checked." Small, repeatable behaviours build trust. Veterans often carry a habit of action; channel it into these predictable kindnesses.

Symbolic Acts: Small Actions, Big Impact

This section explores how seemingly minor symbolic gestures can influence perception and motivation.

Think inside-joke tokens: a patch sewn into a jacket hem, a play list named after a deployment nickname, a tiny rock from a favourite campsite glued into a keyring. These items don't need to be expensive — they need to signal shared meaning.

The 'Love Tank' Check — Physical Touch

End the day with a tactile check-in: hold hands for thirty seconds, a shoulder squeeze while watching TV, or a five-minute cuddle before lights out. Physical touch is fast-acting medicine for stress; it lowers pulse and interrupts spirals. Make these moments routine so they become the default reset button when things get tense.

Reintegration Reflection

Tonight, pick one non-verbal habit to start and write down how it changed your partner's mood over three days. Share the notes and make adjustments together. Small, steady changes win the long haul.

Home environment design and space curation

Creating a Shared Sanctuary: Designing a Home that Honors Both Partners' Identities

After we've talked about small gestures and non-verbal ways of staying connected, let's turn to the space you share. For veterans and their partners, the home can signal a shift from mission-driven routines to something calmer and more personal. Think of it as building a base of operations where both of you are welcome, comfortable, and free to be yourselves.

Intentional Design for a Civilian Sanctuary

Start with a simple goal: make the house feel like a place you both want to come back to. Use calming colours—soft blues, warm grays, muted greens to reduce the pull of stress. Bring in natural elements: a low-maintenance plant on the windowsill, a woven rug, or reclaimed wood shelves. If you keep service items or photos, place them with purpose—one wall or a single shelf, so the veteran's history is honoured without taking over every room.

Concrete idea: create a "memory shelf" with a framed photo, a patch, and a small object that matters. Label it together. That small act recognizes the past while keeping the rest of the home open to both of your tastes.

Balancing Shared and Personal Spaces

Designate zones. A living area set up for conversation and relaxed movie nights, and a separate nook for solo recharge. Shared space: arrange seating face-to-face or in a gentle semicircle so eye contact and talk are easy. Personal space: let each person have a corner,—an office, a reading chair, a small workshop,—where they can lock the door or simply unplug.

Personalizing Individual Spaces

Encourage each partner to style their own zone. Veterans of any gender might use these spots for different self-care practices: one might set up a simple meditation cushion and a small lamp; the other a tool board or a hobby table. Let these be evolving spaces that change with interests and needs.

Fostering Open Communication and Togetherness

Create sight lines that let you check in without interrupting—an open doorway, partial wall, or glass panel between rooms. Ask a few practical questions together:

- Reintegration Reflection: What object in the house makes you feel most like yourself?
- Ranking Needs: Which three features help you relax at home (light, quiet, and privacy)?
- The "Love Tank" Check: Which shared routine this week filled your connection meter?

Design is practical care. When your home honours both identities, it becomes a friendly, usable sanctuary—a place that supports recovery, self-care, and getting close again.

Non-traditional reintegration rituals

Creating Personal Homecoming Ceremonies and Reintegration Rituals

A homecoming can be equal parts joyful and awkward — like slipping back into a pair of boots that aren't quite broken in yet. That's fine. What helps is turning the arrival into something personal: a ceremony that fits your couple's history, sense of humor, and needs. Below are concrete ways to build small rituals and plans that mark the return and ease the first weeks back.

Developing Shared Symbols of Reconnection

Pick one or two tangible things that will act as your "we" signal. Examples:

- A small coin or token you carry in your pocket and put in the same dish when you walk in the door.
- A custom photo frame by the entry with one slot reserved for a new snapshot after each reunion.
- A handshake, phrase, or short song you use when saying goodnight for the first month.

Practical prompt: Sit down together and list three possible symbols. Rank them by how comfortable they make each of you feel, then pick the top choice and give it a name.

Designing Reintegration Maps

A reintegration map is a simple shared plan that sets expectations in writing so surprises are fewer.

Include these headings and fill them in together:

- Goals for the first 30 days (sleep routine, shared meals, family visits)
- Stress-management strategies (who will handle late-night wake-ups, a signal for when someone needs quiet)
- Social re-entry plan (which friends to see first, family visits to postpone)
- Intimacy checkpoints (weekly check-ins about emotional and physical needs)

Example: "Week 1: quiet evenings, no big gatherings. Week 2: one family dinner. Week 3: small get together with two friends.". Reintegration Reflection: What would feel too much right now? What would feel insufficient?

Welcoming Home with a Personal Touch

A welcome package is better than another generic wreath. Ideas to include:

- Favourite snacks or a meal that smells like home
- A soft throw or the partner's well-loved hoodie
- A stack of photos or a short handwritten letter about what you missed
- A small, practical item they need (ear buds, a favourite soap)

Prompt: Make two lists—"must-have" and "nice to haves"—then assemble the package together or surprise them with your top pick.

Incorporating Sensory Experiences

Senses anchor memories. Use them deliberately:

- Light: dim lamps or string lights instead of harsh overhead fluorescents

- Smell: one calming scent like lavender or cedar (use responsibly if someone is sensitive)
- Sound: a play list of three songs that mean something to both of you, or nature sounds for background calm
- Taste: a simple comfort meal warmed up, or a special dessert you only bring out for reunions

Try this: The Five-Minute Homecoming Scene — set the lights, start the play list, place the welcome item in hand, and spend five focused minutes together with no phones.

Re-engaging with Civilian Social Life

Plan a slow ramp-up to social activities:

- Schedule one social thing every two weeks at first — coffee with a close friend, a short volunteer shift, a casual class
- Join a local group tied to a hobby you share (woodworking, running club, photography)
- Host a small, low-pressure gathering at home: two friends, simple food, clear end time

The "Comfort Check": After each social event, spend ten minutes talking about what felt good and what felt like too much. Host a small, low pressure gathering at home: two friends, simple food, clear end time.

These rituals and plans are tools — not rules. Use them loosely, keep checking in, and tweak as you go. The aim is to make coming home mean something personal and practical, so the first weeks back carry warmth, clarity, and fewer surprises.

Community rituals and veterans networks

Discover Your Sense of Belonging Through Community Rituals

If homecoming rituals and partner routines helped ground the first steps of reintegration, community rituals are the wider net that catches you when civilian life feels odd. Humans crave belonging. For many veterans, that need was met by unit cohesion. After service, reconnecting with a group that understands military culture can reduce isolation and give practical support.

Connecting with Veteran Networks

Start local: find a veteran group that meets regularly—weekly coffee meet ups, weekend runs, or monthly support nights. Try one meeting with a low-stakes goal: introduce yourself, listen, and hand out your contact info to one person. Online options work too—forums, Facebook groups, or dedicated app where people swap advice about VA claims, schooling, or just venting after a rough night. Example: a Marine vet joins a local "family BBQ" group and after two meetings ends up mentoring a younger vet through filing for benefits. That's mutual help in action.

Getting Involved in Local Veteran Events

Attend a range of events so you can see what fits your comfort level: casual meet ups, formal honour ceremonies, or volunteer work. Volunteer roles are especially powerful—organizing a stand at a veteran job fair, helping set up chairs for a ceremony, or leading a small workshop on resume-building. These roles create predictable tasks (good for anyone who prefers structure) and quick ways to bond. Quick prompt: pick one event this month and set a simple outcome—meet two people, bring a business card, or sign up to help with logistics.

Branch-Specific Organizations

If you miss the language and rituals of your old unit, branch-specific groups recreate that familiarity. Army, Navy, Air Force, Coast Guard, and Marine organizations often host reunions, technical skill-sharing sessions, and remembrance gatherings. Practical move: call your branch group's local chapter and ask about mentorship programs; many have peer-mentors for transition planning and mental health check-ins.

Building Civilian Connections

Branch out slowly: pick a hobby-centred club, a class, or a volunteer position unrelated to the military. Example: a veteran who loves woodworking joins a community workshop and starts coffee conversations that turn into weekend hikes. For couples, try a joint class—cooking, dance, or ceramics—to practice being partners in a non-service setting. Prompt: list three civilian activities you're willing to try this quarter and rank them by interest.

The Power of Mutual Support

When both partners join community rituals, each gains a safety net. Share responsibilities—one handles RSVPs, the other leads introductions—so attending feels manageable. Try this short exercise: The "Belonging Check"—each week, tell your partner one thing you liked about a group event and one thing you'd change. That simple exchange builds teamwork, increases confidence to attend more events, and strengthens individual and couple resilience.

Case studies of effective reintegration rituals

Reintegration Rituals: Honoring Service and Rekindling Connection

Reintegration after deployment is its own kind of mission—lots of paperwork, new routines, and the slow, meaningful work of getting close again. Rituals give you permission to slow down and mark transitions instead of pretending nothing changed. Below are real, doable ways couples have turned "welcome home" into something that actually helps rebuild intimacy and teamwork.

Creating Shared Homecoming Traditions

Start simple and repeatable. Two examples that work in living rooms and barracks alike:

- The Candle and Check-In: Light a candle together at the kitchen table on the first night home. Each person takes five minutes to say one high and one low from the last week. No problem-solving—just listening.
- The Weekend Reset: Plan a short "decompression weekend" within the first month—no heavy planning, just one night away or a technology-free day to reconnect.

Reintegration Reflection: What two small actions could you repeat each homecoming to signal reunion? Pick one for logistics (time/place) and one for feelings (words/ritual).

Symbolic Gestures: Reinforcing Marital Bonds

Small, consistent acts become emotional anchors. Try:

- Exchange of Letters: Write a short note to leave in a boot, a sock, or taped to the bathroom mirror. Make it a ritual to read them aloud together on the first night back.

- Flag or Memory Display: Create a small shelf with a folded flag, a photo, and a mission patch. Spend five minutes together adding a note or memory after each deployment phase.

The 'Love Tank' Check: Once a week, rate how full each other's tank is (0–10). If below 7, pick one small gesture from the list below to top it up.

Establishing New Shared Routines

Routines say, "we're a team again." Ideas that stick:

- Biweekly Date Night: Rotate who plans it; keep to a budget and a time limit so it's sustainable.
- Shared Hobby Slot: Gardening, woodworking, or a two-person workout—schedule 60–90 minutes weekly where phones are off.

Adapting Existing Rituals

Old rituals may need tweaks. If a pre-deployment ritual was reading scripture together every night, try shortening it to five minutes with a focus on gratitude and update moments that reflect life now. Or transform a pre-deployment "care package" habit into a "mailbox of memories" you open together.

The Power of Small Acts

Never underestimate a well-timed casserole, a sticky note with "I saw this and thought of you," or a planned 10-minute check-in after dinner. These are low-effort, high-return rituals that rebuild trust and presence.

Bridging Emotional Distance

Create rituals that acknowledge the service itself: a monthly photo review, a memory book you update together, or a quiet moment on the anniversary of deployment milestones. These acts make space for grief, pride, and ordinary life to sit together.

Reintegration Reflection: Which ritual could help you say: "Your service mattered, and so do we"? Choose one to try this week and schedule a follow-up to talk about how it felt.

Foundations, Prompts, and Practical Tools

Foundational Discovery and Love Languages

We often want our partners to truly know us, not just the surface presentation, but the core of who we are. This deeper recognition frequently hinges on how we express and receive affection—our individual "love languages." Understanding these unique codes can clarify many small frictions and reveal paths to greater closeness.

This next part focuses on making those languages clear. We'll look at how you naturally offer and accept care, and how your partner does the same. We'll also examine your emotional connection, using the "love tank" metaphor to gauge its fullness. Service life presents distinct hurdles and requires specific adaptations in how we show love, and we'll consider those unique pressures. We'll assess where your "love tank" currently stands and pinpoint actions that either fill or deplete it, for both yourself and your partner. We'll also rank your current preferences for receiving love, acknowledging how military experiences might have shifted these needs, and discuss how your service shaped your view of connection. Finally, we'll look at how shared duties and civilian tasks express love, and how quality time and gifts can be deliberately used to strengthen your bond, particularly as you adjust to life after service.

Love languages overview

You and your partner both want to be known. Not the polished, surface-level version that shows up for ceremonies and holidays, but the real kind—the one that feels like someone finally figured out which lever to pull when your mood tanks. That lever often lives in the way we give and receive affection: our love languages. Gary Chapman named five of them—Words of Affirmation, Quality Time, Receiving Gifts, Acts of Service, and Physical Touch—and once you can read them, many small tensions start to make sense.

Foundational Discovery: What Are Love Languages and Why They Matter

Think of love languages as different radios broadcasting love. If you're tuned to Words of Affirmation but your partner only broadcasts Acts of Service, you'll miss each other's signals. That mismatch is not about intent; it's about code. Your primary love language is the code you default to—the way you naturally give and feel loved. Do you write sticky notes that say "You got this" or leave voice mails? That's likely Words of Affirmation. If you plan a weekend hiking route because you want undivided attention, that's Quality Time.

Discovering Your Primary Love Language: How You Naturally Give and Receive Affection

Try this short exercise: list three things you do without thinking when you want someone to feel loved. If they are compliments, encouraging texts, or praise at the end of the day, check Words of Affirmation. If they're fixing something, cooking, or running an errand, Acts of Service is probably close. If gifts show up for anniversaries or just because moments, Receiving Gifts. May be yours. Physical Touch could be hugs, hand holding, or sitting close during a movie. Use these clues to name your primary language—then tell your partner.

Identifying Your Partner's Primary Love Language: Understanding Their Unique Ways of Feeling Loved

Watch what your partner gives freely and what they complain about when they feel low, as signals of their needs. A service member who feels most hurt when weekends are cancelled might be signalling Quality Time. A veteran who keeps a care package stash and lights up when receiving letters could be Receiving Gifts. Create a mini-observation log for two weeks: note how they show affection and what they ask for. Then discuss findings over coffee or during a walk—no interrogation, just curiosity.

The "Love Tank" Check: Gauging the Depth of Your Emotional Connection

Your "Love Tank" is the emotional fuel gauge. Full? You operate from calm and trust. Near empty? You react, withdraw, or nitpick. Ask yourselves: "Do I feel seen, heard, and cared for?" Rate each area (Words, Quality Time, Gifts, Service, Touch) from 1–10. Compare scores and prioritize the lowest three. This simple chart becomes a roadmap for where to pour attention next.

Impact of Military Life on Love Languages: Unique Challenges and Adaptations

Service life complicates bandwidth. Deployments, field exercises, and frequent moves interrupt routines that refill tanks—especially for those whose primary is Physical Touch or Quality Time. Practical swaps help: If Physical Touch is absent, send a worn T-shirt with a note or schedule a nightly five minute check-in call focused only on each other. If Quality Time gets eaten by training cycles, carve "mission-free" blocks in calendars and treat them like briefings you can't miss.

Reintegration Reflection

After a deployment or transition, sit down and ask: 'What felt empty while I was away? What actions filled me when I returned?' Write two things you experienced, then share them. These concrete steps—letters, care packages, scheduled date nights, shared chores—are how couples keep the love tank full and stay connected when life demands too much.

Love Tank concept

Understanding the "Love Tank" as a practical tool

Think of the "Love Tank" as an emotional gauge you and your partner can check—like a vehicle's fuel needle, except you can't just pull over and refuel at the nearest chow hall. The idea is simple: when the tank is full, people feel appreciated, safe, and close. When it's low, distance, irritability, and withdrawal start showing up in small ways that add up fast.

The "Love Tank" metaphor: how it helps in concrete terms

This metaphor keeps things simple. If your partner is snappy after a long day of shift work or distant after a deployment, you're seeing a low-tank symptom, not necessarily a personal failure. That perspective helps you act instead of react. For example: if your partner prefers Acts of Service, a cold dinner after a 12 hour shift can be interpreted as a tank draining signal—so bringing hot take out or handling chores that night is a direct, practical top off.

The "Love Tank" Check: quick assessment prompts

Use these prompts alone or with your partner to gauge current levels:

- Do they start conversations or shut down early? (Full vs. Empty)
- Are they quick to hug or avoiding touch?
- Do they thank you or focus on complaints?
- Are they present during discussions or distracted?

Ranking Needs: discover what fills their tank

Ask your partner to rank the five love languages in order of what makes them feel cared for. Keep it visible—on a fridge, a phone note, or taped to a locker. Then pick one low-effort habit you can do weekly to top that tank. Examples:

- Words of Affirmation: leave one short voice note after a tough day—specific praise beats vague flattery.
- Quality Time: schedule a 30-minute device-free check-in on Sunday.
- Receiving Gifts: send small, meaningful items from deployments or local artisan stalls.
- Acts of Service: take over a recurring task for a week—mow the lawn, deal with a bill.
- Physical Touch: 60 seconds of hand holding in the kitchen, no agenda.

What drains the tank: watch for these behaviours

Common tank-drainers show up as criticism, ignoring needs, too much absence, or taking gestures for granted. In military couples, the same stressors—missed milestones, last-minute orders, long separations—amplify the effect. When a partner bristles at feedback, pause: are they tank-empty or reacting to something else? Address the emptiness first, then the behaviour.

Intentional refills: small actions, regular rhythm

Top-offs work best when they're routine. Try these:

- Deployments: a weekly letter with a silly story and one thing you miss about them.
- Training periods: a care-package checklist they can request—favourite snacks, a photo, a short play list.
- Post-service transitions: plan a quiet reconnection night after a big appointment—no agenda, just presence.

Reintegration Reflection (short exercise)

- List three ways your service schedule made it hard to feel connected.
- Pick two small, concrete acts you or your partner can do weekly

to repair those gaps.

- Commit to a 30-day check: note mood changes, not just incidents.

Recharging your own tank: self-care with a mission

You can't fill someone else's tank from empty. Practical self-care options for veterans:

- Move for clarity: a run, ruck, or gym session to offload stress.
- Keep friendships: a monthly coffee with a civilian friend to practice conversational skills outside the military bubble.
- Creative time: woodworking, writing, or a music session to process emotions.

Final prompt: The "Love Tank" Action Plan

- Rate your current tank from 1–10.
- Share that number with your partner tonight, and ask theirs.
- Pick one action from this chapter to use tomorrow; repeat weekly.

Small, consistent refills beat dramatic apologies. Start there, and watch the tank needle rise.

Ranking needs exercise

Understanding Your Love Languages: A Path to Deeper Connection

If the "Love Tank" helped you notice when feeling low or full, love languages show you the best tools to refill it — for you and for your partner. Below are focused steps that help you rank preferences, prioritize needs, and account for how military service can shift what matters most.

Identifying Your Top Two Love Languages

Start simple: pick the two ways you most like to receive affection. Use a quick mental checklist or take a short quiz online. Then try this Ranking Needs prompt.

Ranking Needs

- On a sheet, list the five languages. Beside each, write one recent memory that felt truly loving (big or small).
- Circle the two that come up most often. These are your top two.

Example: A female veteran might list "Quality Time" because her partner sat up late talking after a hard day, and "Acts of Service" because he fixed her truck so she didn't miss a workday. For a male vet, the top two could be "Words of Affirmation" after receiving a heartfelt deployment letter, and "Physical Touch" when homecomings included long hugs.

Prioritizing Those Needs

Once you have your top two, put them on the calendar. If Quality Time is one, schedule a weekly phone-free walk or a Sunday "mission brief" where you update each other on the week. If Acts of Service scores high, agree on two chores you'll trade off during stressful seasons. Small, consistent actions beat grand gestures once in a while.

Understanding Your Partner's Love Languages

Open the door to honest talk with a short script: "I want to know what fills your tank most. Is it words, time, gifts, help, or touch?" Follow that with a practical experiment: try meeting their top need for two weeks and compare results.

The "Love Tank" Check

- Ask: Is your partner's tank fuller after a week of focused effort?
- Watch changes: more patience, more warmth, fewer complaints.

If their top language is Words of Affirmation, set a daily habit: one genuine compliment in person or via text. If Physical Touch is primary, add one small contact — hand on the shoulder during TV, a hug before bed.

Military Life and Shifts in Preferences

Deployments, long training blocks, or repeated moves can change what feels most important. During separation many people shift toward Words of Affirmation or Receiving Gifts because physical presence isn't possible.

Reintegration Reflection

- After a deployment or transition, ask: Did your top two love languages change while you were apart?
- Try a short swap: the service member practices the partner's language for two weeks post-return (e.g., more talkative check-ins or extra help with tasks).

Concrete adaptations

- For long absences: schedule regular audio messages or short emails labelled "Today I noticed…" for Words of Affirmation.
- For acrimony after PCS moves: prioritize Acts of Service— the partner's less busy handles housing tasks to reduce stress.

Quick Prompts to Use Tonight

- "What two ways of receiving love matter most to you right now?"
- "Which of my actions this week made you feel closest?"
- Commit to one small change for the next seven days and check in at the weekend.

By ranking your top two languages, actively practicing your partner's needs, and recognizing how service life reshapes preferences, couples can refill each other's tanks more precisely — and with less trial-and-error.

Historical reflection prompts

Reflecting on My Service Path: Moments That Shaped Me

If you've ever held a deployment memento and felt a rush of everything at once—pride, loss, a laugh at some ridiculous field fix—you know how small events stack into the person standing next to you today. Below I lay out specific events and lessons from my time in uniform, and then turn those into prompts you can use with your partner or on your own.

Significant Moments and Experiences

One deployment that sticks with me involved a humanitarian mission after a storm tore through a coastal town. We were there to help clear debris, deliver supplies, and set up a temporary clinic. Watching families sift through ruined homes, and then seeing a child grin at a simple box of crackers we handed out, taught me that compassion is practical—it's bringing water, sharing skills, holding a radio so someone can call a loved one. That day reshaped how I wanted to show up for people: less flash, more doing.

Another pivotal time was when I had to face an injury. Suddenly I went from invincible to immobile, at least for a while. The grind of rehab—early mornings of stretching, the frustration of lost capabilities, the small wins like walking without a limp—taught me persistence and creativity. I learned to ask for help and also to celebrate tiny progress markers that used to feel trivial.

Instances of Strength and Resilience

There were missions where everything seemed stacked against us: bad weather, limited Intel, and equipment that decided to quit mid-mission. What got us through was not heroic solo action, but dependable teamwork. In one operation we redistributed tasks on the fly—medics did commas, logistics people helped secure perimeters, and a quiet radio operator became the liaison with locals. Those moments drilled in me that trust and clear communication beat bravado every time.

Reinforcement prompt: Name one task you delegated during a tough period that turned out better when someone else handled it. Why did that work?

Navigating Hard Times Together

When things got rough, practical planning plus emotional check-ins kept us functional. We instituted a simple nightly check: two minutes, no problem-solving—just one thing that went well, and one hard thing. That tiny habit stopped blame cycles and built a rhythm of accountability and care.

Reflection question: Try a three-night version of the check-in. What patterns show up?

Profound Connections and Camaraderie

The friendships from service are different—built under pressure and often very direct. Those bonds taught me loyalty and how to be present without fanfare. One friend called at 0300 because he needed to talk; showing up to listen was more meaningful than any speech.

Love, Loyalty, and Support at Home

These lessons carried over to my partnership. Acts of service in camp turned into making coffee in the morning or taking the car in for a repair so my partner didn't have to stress. We learned to translate battlefield habits—brief, clear updates—into home life as "status checks" that keep both of us informed without turning dinner into a mission debrief.

Overcoming Post-Service Challenges with My Partner

Transitioning out of the military tested us. The practical stuff—finding health care providers, translating VA paperwork into plain steps—was one side. The other was emotional: figuring out new routines, rediscovering clumsy intimacy after long absences, and handling triggers from old memories. We approached it like a small ops plan: list priorities, assign tasks, set a check-in timetable, and give ourselves permission for slow progress.

Shared Memories and Goals

We kept a tradition of writing letters during deployments and still exchange them on hard anniversaries or when work gets heavy. Those letters remind us why we committed to each other and serve as touch points for goals: more shared weekends, a class to take together, or simply cutting screen time at dinner.

Cherished Memory Exercise

Write one short letter to your partner today—something concrete: a specific moment you appreciated and one small promise (e.g., 'I'll handle the next doctor's call'). Exchange and discuss it within 48 hours.

Closing Reflection

These moments—disasters helped, injuries rehabbed, missions completed, nights spent talking—shaped my values. Use the prompts here as practical tools to capture lessons, strengthen daily habits, and keep your connection active. You're not rewriting history; you're putting useful parts of it to work in the life you're building now.

Partner self-assessment

The Foundation of Connection: Individual Self-Assessment

Before we try to give what we don't have, let's do a quick inventory. Think of this as pre-mission planning for your emotional world. If your checklist is honest, simple, and repeatable, you're more likely to show up for your partner in ways that actually matter.

Understanding Your Personal Needs and Preferences

Start by asking: what makes you feel noticed and appreciated? Are you the type who lights up when someone says, "Nice job," or do you perk up when someone sits beside you without saying a word? Rank three must-haves and two deal-breakers. Example: Must-have #1 — consistent one-on-one time once a week; Deal-breaker #1 — repeated dismissal of service-related trauma.

Quick, practical examples for vets:

- Male vet: Try a nightly 10-minute debrief where you say one thing that went well and one that didn't. It's low-stress and offers words-of-affirmation without a long sit-down.

- Female vet: If acts of service are your thing, accept an offer to handle a task when your partner notices stress—then thank them directly for the help so they know it landed.

Primary Love Language Check

Identify your love language honestly. If it's physical touch, that might mean hand-holding during a tough conversation. If it's acts of service, that might mean folding laundry without being asked. Write your top two and share them aloud once this week.

Assessing Your Current "Love Tank" Level

The "Love Tank" is an emotional fuel gauge. Use this quick pulse-check:

The "Love Tank" Check

- Rate from 0–10 how full you feel (0 = bone-dry, 10 = fully fuelled).
- Note one reason for your score (sleep, work, unresolved tension).
- One small refill action you can take in 24 hours (10-minute walk with your partner, a quick "thank you" text).

If you're near empty, don't try a big repair op right away—start with micro-actions that are sustainable.

Reflecting on Your Patterns of Showing Affection

How do you typically give love? Write three patterns (for example: fixes problems, gives gifts, creates structure) and ask your partner whether those actions feel loving to them. Sometimes the very things you do out of care are missed because they're delivered in a different language.

Extending Reflection to Your Partner's Needs and Preferences

Now flip the scope. Spend a short session where each of you names the other's top two needs and one thing that drains you. Try this prompt:

Reintegration Reflection

- Partner A: "When I'm off-duty at home, I need X and I feel drained by Y."
- Partner B repeats back what they heard, then offers one way they'll respond this week.

This practice trains hearing over reacting. It's simple, tactical, and it rewires daily interactions—from civilian friendships to tough post-service transitions—so both of you feel seen and able to give what the other actually needs.

Now vs Next prompts

Now vs. Next: Charting Your Relationship's Course from Service to Civilian Life

Standing at the threshold of leaving military life means your day-to-day will change—the routine, the roles, even the casual banter. That doesn't erase the bond you built; it changes the context that bond operates in. Use this moment to take stock and decide where you want the two of you to head next.

Assessing Current Strengths and Areas for Growth

Start with a candid check-in. Take a quiet hour with coffee or a beer and answer these questions aloud to each other.

- Reintegration Reflection: List three things your partnership handles well (example: you split household tasks, you give clear warnings before stress peaks, you make time for weekly debriefs). Then list three issues that still trip you up (example: one partner feels invisible at family events, money conversations get heated, parenting approaches clash).
- Ranking Needs: Each partner ranks top five non-negotiables. Compare lists. Where they overlap, put a star. Those starred items become your priority anchors for the next year.

A simple assessment tool: draw two columns, Strengths / Needs Attention. Fill in specific behaviours, not labels. "Good communicator" is vague—write "we use calm tones and pause before answering" or "we interrupt each other and text when annoyed."

Defining Shared Post-Military Goals, Aspirations, and Dreams

Once you've mapped what's working, talk about where you want to steer your life together.

- Goal Grid: One partner lists short-term goals (6–12 months), the other lists long-term (2–5 years). Swap and discuss how you can support each other—practical support includes childcare for classes, flexible schedules for job searches, or splitting networking tasks.
- Career & Life Check: Be explicit. If one of you plans to take night classes and the other is job-searching, agree on who handles dinners and weekend errands for a set period. Put it on a calendar.

Exploring and Articulating Individual Identities

The uniform gave you purpose and a community. Outside of it, you need to name who you are now.

- Identity Inventory: Each of you writes five things you enjoy that have nothing to do with service (hiking, woodworking, baking, coaching youth sports, music). Commit to trying one new thing from your partner's list this month.
- Purpose Reframe: Ask, "What would make me excited to get up on a civilian weekday?" If the answer is vague, pick one small project—volunteering, a class, a side business—and test it for three months.

Examining Love Languages and Communication Patterns

Military patterns—direct orders, mission briefs—can carry over into how you give and take affection.

- The 'Love Tank' Check: Once a week, ask: On a scale of 1–10, how full is your love tank? Give one concrete thing the other could do that week to move it up one point.
- Communication Adaptations: If your default is blunt clarity, practice softening with an opening line: "I need to talk about something—can we sit for five minutes?" If your partner prefers indirect cues, try adding brief direct statements like, "I felt overlooked at the event."

Envisioning and Articulating Your Aspirational Love

Paint a short, shared description of what you want your relationship to feel like in two years. Make it specific—no vague platitudes.

- Shared Vision Prompt: Each writes a one-paragraph picture of your life together (daily routine, friendships, weekend rituals). Read them out loud and combine into a single paragraph you both like.
- Action Steps: From that paragraph, choose three concrete habits to start this month—weekly date night, one tech-free hour each evening, or alternating who plans a Sunday activity.

Small, practical moves now make the transition less rocky and more intentional. You've navigated hard missions together; this is another mission with different terrain. Treat it with the same clear-eyed teamwork.

Love language prompts: Words of Affirmation

The words we choose in a relationship can be like field rations: simple, dependable, and surprisingly sustaining when you're running on fumes. After you've sketched out your shared vision and clarified identities, it's time to talk about how you verbally build each other up on a daily basis. This section focuses on practical ways to use affirmation, gratitude, listening, and encouragement to strengthen a post-service life together.

Verbal Affirmation: Call Out the Specifics

Generic praise can feel like a salute without a name tag. Make compliments specific and tied to actions or character. Try this:

- Instead of "You're great," say, "I'm proud of how calmly you handled that call with the landlord today."

Thank you for staying up late with the kids so I could finish my resume; your support helped me stay focused.

Quick Practice: The Specific Compliment Drill

Tonight, each partner names two things the other did this week that made life easier or showed character. No vague statements. Keep it to 60 seconds each. Small habit, big return.

Celebrate Strengths and Efforts

Recognition isn't just for medals. When one of you makes a shift — starting therapy, applying for jobs, reconnecting with friends — put words to the effort. Statements like, "I noticed how steady you were at that meeting; you listened and spoke up when it mattered," validate the work behind the action and fuel more of it.

Expressing Gratitude: Make It Habitual

Gratitude works best when it moves from "sometimes" to "expected." Create low-friction rituals:

- Morning gratitude text: one sentence naming something your partner did or a trait you value.
- Weekly gratitude check: over dinner, each person lists one contribution the other made that week (no repeats allowed).

Offering Encouragement and Validation During Tough Patches

When stress spikes—job hunting, VA appointments, or holidays that used to involve full uniforms and old routines—words can steady a person. Try these scripts:

- "I see how hard you're trying right now. It's OK to be exhausted."
- "You're making progress, even if it doesn't feel like it today."

Active Listening: The Tactical Pause

Active listening is less about solving and more about holding space. Use the Tactical Pause:

- Stop and face each other.
- One person speaks for up to three minutes while the other only listens.
- The listener reflects back what they heard in one sentence before asking a question.

Reflection Prompt — The Tactical Pause Practice

Schedule a 10-minute Tactical Pause this week. Afterward, each of you names one thing you felt heard about and one thing you still want to say.

Reinforcing Identity Beyond the Uniform

Words can help untether a person from their military role and reconnect them to hobbies, talents, and values. Say things like:

- "I love how passionate you are about woodworking; your bench looks amazing."
- "It's impressive how you coached that soccer game — you've got real patience."

Activity — Identity Statements

Write three identity statements for your partner that are unrelated to service (e.g., parent, baker, volunteer). Share them aloud and stick one on the fridge as a reminder.

Small daily verbal practices add up: specific compliments, regular gratitude, encouragement in rough patches, active listening, and affirmations of identity. These verbal tools aren't complicated, but they require intentional use — the same disciplined attention you gave to mission plans can be re purposed here to keep your connection strong as you build civilian life together.

Reintegration Reflection

- What two phrases would make you feel more seen by your partner this month?
- Where can you add a one-sentence gratitude ritual into your week?

Small daily verbal practices add up: specific compliments, regular gratitude, encouragement during rough patches, active listening, and affirmations of identity. These verbal tools aren't complicated, but they require intentional use — the same disciplined attention you gave to mission plans can be re purposed here to keep your connection strong as you build civilian life together.

Love language prompts: Acts of Service

Understanding the Acts of Service: How Military Partners Express Love Through Actions

If compliments and gratitude are the verbal fuel for a partnership, acts of service are the toolbox you both reach for when life gets operational. For many military couples, love showed up as the person who took the late shift with the kids during field training, who packed the deployment care package that included socks and a favorite snack, or who stayed up organizing medical appointments when the other was overseas. Those actions carried meaning: they kept daily life running and told the other person, plainly, 'I've got your back.'

Reflecting on Shared Duties During Service: How Did You Support Each Other Operationally?

Reintegration Reflection: Set aside 10 minutes with a pen and share answers aloud.

- What specific tasks did your partner pick up when you were gone? (Child care, paperwork, house repairs, car maintenance)
- Which of those felt like the clearest sign of care?

Concrete example: One partner handled all school pick ups and teacher emails during a deployment. That logistical consistency made reintegration smoother because the returning partner didn't have to catch up on every missed detail. "Naming that kind of support out loud helps both people see it as love, not just 'what had to be done.'"

Identifying Current Daily Tasks that Feel Like Acts of Service in Civilian Life

The "Love Tank" Check: Each week, list three small tasks your partner did that filled your tank. Swap lists.

Daily tasks that often double as quiet devotion:

- Cooking a meal when the other gets home late.
- Scheduling a doctor's visit and driving the partner there.
- Fixing the lawn mower or sorting the mail pile.

Actionable tip: Turn one of those tasks into a mini-ritual. If making dinner is often an act of service, alternate "chef nights" and leave a sticky note of appreciation on the fridge the morning after.

Brainstorming Ways to Alleviate Each Other's Post-Service Burdens Through Action

Ranking Needs: Together, rank the top three post-service stressors (job search, health care, paperwork) and pick one small, concrete action you can take for each.

Examples:

- Job search: Offer to proofread a resume and role-play an interview for 30 minutes.
- Health care: Book specialist appointments by phone or drive to the first appointment.
- Paperwork: Set a two-hour "admin sprint" to sort VA forms, with snacks and a timer.

Recognizing and Appreciating "Invisible" Tasks: The Unseen Labour of Love

Invisible work keeps the household and your lives functional. Make a habit of calling these out weekly. A simple, 'I noticed you handled the insurance questions—thank you.'.

Recalling Moments of Unexpected Help: What Acts of Service Made a Significant Difference?

Reflection prompt: Each partner names one unexpected help moment from the last year and explains why it mattered emotionally. These stories reinforce trust and make it easier to ask for help later.

Planning Small, Consistent Acts of Service to Nurture Your Partnership Moving Forward

Small, steady actions beat sporadic grand gestures. Choose one tiny habit for the month—packing lunch one morning a week, rotating car maintenance, or an agreed "quiet hour" where the other handles kid duties. Check in every Sunday: what worked, what felt like support, what didn't?

Practical closing: Keep a running list titled "Acts That Matter" on the fridge or phone. Add items when something helps you breathe easier. Then, when stress ramps up, you have a ready menu of ways to help each other—specific actions, not vague promises.

Love language prompts: Quality Time

Reconnecting with the Meaning of "Quality Time" as a Couple

If deployments, TDYs, and training cycles taught you one thing, it's how precious a few uninterrupted minutes together can feel. That muscle — appreciating time with your partner — may be sore after service, because civilian life brings different rhythms and expectations. The task now is to redefine what quality time looks like for both of you, not to chase an idealized version from the past.

Understanding the Impact of Military Life on Quality Time

Military schedules train you to maximize togetherness when it appears: a single weekend, a few phone calls, a surprise return. Those intense bursts can set the bar sky-high. Post-service, you might expect the same fireworks every evening and get frustrated when routine sets in. Stress, sleep issues, or lingering hyper vigilance can also make being "present" harder. Name those pressure points out loud with your partner — that clears space for practical fixes rather than blame.

Mini-Date Ideas: Small Blocks, Big Connection

You don't need a whole afternoon to reconnect. Treat mini-dates like tactical ops: short, planned, and with a clear objective — to connect.

- 15-minute morning coffee debrief: share one good thing and one worry before the day begins.
- A 20-minute walk after dinner — no phones, no planning talk, just what you noticed today.
- Cook one new recipe together on week nights; assign one person to be sous-chef and the other head chef for the night.

These are easy to schedule and consistently doable. Log five mini-dates this month and compare how you felt after each one.

Shared Activities that Create Presence

Choose activities that demand attention together rather than parallel scrolling. Try one of these and commit to doing it for a month:

- Take a single cooking class (in-person or virtual) and recreate the dish at home the following week.
- Attend a beginner's yoga or meditation session twice a week — even veterans who think "meditation" sounds soft often report improved sleep and calmer conversations.
- Pick a "try-new-food Saturday": each month one partner chooses a cuisine neither of you usually eats.

Shared learning gives you new, neutral ground to talk about and laugh over.

Prioritize and Protect Dedicated Time

Treat your quality time like an appointment with a commander: put it on the calendar and enforce boundaries.

- Block two hours on a weekend as protected couple time. If work intrudes twice, renegotiate immediately.
- Create a tech-free 30-minute buffer when you get home from work so transition stress doesn't bleed into the evening.
- Agree on "no-response" rules for work messages unless it's a true emergency.

These safeguards reduce sneaky intrusions and make the time you do have more meaningful.

Create Distraction-Free Moments

Distraction-free doesn't mean dramatic. It can be a five-minute ritual that signals "we're together now."

- The "Five-Breath Reset": sit facing each other, breathe together for five full deep breaths, then name one thing you're grateful for.

- Try a weekly "gratitude swap": each person lists one thing they appreciated in the other during the week.

These small practices sharpen presence and increase positive interactions over time.

Cherish and Safeguard What Matters

Quality time builds memories and trust when you protect it. Keep a shared jar or note file: after a mini-date, jot one sentence about what felt good. Revisit the notes when life gets hectic — it's a quick reminder of what you're protecting and why it matters.

Reintegration Reflection

- What did quality time look like when you were in service? Which bits felt realistic to keep?
- Rank three mini-dates you'd be willing to try this month.
- The "Love Tank" Check: on a 1–10 scale, how full does your tank feel around presence and shared time? What one small action could raise it by one point?

These steps are practical, low-friction ways to reconnect. With intention and a little planning, you can build steady, meaningful moments — the kind that outlast stress, schedules, and change.

Love language prompts: Receiving Gifts

Understanding the Language of Giving and Receiving: Gifts as Expressions of Love

If words sometimes get clipped in the transition from uniform to civilian life, gifts can say what a conversation might miss. For many couples who've lived through deployments, long separations, or high-stress assignments, a small object can become a carrier of care, memory, and reassurance. Here we look at how to read that language—and use it on purpose.

Recalling Treasured Gifts: Military and Civilian Examples

Start by thinking back to the items that still make you smile. Maybe it was a handwritten letter stashed in a helmet, a wristwatch that kept time through multiple time zones, or a simple backup pair of socks slipped into a duffel. On the civilian side it might be a handmade coupon for a free night of babysitting, a mixed tape (yes, those exist in spirit), or a hand-stitched patch on a jacket.

Reflection prompt: Reintegration Reflection

- List three gifts—military or civilian—that you still remember clearly. What about each one felt important? Timing, effort, utility, or the exact words written on a tag?

Finding your partner's "found" gift preferences

"Found" gifts are the small, surprising things that say you were paying attention. For someone who misses routine, a thermos with their favourite roast can be gold. For a partner who values practicality, a multi-tool with an engraved date can hit the mark. The trick: notice what they reach for when they're stressed, what they mention in passing, and what they keep near at hand.

Action exercise: The 'Love Tank' Check

- For one week, quietly note three items or moments your partner reacts to positively (a snack, a song, a gesture). Rank those three from "most likely to light them up" to "least." Use the top item for a surprise the next week.

Integrating gift-giving into your reconnection plan

Make gift-giving deliberate and low-pressure. Set a calendar reminder to drop a small token into their work bag, or create a mini tradition—like trading a single note on pay days. For couples adjusting after deployment, consider ritualized small gifts: a postcard from a deployment-support location, a jar of "open when" notes, or a matching key fob that signals "I'm thinking of you" during rough patches.

Concrete habits to try:

- Weekly micro surprise: favourite coffee, a single flower, or a sticky note compliment.

- Weekly micro surprise: favourite coffee, a single flower, or a sticky-note compliment.

- Monthly "found" hunt: each partner brings a small, surprise item that connects to a memory.

Gifts as Symbols of Deeper Affection

A well-chosen gift does more than please the eye; it signals that you heard your partner, that you prioritized their comfort or joy. When gifts are tied to shared meaning—an inside joke, a hardship overcome, a promise kept—they become anchors for rebuilding closeness.

Conversation prompt: Ranking Needs

- With your partner, list five non-material ways you feel loved (time, touch, help with chores, words, gifts). Then assign each one a realistic gift-action you can do in the next month.

These small practices turn giving into a steady, thoughtful way to reconnect—not a one-off grand gesture, but a string of tiny "I see you" moments that add up.

Love language prompts: Physical Touch

Understanding Physical Touch: The Power of Connection in Military and Civilian Life

Physical touch is one of those things you don't fully appreciate until you're missing it—think of the first hug after a long deployment and how it rewires everything. For anyone who's spent time apart due to service, touch has a specific gravity: it communicates comfort and safety faster than words. Below are practical ways to think about touch, talk about touch, and bring touch into everyday life without making it awkward.

The Power of Touch: Communicating Support and Empathy

Touch triggers oxytocin and quiets stress; that's biological, not woo. A hand on the shoulder, a hug after a rough day, or a palm on the small of the back can trigger oxytocin and quiet stress. That's not woo—it's biology. For couples with one or both partners who served, use touch intentionally as part of reintegration: a five-second hug when saying goodbye, a squeeze of the hand in a crowded room, or a calming back rub after a tense breakfast conversation. These small moves send "I'm here" more clearly than long explanations.

Identifying Comfortable Touch: Discussing Preferences and Boundaries

Comfort with touch changes. Someone who was fine with long cuddles before deployment might shy away afterward because of stress responses or simply relearning closeness. Schedule a short check-in—five minutes with no devices—where each person answers three quick prompts:

- Reintegration Reflection: What kinds of touch felt good before your time away? Which feel different now?

- Ranking Needs: Rank these from 1 (most wanted) to 5 (least): holding hands, hugs, cuddling, back rubs, intimate touch.
- The "Love Tank" Check: How many supportive touches a day/week do you need to feel connected?

Use these answers to set clear boundaries. Example: "I'm okay with hugs and holding hands in public, but I need a heads-up before more intimate touch tonight." Keep the language simple and kind.

Building Safety Through Touch: Fostering Security and Emotional Safety

For veterans who carry stress or trauma, touch can either calm or trigger. Create a safety plan: agree on a safe word or gesture that means "pause," and learn calming touch techniques together—slow breathing while holding hands, or a non-invasive shoulder squeeze. If one partner needs space, make a ritual that still signals care: a brief text like "Thinking of you" or placing a hand over the other's on the armrest. Small rituals preserve connection while honouring boundaries.

Integrating Touch into Daily Life: Practical Ways to Reinforce Connection

Turn touch into habit without making it robotic. Try these concrete moves:

- Morning check-in: a two-second forehead touch or a "five-count hug" before you both get out of bed.
- Transition touch: an intentional hug when one returns from a shift or training.
- Walk-and-hold hands during neighbourhood walks or while running errands.
- Public affection micro-habits: a quick hand squeeze in line at the grocery store—low drama, high signal.

Adapting to Individual Comfort: Respecting Unique Needs and Preferences

Every service member and partner have a different tolerance rail. Be curious and patient. If one of you prefers non-sexual touch most days and more intimate contact on select nights, plan for that. Pair touch goals with practical timing: after a shared meal, during a 10-minute wind-down, or before sleep. Check in monthly—what worked? What felt off? Adjust.

Quick Partner Prompt

Tonight, sit across from each other for three minutes and try this.

- Each person names one touch they liked this week and one they'd like less of.
- Agree on one small touch to do every day for the next week.

Write it down and revisit after seven days.

Physical touch is a muscle—use it thoughtfully, listen carefully, and watch how tiny changes can make a big difference in feeling safe, close, and seen.

Reflection and journaling prompts

Approaching Self-Discovery with an Open Heart

You've practiced bringing touch into daily life and talking about boundaries. Now turn some of that attention inward. Self-discovery is practical work, not a therapy buzzword. Think of this as doing a personal inspection—like checking the rigging before a long trip—so your emotional reserves hold up when things get challenging.

Reintegration Reflection

- Set aside 15–20 minutes with a notebook. Breathe, sit still, and answer: What makes me feel most cared for? Jot examples from the last month. Be specific—"Sunday morning coffee and a hand squeeze" beats "affection."

- If you've been deployed, note one moment during reintegration when you felt connected and one moment when you felt distant. What were the actions, words, or lack of them that made the difference?

Foundational Discovery: Identifying Your Primary Love Language

- Quick quiz for yourself: When you're low, what fills you fastest—time alone together, someone doing a chore you hate, a clear compliment, a thoughtful gift, or physical touch?

- Try this concrete experiment for a week: ask your partner to intentionally use one love language (for example, do a household task without being asked). Track how energized your "love tank" gets on a scale of 1–10 each day. That data is honest and useful.

Understanding Your Partner's Love Language

- Use active listening: ask your partner, "What made you feel taken care of this week?" Mirror back what you hear—this shows attention more than a perfect solution.

- Try a role-reversal night: each person practices showing love in the other's primary language. If your partner's main language is acts of service and yours is physical touch, spend the evening doing a dinner-and-kitchen clean-up while asking for a hug after. Note what felt awkward and what felt real.

The "Love Tank" Check

Take five minutes each week for a "tank readout." Each partner states a number from 0 to 10 and names one specific thing that would raise their number by two points.

- Take five minutes each week for a "Love Tank" readout. Each partner states a number (0–10) and one specific thing that would move the number up two points. Keep requests small and doable: "Ten-minute walk" or "I need one compliment after work."

- If tanks are low repeatedly, consider whether timing, PTSD, or stress is draining capacity. Low tanks are not moral failures; they're signals to adjust routines or ask for help.

Reflecting on Past Expressions of Love Given and Received

- Make two columns in your journal: "When I Felt Most Cherished" and "When I Showed Love and It Landed." Under each, list exact behaviours (not vague praise). These patterns reveal both needs and strengths you can repeat.

Journaling About Service Experiences

For veterans, write three sentences linking a specific service event—such as a deployment—to your current emotional response. Example: "During deployment I learned to shut down after bad news; at home I go quiet instead of asking for comfort."

Connecting Service Life to Current Dynamics

- Discuss with your partner one way military life shaped how you argue, apologize, or cuddle. Use "I" statements: "I learned to be brief under stress, so I may seem cold when I'm actually overwhelmed."

Visualizing Your Ideal Post-Service Connection

What three rituals are present— a routine hug, a check-in over coffee, and a joint chore schedule?

- Guided prompt: Close your eyes and picture a weekday evening two years from now. What three rituals are present (a routine hug, a check-in over coffee, a joint chore schedule)? Share this vision aloud and pick one small step to take this week toward that picture.

Practical Self-Love Techniques (Examples)

- For men: after a rough day, schedule a solo 20-minute routine—walk with ear buds, list three wins from the day, then text one good observation to your partner.
- For women: build a "reset box" with a favourite mug, a play list, and five index cards of calming prompts. When triggered, use the box for a purposeful break.

Pair up these personal reflections with weekly partner check-ins. Keep them short, honest, and action-focused. The goal is not grand transformation overnight, but steady, practical adjustments that keep both of your love tanks fuller and your shared life steadier.

Inclusive perspectives and diversity

Celebrating Every Veteran Story

No two service records are identical. Your path through training, deployments, station moves, and post-service life is shaped by family history, region, faith, gender identity, branch, and the people you served with. That variety is a strength. It adds texture to your partnership—sometimes the good kind, such as oddly specific inside jokes, and sometimes the playful kind, like the classic "why are we arguing about socks?" Debate. The point is to notice and respect those differences, not to try to make everyone fit a single mold.

Cultural Backgrounds and How You Say "I Care"

How we show affection often comes from where we grew up. Some households put direct words on a pedestal—"I love you" said plainly—while others prefer showing care through quiet actions or indirect signals. If you grew up where feelings were discussed openly, you might lean into conversations; if your family communicated through doing—fixing a leaky Faust, bringing extra rations to the table—you might send love in the same way.

Quick Prompt — Reintegration Reflection

- List one thing from your family or cultural background that shaped how you show care.
- How does your partner express love differently? One sentence each.

Valuing Unique Contributions

Everyone brings something useful from service into civilian life: discipline, an eye for detail, the ability to stay calm under pressure, or a talent for organizing group BBQs. That includes women and men, LGBTQ+ vets, and folks from varied ethnic and religious backgrounds.

Name these strengths in your household. Call them out when you see them—'Hey, thanks for sorting the car maintenance; your planning saved us a weekend of stress'—and watch gratitude refill your love tank.

Inclusive Self-Love Practices for Everyone

"Self care doesn't have to look like a spa ad." Here are practical examples that work across genders and identities:

- For someone who prefers action: schedule a weekly "mission"—a three mile run, a gear-clean session, or targeted strength workout—then mark it done.

For someone who prefers solitude: a 20 minute unplugging ritual with a play list that soothes or a guided breathing app.

- For someone needing social contact: a monthly dinner with veteran friends, alternating hosts.

These are adaptable—mix, match, and agree with your partner on non-judgemental check-ins.

Prompt — The "Love Tank" Check

- Rate your emotional tank (0–10). What one action fills it by two points this week?

Family Structures and Relationship Models That Fit You

Solo parents, poly households, same sex couples, and multi generational homes.

Family Structures and Relationship Models That Fit You

People come in many family structures—solo parents, poly households, same sex couples, multi generational homes—and each brings unique logistical and emotional needs; for instance, if your partner's family dinners include five cousins and a poodle, plan for the higher energy output than a quiet two person weekend, and make plans that honour those differences rather than erase them.

Communication Strategies That Work

Military communication often values clarity and brevity. Civilian partners might prefer more context or emotional detail. Try a short, practice drill:

- Tactical Check-in (2 minutes): State your main need ("I need help with childcare tonight.").
- Debrief (5 minutes): Offer feelings behind the need ("I'm wiped and want to feel supported.").

This keeps messages clear and gives space for feelings without turning every talk into a briefing.

Prompt — Ranking Needs

- Practice the Tactical Check-in with your partner tonight.

Intimacy and Physical Connection, Your Way

Intimacy looks different across people. Some need touch; others need words; others need shared tasks. Start a weekly "connection experiment": one week is a cuddle-only night, another week is a shared chore with focused eye contact, another week is a love-note swap. Track what actually increases closeness, not what theory says should.

Final Thought

When you honour backgrounds, identities, and personal rhythms, your partnership becomes a practical alliance built on mutual respect and real strategies. Use the prompts, try small experiments, and give one another credit for the ways you both contribute—visible and invisible.

Practical Tools, Journaling, and Prompts Library

The shift from military service to civilian life is more than just a change of address; it's a profound recalibration of daily life and partnership. Having already explored the foundational elements of how you connect – understanding each other's affection codes and assessing your emotional reserves – we now move to the practical implementation of that knowledge. This section provides you with a toolkit, a series of actionable guides and structured conversations, designed to solidify your preparedness for civilian living and deepen your connection. You'll find specific methods to assess your joint readiness for this new phase, tools to identify areas where your partnership can flourish, and frameworks for planning your collective future. We will also address how to adapt the directness of military communication for civilian dialogue and how to intentionally preserve and celebrate your shared experiences as a couple. Prepare to acquire practical strategies that will help you build a strong and connected partnership as you embark on this new chapter.

Ready-to-use check lists and templates

Transitioning out of service brings practical to-dos and emotional check-ins—both matter. Below is a compact, usable Transition Readiness Checklist for couples, designed to help you talk, plan, and act together without turning every conversation into a briefing.

Transition Readiness Checklist for Military Couples

- Relationship Strength Assessment
- Quick exercise: each partner rates these on a scale of 1–5, then compare answers.
- Communication: How often do we talk about feelings vs. Logistics?
- Trust: How confident are we that the other has our back when stress spikes?
- Emotional intimacy: Do we make time for non-mission talk?
- Reintegration Reflection: If one score is a 3 or below, schedule a weekly check-in for four weeks. Use that time to practice active listening—one person speaks for five minutes without interruption while the other reflects back what they heard.
- Love Language Preference Inventory
- Short tool: list your top two love languages from Chapman's five (words of affirmation, quality time, receiving gifts, acts of service, physical touch).
- The "Love Tank" Check: each week, pick one action that fills your partner's tank. Examples:
- Words of affirmation: leave a sticky-note on their gear bag with a specific thank-you.
- Quality time: block 30 minutes after dinner—no screens, just a

walk or coffee.

- Acts of service: handle a chore they hate for a week (garbage duty, paperwork).
- Receiving gifts: small, meaningful items tied to recent conversations.
- Physical touch: brief, consistent gestures—hand on the small of the back when passing.
- Reflection prompt: Which action was easiest? Which felt awkward? That tells you where habit needs adjustment.
- Communication Adaptation Template
- Ground rules to try: 1) Use "I" statements, 2) Pause before replying, 3) Ask one clarifying question before defending.
- Script example for tense topics: "I feel anxious about X. Can we spend five minutes listing solutions before we decide?"
- Role-play drill: once a week practice a tough conversation where one partner plays the worried civilian version and the other answers as the veteran adjusting to new schedules. Switch roles.
- Practical Considerations for Transition
- Housing and relocation: Have a short list of three possible towns with pros/cons (jobs, schools, commute, community). If planning a PCSstyle move, create a moving checklist with deadlines—research neighbourhood: 60 days; visit: 30 days; secure lease/sale: 15 days.
- Employment and education: Each partner drafts a 90-day career plan—target job types, networking steps, certifications needed. Example: former mechanic signs up for a commercial driving course, books two informational interviews, and applies to five openings in 90 days.

Financial Planning: Build an emergency fund target (three months of essentials). Create a joint budget the first month out with categories: housing, food, healthcare, debt, savings. Use one app or a paper binder—

whatever you actually use.

- Healthcare and insurance: Gather current medical records, list medications, and check TRICARE transition dates. Book primary care and mental health intake appointments within 90 days of separation.

Final prompt for the two of you: Rank your top three immediate needs (shelter, income, healthcare, emotional support, legal paperwork). Call this "Ranking Needs" and put it on the fridge. Revisit in 30 days and see which moved up or down. Small, regular checks cut down on emergency scramble, and increase calm control—exactly the kind of mission planning that works in civilian life too.

Conversation scripts and communication guides

Intentional Communication: Structured Conversation Scripts for Military Couples

Think of structured conversation scripts as a compact formation drill—rules, roles, and a clear plan, so neither partner gets caught in unintended conflict from a stray comment. These scripts give you words to start with, ways to listen, and steps to finish without leaving emotional debris in the room.

Quick Script: The Check-In (5–10 minutes)

- Leader: "Right now I'm feeling ___ about ___." (name the feeling and the subject)
- Partner: Paraphrase: "What I hear you saying is ___." (no rebuttal)
- Leader: Add one need or request: "I need ___ from you this week."
- Partner: Respond with one doable action: "I can ___ by ___."

Why this works: short, direct, and limits spirals. Try it weekly during coffee or while packing a deployment bag.

Love Languages Applied: Small, Specific Moves

Use your language list and try concrete acts for a week. Keep it playful and measurable.

"Text one specific praise each day—'I was impressed when you fixed the fence.' Not vague; names, actions, why it mattered."

- Quality Time: Block 90 minutes and do zero planning except a shared play list and one old photo album.
- Receiving Gifts: Pick something under $15 that maps to a

memory—MRE snack, an old unit patch, a paperback from a base exchange.

- Acts of Service: One offer that gets logged: "I'll take the car in for inspection Saturday at 10.""
- Physical Touch: Start with non-sexual contact routines: two hugs after work, hand on the shoulder during TV, ten-second hold when saying goodbye.

Shared Post-Military Goals: One Conversation Sheet

Use a single sheet with three columns: Short-Term (1 year), Medium-Term (3–5 years), Non-Negotiables. Fill it together in 20 minutes, then pick one joint action for the month. Example prompts:

- What job or training will we pursue?
- Where are we willing/unwilling to live?
- Which family needs come first?

Individual Identity Beyond the Uniform

Losing the uniform doesn't mean losing self. Make a "Me Map": three boxes—Hobbies, Strengths, Roles I Want. Spend 15 minutes each and swap maps. Concrete examples:

- Hobbies: Relearn a musical instrument, join a veteran woodworking class.
- Self-care: Sleep schedule, weekly therapy, 30-minute solo runs or yoga.
- Personal growth: Enrol in a certification, volunteer at a youth program.

Understanding Giving Styles

Name your giving style out loud—Practical, Emotional, or Experiential—and give one example of how you give and how you prefer to receive. Try a week where each partner intentionally gives in the other's style at least twice.

The "Love Tank" Check

A quick weekly ritual:

- Each partner ranks their tank 0–10 and names one thing that filled it this week and one thing that drained it.
- Reflection questions: What small support would raise your tank by two points? What can we stop doing that costs points?

Adapting Communication for Service-Specific Challenges

Customize scripts to your experiences. Example for someone with long deployments:

- Pre-deployment script: Top three stress triggers, top three support actions needed, emergency contact plan.
- Post-deployment reintegration script: One daily question for two weeks—"How are you sleeping?"—And one shared task to rebuild routine.

Symbolic Gestures That Stick

Create rituals with meaning: a departure coin exchange, a "welcome home" play list, or a monthly ritual dinner where one partner cooks a recipe from the other's original hometown. Small, consistent rituals anchor connection when schedules get messy.

Reintegration Reflection (prompt)

- What one communication habit would make coming home less tense?
- Which giving style feels most natural to you, and how will you try the other partner's style this month?

These tools are short, repeatable, and practical—designed for people who like check lists but also want emotional safety. Try one script and one ritual this week, compare results, and adjust.

Decision-making templates

Establishing Collaborative Decision-Making Frameworks

Okay—so you've talked about love languages, rituals, and keeping each other's "love tanks" topped off. Now for the things that actually keep a household running: decisions. Big ones. Small ones that spiral into big ones. Putting a simple, repeatable framework in place turns disagreements about where to live or how to spend a bonus into teamwork instead of turf wars.

Aligning Future Aspirations: The Shared Goals Template

Start with a short, concrete template you can fill out together on a weekend afternoon (bonus points if there's good coffee or your favourite take out). Each partner lists:

- Three individual hopes for the next 1–3 years (career, school, travel)
- Two values that matter most (stability, adventure, proximity to family)

One non-negotiable

Keep the document somewhere visible—on the fridge or a shared document—and review it every six months.

Quick prompt: Reintegration Reflection — After a deployment or PCS, take 30 minutes to update this template together. What changed? What stayed the same?

Developing Joint Financial Planning Tools

Money talks can sound like enemy fire. Make them short and tactical.

Budgeting: List net income, fixed monthly bills, and three variable categories (food, transportation, fun).

- Debt Management: List debts highest to lowest interest. Agree on monthly payoff amounts and which one gets the extra payment when there's spare cash.
- Investment Strategy: Decide risk level (conservative, moderate, aggressive) and choose one automated action—monthly contributions to a retirement account or brokerage.

Practical example: If one partner has VA education benefits coming, plan how that will affect income and timeliness before starting a degree.

Constructive Conflict Resolution Templates

When tempers flare, use a short Conflict Resolution Template:

- Identify the Issue (one-sentence statement)
- Each person states their perspective for two minutes—no interruptions

Ask: What do we each need right now? Ranking Needs exercise

- Brainstorm two options and pick one to try for 30 days
- Check-in date: calendar it now

Keep it tactical: if the disagreement is about childcare or chores, assign specific tasks for two weeks, then revisit.

Intentional Family Time Planning Template

Monthly: One planned outing or date night (pick a date now).

- Weekly: Two 30–60 minute windows for focused connection (phones off)
- Activities: Rotate who picks the activity—hike, board game, and couch buddy workout.

- Goal: Name one aim for the time (laugh together, discuss plans, teach the kids a skill).

The 'Love Tank' Check: At each weekly check-in, rate emotional capacity 1–5. If anyone is under a 3, prioritize recovery actions—rest, small acts of service, or a quiet hour.

Putting it into practice: pick one framework (goals, finances, conflict, or family time) and spend 45 minutes implementing it tonight. Small systems reduce stress, cut down arguments, and get you moving toward the life you both want—post-service or not—with much less friction.

Relationship-building activities and mini-dates

Cultivating Connection Through Intentional Activities

Transitioning out of service often brings a shift in how partners spend time together. Small, deliberate acts of connection can make that shift less rocky and more rewarding. Below are practical ways to re-center your partnership around shared moments—ones that fit into civilian schedules and honor what you've both been through.

Rediscovering and Forging Shared Interests

Start with a list: each person names three things they loved doing in service and three things they'd like to try now. Compare lists and pick one match and one new activity to try each month. Concrete examples:

- If both enjoyed being outside, sign up for a weekend taking clinic together.
- If one misses organized team structure, try joining a Saturday recreational softball team or an adult league at the local YMCA.
- If food connected you during deployments, take a hands-on cooking class—choose a cuisine neither of you has made before.

Mini-Tasks

- Reintegration Reflection: What activity from your list felt most "you" when you tried it together? Write a one-sentence note about why.
- Plan one shared outing in the next two weeks and mark it on both calendars.

Mastering the Art of the "Mini-Date"

Not enough evenings free for a three-hour date? Good. Short, meaningful interactions often carry more punch. Examples that fit into tight schedules:

- A 30-minute sunrise coffee ritual on weekdays before work, no phones.
- A surprise picnic during a lunch break at a nearby park.
- A 45-minute "theme night" at home: one cooks, one sets the vibe (music, lighting), then 30 minutes of catching up without interruptions.

Quick prompts

- The "Love Tank" Check: After a mini-date, each person names one thing that filled their tank. If one answer is "nothing," schedule a longer, focused session to troubleshoot.

Tailoring Love Languages to Military Realities

Love languages work if you get creative with the constraints of military life. Ways to adapt:

- Words of affirmation: leave sticky notes on the coffee maker or send a short voice memo between shifts.
- Acts of service: handle a task that triggers stress—renew car tags, call the insurance company, or prep lunches for the week.
- Physical touch: brief daily rituals like a hallway hug, a five-minute hand-hold while watching TV, or a quick back rub before bed.
- Quality time and gifts: build care packages for deployment anniversaries or plan surprise visits that honour work schedules.

Prioritizing Dedicated "Us" Time

Block it in the calendar like a medical appointment. Protect that slot. Examples:

- Weekly "us night" every Thursday from 7–9 p.m., device-free.
- Monthly check-in brunch on the first Saturday: talk finances, plans, and one non-work dream.

Active Listening in Shared Moments

When you're in a dedicated moment, listen with intent. Put the device face down, mirror one sentence back, ask a follow-up question. Try this exercise:

- Listening Drill: One partner talks for three minutes about a current stress or; the other repeats back what they heard, then asks one clarifying question. Swap roles.

Crafting Symbolic Gestures of Your Journey

Small rituals honour service and civilian life together. Ideas:

- Create a memory book with photos, patches, and ticket stubs; add an annual entry on your transition anniversary.
- Design a simple ceremony to mark leaving service—light a candle, share a short statement, or exchange a meaningful token.
- Pick a shared symbol (a bracelet, coin, or plant) that you care for together as a reminder of your bond.

Reflection prompts

- Ranking Needs: Which of the activities above would most help you reconnect this month? Rank top three and schedule one.
- Reintegration Reflection (partner version): How did your service influence the way you prefer to receive affection now?

Those small, intentional moves add up. They create a visible trail from uniformed life to partnered life—one moment at a time.

Journaling prompts for transitions and gratitude

Reintegration and Rediscovery: Navigating Life After Service

Transitioning out of service brings a mix of awkward moments and small victories — like figuring out whether jeans still fit (or don't), and realizing you now have to choose your own uniform: business casual or pajamas? Let's get practical about the actual hurdles and the actual wins.

Challenges and Triumphs of Reintegration

- Identity shift: That clear role you had—mission, rank, routine—doesn't just vanish overnight. You might wake up wondering who you are without it. That confusion is normal; think of it as an invitation to try on new versions of yourself rather than a failure.
- Civilian rhythm: Civilians run on different schedules and social rules. Saying no to weekend invitations because you need downtime is okay — and sometimes necessary.
- Mental health: Old or new symptoms like anxiety, sleep problems, or flashbacks can resurface. Professional help, peer groups, or trusted friends are practical options, not signs of weakness.

Wins you can rely on

- Resilience: The grit you built in service helps you adapt. When a civilian job or relationship goes sideways, you know how to keep showing up.
- Transferable skills: Leadership, clear briefs, problem-solving — those are assets at a job interview and in family decision-making.
- Support networks: A small circle of people who get it will make reintegration less lonely. That could be fellow vets, an empathetic neighbour, or a partner who's learning alongside you.

Lessons Learned and Skills That Stick

Leadership and teamwork translate into being a reliable partner or project lead at work. Adaptability helps when plans change — practice by volunteering for one new small responsibility at home each month (take over the laundry schedule, manage the grocery list, or lead a weekend plan). Time management and discipline: set one non-negotiable daily routine—exercise, quiet time, or a 20-minute reading block—and treat it like a mission.

Love Languages and Personal Growth: Practical Applications

- Acts of Service: For a male veteran who shows care by fixing the car, try swapping roles: schedule a weekly kitchen night where you make dinner together as an act of service to the household. For a female veteran who prefers actionable support, leave a note listing three things you'll handle this week.

- Quality Time: Block out a 45-minute "no screens" window twice a week. Use it for a shared hobby, a quick walk, or a check-in about how reintegration is going.

Shifts in Identity and Core Values

A sense of purpose may feel muted at first. Rebuild it with small goals: mentor a younger vet, join a community class, or volunteer where your skills matter. Value the friendships that came from service; they're anchors. Celebrate your adaptability when plans change and you still make it through the day.

Reflection Prompts

- Reintegration Reflection: What part of your service identity do you miss most? Which habit from service helps you now?

- Ranking Needs: List three personal needs (purpose, calm, connection). Rank them and pick one to address this week.

- The "Love Tank" Check: On a scale of 1–10, how full is your partner's emotional tank? Name one concrete thing you can do this week to add two points.

Celebrate progress. Take a slow step, try a small adjustment, share the outcome with your partner. You're not alone in this next chapter; there are practical moves and prompts to help you find footing and meaning again.

Memory-keeping and memorabilia activities

Create a Shared Memory Box: A Hands-On Ritual for Two

If you've been living off duty for a while, you probably have a stack of loose photos, a drawer full of odd keepsakes, and maybe a shoe box somewhere labeled 'misc.,' Turning that clutter into a shared memory box is a low tech, high feel way to collect the concrete pieces of your life together—what you did, where you went, and who you became as a pair.

Why it matters

A shared memory box does more than hold stuff. It anchors moments you might otherwise lose—letters sent during deployments, the concert ticket you almost forgot to keep, the key fob from the first place you lived together. When stress or old habits creep back in, pulling the lid off the box is an instant map to "we've done hard things and made it." It also gives you a simple ritual to reconnect: pick a time, open the box, and narrate the back stories.

Gathering items: specific ideas

- Photos: one printed 4x6 from a deployment homecoming, one candid from a family BBQ, one selfie from a late-night shift swap.
- Paper keepsakes: handwritten notes, hospital bracelets, program booklets, or a folded boarding pass.
- Small objects: a coin collected on a road trip, a single earring found at a wedding, a unit patch that eventually came off a jacket.
- Tokens of ordinary life: a dried flower from a prom corsage, a restaurant receipt with your favourite dessert, a small tool or memento from your first civilian job.

Practical tips for building it together

Make it a team mission: Schedule a two-hour "box date"—snacks, music you both like, maybe one glass of water or your favourite beverage. Each partner brings items and tells a quick story about one piece they place inside.

- Tell the story: Add a short note (even a sentence) to each item explaining why it matters. For example: "Letter from T—wrote this the night before deployment; read it when I missed home."
- Keep it tidy: Choose a sturdy container with a lid. Use envelopes or small zip bags and label by year or theme ("Homecomings," "First Apartment," "Kids").
- Accessibility: Store the box where you can get to it without climbing a ladder. If it becomes an annual ritual, you'll want it handy.

Make it a ritual

Set a calendar reminder—quarterly or yearly—to add new items. Use this time intentionally: review old pieces, laugh, cry if you need, and add a new memory. Try one twist: at each anniversary pick one item from the box to tell your children or a close friend the story behind it.

Prompts for reflection and dialog

- Reintegration Reflection: Which item in the box best shows how we handled a big change together?
- The "Love Tank" Check: Which object makes each of us feel most seen—why?
- Ranking Needs: Pick three items and rank them by how important they feel to your shared history.

This box becomes a living collection: physical proof that your shared life—military years and civilian days—has meaning and momentum. Treat the process like you would a mission brief: clear goal, shared effort, and a reminder of why you keep showing up for each other.

Self-love exercises for male/ female veterans

Embrace Your Unique Self-Love Roadmap

You've created a shared memory box—great work. Now let's turn some attention inward. Transitioning out of service can shake up who you think you are. That's normal. What matters is giving yourself time, patience, and a plan to re-establish a steady sense of self. Below are practical ways to do that, plus prompts to use solo or with your partner.

Rediscover Your Core: Values and Strengths Outside the Uniform

Start with small, concrete steps. Grab a notebook and spend 10 minutes answering these prompts.

Reintegration Reflection

- What three values will I carry forward whether I'm in uniform or not? (Examples: discipline, loyalty, fairness.)
- Which two strengths are mine even when nobody assigns me a rank? (Examples: quick decision-making under pressure, calming others in crisis.)

Example: If you notice "service" is a core value, you might volunteer at a veteran centre or mentor young people. If "precision" is a strength, consider trades, technical certifications, or roles where attention to detail pays off.

Nurture Your Inner Champion: Mindful Self-Compassion

Self-compassion isn't soft — it's tactical. Try this daily routine that takes five minutes.

The One-Minute Reset

- Sit, breathe for 30 seconds.
- Repeat an affirmation: "I did hard things today." Or, for female veterans: "My strength includes my sensitivity." for male veterans: "I am capable and worthy of rest."
- Notice one small win from the day, out loud.

Pair Prompt: Tell your partner one win at dinner—no matter how tiny. They'll be surprised how much that sharing fills the room.

Ignite Your Passions: Hobbies that Stick

You don't need a big budget or a full schedule—just curiosity and a little structure.

Hobby Test Drive (two weeks)

- Week 1: Try three activities for 60–90 minutes each (a painting night, a solo hike, a guitar lesson).
- Week 2: Pick the one that felt easiest to return to and schedule two sessions.

Example projects: Join a weekend woodworking class, sign up for a mixed-level running group, or commit to a community band. For couples: take different classes and swap what you learn—it builds new conversation and respect.

Honor Your Vessel: Body-Focused Habits

Example projects: Join a weekend woodworking class, sign up for a mixed level running group, or commit to a community band. For couples, take different classes and swap what you learn—it builds new conversation and respect.

Quick Body Check (daily)

- Spend a glass of water within 30 minutes of waking.
- Spend 20 minutes moving in a way you enjoy (walk, lift, dance).
- One sleep habit: consistent bedtime, use blackout curtains, or a 15 minute wind down without screens.

Action for partners: Commit to a joint 20-minute walk, three times a week. It's low-pressure and great for talking.

Empower Your Boundaries: Protecting Energy

Boundaries are one of the clearest ways to care for yourself.

Boundary Drill

- Choose one situation where you often overcommit. Practice saying: "I can't take that on right now." Offer an alternative: "I can help next month" or "I can do X instead of Y."
- Rank needs with your partner: each lists top three non-negotiables (sleep, solo time, date night) and compare.

Acknowledge Your Triumphs: Celebrate Often

Keep a small wins jar. Every time you complete a task, master a hobby move, or get through a tough day, write it down. Read them monthly.

Build Your Tribe: Find People Who Get It

Practical ways to connect:

- Join a veterans' meet up around a hobby.
- Attend a civilian class with a different crowd; practice explaining one military habit and one civilian interest.
- Host a low-key dinner with two civilians and one veteran friend—mixing groups lowers social pressure.

The "Love Tank" Check (for couples)

- Weekly, each answers: "What filled my tank this week? What drained it?" Use that to plan the next seven days.

Closing prompt: Pick one small action from any section and do it in the next 48 hours. Jot the result in your notebook and share it with your partner at the next meal. Small consistent moves add up faster than heroic leaps.

Non-sexual touch ideas

The Power of Gentle Touch: Rebuilding Connection and Safety

Touch is often underrated in recovery work, but for many who served, it can act as a fast track back to feeling safe with someone else. Physical contact does more than feel nice; it signals support in ways words sometimes can't. Below are practical, low-pressure ways to use gentle touch to rebuild closeness with your partner—no marching orders required, just human closeness.

Holding Hands: A Grounding and Connecting Habit

Holding hands is simple, but it's also a quick way to switch from 'on duty' mode to "we" mode. Try these concrete moments:

- During a short walk after dinner, make it a habit to link fingers for five minutes. No small talk required—just presence.
- When cooking together, tap your partner's hand and hold for three breaths before moving on to the next step.

Reintegration Reflection: Which five-minute routine could you add to your day that involves hand contact? Try it three times this week and note how your stress level shifts in a journal.

The Gift of a Comforting Back Rub

A back rub can be practical therapy. If you don't know how to give one, here's a basic plan:

- Have the receiver sit or lie comfortably. Use light oil or lotion if it helps.
- Start with long, slow strokes from shoulders down the spine (not on the spine). Spend two minutes warming the muscles, then apply gentle kneading on the shoulders for another two minutes.
- Check in: "Pressure okay?" Small adjustments prevent discomfort.

Action Prompt: Trade 5-minute back rubs after a stressful day for one week. Track which pressure and timing feel best for each of you.

The Power of a Pat on the Shoulder

A quick, intentional pat can be built into everyday life:

- After a briefing-style update about a day at work or a small win, deliver a short, firm pat and a nod. It's an acknowledgment ritual that says, "I see you."

The 'Love Tank' Check: Who in your household responds better to this kind of small, public recognition? Try using it following one accomplishment per day.

Casual Physical Closeness: Sitting Close on the Couch

Proximity without performance—this is where comfort grows. Try these low-pressure experiments:

- Start a "couch minute": on commercial breaks, scoot closer and rest a shoulder against the other. No forced conversation.
- Create a "snuggle signal"—a light elbow bump or a hand on the knee—to invite closer seating.

Reflection: Over a week, notice whether these micro-moments increase your desire to be together in non-task times.

The Reconnection Power of a Warm Hug

A genuine hug at reunion times—walking through the door, leaving for a shift—releases oxytocin and resets tension. Make a quick ritual:

- Two second squeeze on arrival; three second squeeze on goodbyes. Keep it consistent.

Prompt: Try the arrival hug for two weeks and record mood changes on reunion days.

Comforting Touch During Stressful Moments

When stress spikes, a small, steady touch can stop escalation:

- A palm to the forearm, slow strokes on the wrist, or a steady hand on the back of the chair—simple, grounding.

Communication Adaptation: Ask your partner, 'Do you want touch when stressed, or space?' Honour their answer and have a fallback phrase like, "Touch check?" to request permission.

Small physical acts, done with intention and consent, rebuild safety. Try one of these tactics this week, then discuss what landed and what didn't. These are not fixes; they're ways to practice being close again.

Gift ideas and etiquette for veterans

Gifts That Honor Service and Branch Pride

If you want to nod to someone's service without being overly saccharine, pick something that signals you see and respect that chapter of their life. Concrete ideas: a custom challenge coin with the unit patch and a short engraved line from a ceremony, a framed rendition of their MOS patch with dates of service, or a faild issue style watch band in branch colors. For milestone moments — think boot camp graduation, first deployment return, retirement — consider a shadow box with a nameplate and a few meaningful mementos (dog tags, a ribbon, a photo). Small touches matter: include a handwritten note that names one specific quality you appreciated during their service.

Practical Gifts for Everyday Life

Transitioning out of uniform often means being grateful for the little things that make civilian life smoother. Practical but thoughtful: a travel coffee maker that fits an 8-hour shift pattern, a durable multi tool with a laser-engraved message, or a "starter apartment" kit with cookware, bedding, and a quick-guide binder (insurance, VA contacts, resume help). Subscription picks work well: meal-kit deliveries for the early weeks back home, a monthly sock or underwear club (practical and low-fuss), or a car maintenance plan voucher. These gifts signal you see the practical load they're carrying.

Gifts that Encourage Shared Hobbies and Relaxation

Shared activities rebuild connection faster than any speech. Sign up together for a local cooking class (BBQ skills are very popular), buy a beginner-friendly acoustic guitar plus a few lessons, or order a two-person painting kit and set aside an evening with snacks. For unwind time: a massage certificate, a guided-meditation app subscription, or a weighted blanket paired with a curated movie night kit. These gifts create neutral ground where both partners can relax and laugh.

Personalized Gifts with Emotional Weight

When you want the gift to carry emotional meaning, personalize it. Ideas: a photo album that chronicles pre-, during-, and post-service life with captions that tell the story, a handmade quilt made from uniform pieces, or a map with push pins marking important locations and a captioned key. Consider including a short letter describing one memory you'll never forget — specific beats build emotional impact.

Action Prompts

- Reintegration Reflection: Sit down with your partner and list three small tasks that would make their civilian days easier; pick one to gift this month.
- The "Love Tank" Check: Ask, "Did that present make you feel seen, supported, or relaxed?" Rank the effect 1–5 and talk about why.

Thoughtful giving isn't about cost. It's about choosing items that match a person's past, present needs, and the future you want to share.

Deployment debrief scripts

Deployment Debrief: A Collaborative Processing Framework for Couples

Coming home is a relief — and often a mess. The emotional unpacking after deployment can sneak up on both partners: one returns with memories and tension, the other has been holding the fort and carrying worry. A short, structured debrief you do together can help move from reactive to intentional, so both of you get heard and can begin the practical work of reconnecting.

Structured Debrief Questions: Guiding Conversations About the Military Experience

Set aside 30 to 60 minutes, no tech, no interruptions. One person speaks for a set time (try 10–12 minutes), the other listens without interrupting, then switch. Use these prompts as a starting point:

- What were the toughest parts of your deployment?
- How did you handle stress or hard days?
- What felt most like a success — big or small?

Practical example: sit with a timer and a notebook. As the returning partner speaks, the listener writes one sentence that captures the feeling — no judgment, just words. After both share, read the sentences aloud to check for accuracy.

Exploring Shared Emotions and Deployment Impacts: Understanding Each Other's Feelings

When feelings are messy, a simple framework helps keep things constructive.

Active listening: Practice the "reflect and validate" move. After your partner finishes, summarize what you heard and add, "That must have been…" then name an emotion. If your partner corrects you, listen again.

Empathy: Try this micro-exercise: swap two minutes and explain, in first person, how you think the other felt during a specific event. It's awkward but useful.

Validation: Don't fix. Acknowledge. "I can see why that would make you anxious" is more healing than problem-solving right away.

Identifying Strengths and Lessons Learned: Highlighting Growth and Positive Takeaways

Deployments aren't only stress. They sharpen coping skills, test patience, and reveal strengths.

Reflection prompts:

- Which coping strategies worked? (Example: nightly calls, humour, running)
- What skills did you build? (Example: patience with uncertainty, improved budgeting).
- What can you celebrate? Write three wins — even tiny ones — and read them together.

Acknowledging Challenges and Identifying Support Needs: Opening Dialogue for Mutual Assistance

Be blunt but kind. Make a short list: communication issues, emotional triggers, household pain points. Then rank them together — highest priority first.

The "Ranking Needs" prompt:

- Each partner lists three needs (emotional, practical, social).
- Swap lists and mark which items you can help with and which need outside support.
- Create a 30-day plan with one practical step per week (e.g., schedule a couples check-in, contact a local vet support group, try a communication technique from this book).

Navigating the Transition Back to Civilian Life: Reintegrating After Deployment

Rebuilding rhythms takes time. Focus on routines, social reconnection, and realistic expectations.

Reintegration Reflection:

- What routines do you want back? Which new routines would help?
- Who in your circle can you reconnect with this month?
- What professional or peer supports might you try?

Small actions matter: plan a "normal" Saturday together, set one weekly friend meet up for the non-deployed partner, and pick one community resource to call this week. Use the debrief framework again in six weeks to track progress and adjust the plan.

Inclusive resources and LGBTQ+ considerations

Inclusive Resources and Support Networks

When you and your partner are sorting out how to get through the next phase—whether it's post-deployment catch-up, dealing with military-related stress, or just finding people who "get" you—affirming support matters. Below are concrete places and options to plug into, plus short exercises to help you pick what's useful.

Support Groups and Community Networks

- The Trevor Project: Useful if you or a younger partner need immediate crisis support or safe conversation at odd hours. Practical tip: save their number in your phone under "Safe Line" and share it with each other so both partners can reach out if one feels overwhelmed.

- NAMI Veterans Resource Centre: Offers group meetings and education tailored to veterans and their families. Action step: attend one group session together and then do a short debrief—what felt helpful, what felt awkward? Use "Reintegration Reflection" below to guide that talk.

- Human Rights Campaign (HRC) Military and Veterans Affairs program: Provides materials and referrals that are specific to service members and their families. Try their local listings to find community events where you can meet other couples.

Online Resources and Hot lines

- VA LGBTQ+ page: A starting point for benefits, health care, and local VA contacts that are LGBTQ+ aware. Practical use: print or screen shot the nearest LGBTQ-affirming VA clinic info and tape it to your fridge or keep it in a shared notes app.

- NCTE Veterans and Military Families program: Especially helpful for transgender veterans and partners navigating paperwork, access to care, or legal name changes. Action example: make a checklist from their resources and schedule one small thing to do this month (call, gather documents, or book an appointment).

- GLBT National Hotline: 24/7 support if you need a non-judgemental voice late at night. Keep the hotline number in a "crisis" entry alongside the Trevor Project number.

Importance of Affirming Resources

Having an affirming group or contact cuts isolation fast. For many LGBTQ+ veterans, finding a space where the military-influenced experience is understood—where uniforms, rank, trauma, and pride are part of the conversation—makes reaching out feel safer. Ask yourselves: Who on this list feels like a "safe first call"? Rank those options in the "Ranking Needs" exercise below.

Unique Challenges and Triumphs

LGBTQ+ veterans often face extra hurdles: past military policies, civilian misunderstandings, or family push back. But they also bring strengths—resilience from service, an ability to create tight bonds with chosen family, and skills in adapting under pressure. Try this short partner task: each person names one challenge they still face and one strength they bring from service. Then do the "The 'Love Tank' Check"—rate how supported you feel by your partner on a 1–10 scale and write one small action to move that score up by one point this week.

Prompts for Action

- Reintegration Reflection: After attending a support session, share three takeaways and one thing you'll try differently at home.
- Ranking Needs: List the resources above, rank them by comfort level (1 = would call today), and agree who will contact which service.
- The "Love Tank" Check: Weekly, both partners rate support and commit to one concrete, timed action (text check-ins, a shared

appointment, or attending a group together).

Finding affirming networks is practical work—phone numbers, appointments, and small check-ins—not a romantic ideal. Take one step this week: pick a resource, mark a time, and treat it like any other maintenance task for your health and your bond.

Glossary of military terms and recommended readings

Glossary and Practical Reading List

Before we move into exercises and prompts, here's a compact glossary and a short reading list to keep on hand. Think of this as a field manual for words and programs you'll see during transition check-ins, benefit appointments, or after a community meeting.

Military Terms (Quick Definitions)

- ASAP — As Soon As Possible; used when something is urgent and needs action now.
- CO — Commanding Officer; the person in charge of a unit.
- Deployment — Movement of troops to an operational area; often a major stress or for couples.
- FUBAR — Fouled Up Beyond All Recognition; blunt slang for a situation gone sideways.
- MOS — Military Occupational Specialty; your specific job code in the service.
- NDA — Non-Disclosure Agreement; legal limits on sharing certain information.
- OPSEC — Operations Security. Keeping sensitive info from reaching the wrong audience.
- PT — Physical Training. Scheduled fitness sessions and testing.

Post-Service Acronyms (What you'll run into after leaving)

- TAP — Transition Assistance Program; classroom and counselling sessions that walk service members through benefits, resumes, and civilian employment basics.

- GI Bill — Education benefits for veterans; covers many degrees and training programs.
- VA — Department of Veterans Affairs; handles healthcare, disability claims, and more.
- VSP — Veterans' Service Provider; community organizations or individuals who help with benefits, paperwork, and referrals.

Practical Reading and Self-Help Picks

Books on trauma:

- The Body Keeps the Score — A clinical yet readable look at trauma's effects and treatment.
- Trauma and Recovery — A foundational text on coming back from traumatic experiences.

Books for partners and couples:

- The Gottman Institute materials — Research-based tools for conflict, friendship, and repair.
- Attached — A concise guide to adult attachment styles and how they show up in partnerships.

Self-care and reflection:

- The Gifts of Imperfection — Short, actionable ideas for reducing self-criticism.
- Daring Greatly — On vulnerability as strength; good for veterans learning to ask for help.

Suggested Journals

Five-Minute Journal — Daily prompts that take little time but build habit.

- Morning Pages Journal — Three pages of free writing to clear the head and spot patterns.

Action Prompts and Reflection Questions

Reintegration Reflection: Sit with your partner for 10 minutes. Each names one thing that felt hardest post-service and one small win from the last month. No interruptions.

Ranking Needs: List five needs (e.g., rest, routine, social time, paperwork help, intimacy). Rank them together and pick one to tackle this week.

The "Love Tank" Check: Each partner names one behaviour that fills their tank and one that drains it. Try one fill-the-tank action within 48 hours.

How to use this list: Carry the glossary on your phone or print it for benefit appointments. Keep one of the journals with your bedside. Use the prompts at the start of couples' check-ins or when stress spikes. These small, concrete steps help translate knowledge into action - and make the path after service a bit more manageable.

Appendix: translation cheat sheets for civilian partners

Decoding Military Jargon: A Civilian's Guide to Common Acronyms and Terms

If you've ever stood in a room where someone said "ROTA" and everyone else reacted like it was a punchline, you're not alone. Military talk moves fast because lives sometimes depend on quick clarity. Below is a compact, usable guide to help civilians make sense of frequently heard acronyms and phrases. Read it and file it away — or print and hand to a friend who still thinks "KP" is a brand of protein powder.

Common Military Acronyms

- ASAP — As Soon As Possible. Not a suggestion.
- CO — Commanding Officer. The person whose word matters on that base.
- ETA — Estimated Time of Arrival. Works for flights, convoys, and reunions.
- FUBAR — Fouled Up Beyond All Recognition. Said with resignation and dark humour.
- HOOAH — An all purpose shout of agreement, motivation, or morale. Think of it as military "you got this."
- IDK — I Don't Know. Yes, even the military uses internet shorthand.
- KP — Kitchen Police. The folks stuck cleaning up after chow.
- MOS — Military Occupational Specialty. Your job code in uniform.
- NCO — Non-Commissioned Officer. The glue between

leadership and troops.

- OIF — Operation Iraqi Freedom. Historical shorthand for a specific deployment era.
- PT — Physical Training. Runs, callisthenics, and the occasional group groan.
- ROTA — Rotation. The schedule that determines where and when people move.

Common Phrases That Matter

- “Roger that”: I heard you and I’m on it.
- “Copy”: Got the info.
- “Say again”: Repeat, please.
- “Over”: I’m finished talking, awaiting reply.
- “Out”: Conversation finished, radio off.

Communication Style: What Civilians Should Know

Military speech often skips small talk. That’s not rudeness; it’s efficiency. In tense situations, brief, direct exchanges reduce mistakes. For civilians, this can feel blunt. Try to view it as functional honesty rather than a personal slight.

Practical Tips for Civilians

- Ask questions. A simple “Can you explain that?” Is better than nodding and guessing.
- Listen to context. Acronyms mean different things in different settings — “CO” at a unit picnic is still command, but tone changes.
- Don’t fake it. Using jargon incorrectly can sound worse than asking for clarification.
- Be patient. Quick answers often come with blunt delivery.

Reintegration Reflection

Take five minutes with a partner or friend:

- List three acronyms you hear most often from your veteran partner.
- Which term makes you curious or uneasy? Ask about it and write down the explanation.

Quick Practice: The "Say Again?" Drill.

Partner A speaks a short story about their day using two acronyms. Partner B practices "say again" and "copy" until it feels natural. Swap roles. This builds patience and mutual fluency without awkwardness.

These small steps reduce misunderstanding and build rapport. When civilians learn the basics and veterans slow down a beat to clarify, conversations get smoother and home life gets a little easier.

Carrying Forward the Strength Within

We have walked through the significant shifts that follow military service, from the initial disorientation of reintegration to the specific challenges and triumphs faced by those who served in different branches. We have acknowledged the unique paths men and women take in rediscovering themselves after the uniform comes off, and the critical importance of self-care in this process. The connections we build, both with those who share our military background and those who do not, have been a central theme. The strains that post-service life can place on couples, and the ways to strengthen those bonds through shared purpose and understanding, have been laid bare. We've considered how communication might need to adapt, and the comfort and meaning found in shared rituals and symbols as we return home. Our exploration also touched upon the foundational work of discovering our inner selves and understanding how we give and receive affection, providing practical methods for ongoing self-reflection.

The purpose behind this work has been to offer a guiding light for those navigating the often turbulent waters of transition. It is a recognition that the skills and experiences gained in uniform are valuable, but their application in civilian life requires conscious effort and adaptation. This book has been a companion, providing insights and tools to help individuals and their loved ones move forward with clarity and confidence. It is an acknowledgment that while the external structure of military life may dissolve, the internal strength and resilience cultivated within it can be a powerful force for continued growth and fulfilment. The experiences of those who have served are rich and varied, and the path ahead is not always clear. This book aimed to illuminate that path, offering not just understanding, but also a sense of possibility.

The lessons presented here are not meant to be static directives, but rather adaptable principles. The journey of post-service life is an ongoing one, marked by continuous learning and adjustment. The self-love that was encouraged is not a destination, but a practice. The ways we connect with others and build our lives beyond the service will continue to adapt. The challenges faced by couples require ongoing attention and communication, and the discovery of shared goals provides a compass for future endeavours. The tools offered are intended to be utilized and adapted, serving as springboards for personal development and stronger connections. The strength found within each individual, forged through their military service, is the most potent resource they possess. This strength, coupled with intentional effort and supportive connections, allows for a continued flourishing in the civilian world. The insights and practices shared within these pages are meant to empower you to carry forward the discipline, the commitment, and the character that defined your time in service, and to apply them to building a meaningful and satisfying life ahead. The next chapter is yours to write, and it can be one of great purpose and connection.

www.ingramcontent.com/pod-product-compliance
Lightning Source LLC
LaVergne TN
LVHW010222110826
845148LV00022B/1241
9798903298617